William J Phillips

4-6-10

"Bill Phillips reminds us all of what it is that makes America great! He is a classic entrepreneur who has used his talent, perseverance, willingness to take risks, and strong work ethic to create something bigger than himself. He is an incredibly successful business leader who has never forgotten where he came from…and, thankfully, reminds us all that it is 'all about the chocolate milk'!"

—*David Brandon, Chairman and CEO*
Domino's Pizza, Inc.

"This is one of the best books around on the power of the free enterprise system by one of America's great business innovators. Bill Phillips shares his thoughts and business acumen in an interesting and insightful way—a must-read!"

—*Rodger D. Young*
Founding Partner of Young & Susser, PC
Former U.S. Ambassador to the United Nations General Assembly

"A memoir that is both candid and insightful. Every entrepreneur and would-be entrepreneur will enjoy it. Bill Phillips' journey from pauper to millionaire is a great read. Bill managed to balance his business acumen and family values to build a multimillion-dollar business and to raise a wonderful family, resulting in a great family business."

—*Paul Bernhard*
Director of Family Business
Plante & Moran, PLLC

"There are all kinds of entrepreneurs. Most have a passion for what they do and a drive to succeed. Bill Phillips has gone beyond those basics and incorporated values of honesty and integrity into his business. It takes a special talent to build values into a big business. He is the kind of entrepreneur we need in this great country. He treats his employees with honesty and truth and expects the same in return, with no exceptions. Employees who do not maintain these values in their daily work are not kept on as a part of his company. On these important values sits a strong foundation for all his business transactions. When he purchased my company, we were looking for a buyer with the right fit for my employees. We wanted to find a buyer who would carry on our tradition of honesty and integrity. It was a pleasure to sell my business to Bill Phillips and see the company I had so carefully managed benefit from his expertise. He has continued to grow and improve my business, even through a few difficult years. I have had the privilege of getting to know Bill since the purchase. His generosity has been a blessing to my family and me. He is a man of his word. Many years later, it is a real pleasure to know that my company is in good hands—the honest hands of Bill Phillips."

—*Charles Walker*
Former Owner, Evana Automation

"I take this opportunity to focus on the positive impact of William Phillips on this family, countless others, the City of Livonia, Michigan, and our nation. Much of my career has been in the public sector working with a variety of business leaders and executives. Bill is a leader among leaders. As you read his life story, know that his many successes were the result of a unique skill set and unusually keen entrepreneurial insight, in addition to Bill being very bright. Bill Phillips didn't wait for circumstances to shape his life. He saw opportunities overlooked by many and worked hard to bring them to reality. His business ventures have been complex and required a mastery of engineering sciences, a trained work force and managerial team, and well-crafted business plans. They were moved forward with Bill's close, personal involvement and high moral and business standards. With all that going on in their lives, Bill and his wife, Betty (who are no-nonsense parents), have remained close to their eight children and twenty grandchildren, and have provided generous support to Madonna University, St. Mary's Hospital and numerous other community organizations and activities. As a job creator, he has provided employment to hundreds of individuals, adding to their quality of life. Although Bill is strictly business in his oversight of Phillips Service Industries, he has a great sense of humor and truly cares about those around him. Livonia is a great city because of people like Bill who are willing to share their success. I'm proud he is my friend."

—*Mayor Jack E. Kirksey*
City of Livonia, Michigan

"William Phillips' constant awareness of diversity is supported by his ardent devotion to his faith, his family, his friends, his country, and his business. His strong values have been inculcated in him by his religion, his appreciation of diversity in the many aspects of his industries, and in his relations and friendships to people of all races, religions and cultures. He lives this awareness in his love of his faith, his family, his friends, his industries and his country. In all of these, there is also the constant presence of joy."

—*Bishop Moses B. Anderson, S.S.E.*

"In this book, you will witness the evolution of a young man's hopes and dreams into an incredible business dynasty. Bill Phillips is a man confident enough to share his business strategy, his faith in God and his love of family."

—*Sister Mary Giovanni, President/CEO*
Angela Hospice, Livonia, Michigan

"Bill Phillips' story is that of a fortune built on sales, manufacturing and plain hard work by a man of character with the innate gifts to 'read' an individual quickly, to set someone at ease at the first introduction, and to feel as comfortable jetting to Portland, Maine, for a lobster dinner with his wife as he is in the trenches, hammering out a deal with top industry executives. Bill Phillips is a man enthralled with free enterprise, who owns far-flung businesses and properties and has experienced life on the financial edge. He has at his disposal a personal jet to quickly fly himself and his associates to the next 'hot deal' or just a regular visit to one of his plant sites. Yet this same magnate of industry is a simple man from humble beginnings, who is known to his many friends as 'WTP,' or simply 'Bill.'"

—*Frank Lampi, Chief Pilot*
Phillips Service Industries, Inc.

An
AMERICAN
Entrepreneur

An
AMERICAN
Entrepreneur

William T. Phillips

Phillips Service Industries, Inc.

Book design by:
Arbor Books, Inc.
www.arborbooks.com

Printed in the United States of America

An American Entrepreneur
William T. Phillips

1. Title   2. Author   3. Biography

Library of Congress Control Number: 2009913866

ISBN 10: 0-9844008-0-X
ISBN 13: 978-0-9844008-0-5

TABLE OF CONTENTS

This book is dedicated to my wife, Bridget, for all of the support she has given me over the years and because without her, none of this would have been possible.

ACKNOWLEDGMENTS

I think it's safe to say that no one gets anywhere in life without the help and support of others. And, when you've lived a life as long, as varied and as full as mine, that's not just true, it's gospel. So, to all my family, friends, colleagues, coworkers and associates, I want to say thank you so very much. And, a special thanks goes to my kids, Lynn, Terry, Lisa, Donna, Amy, Scott, Sean and especially my son Bob, whose encouragement and advice was invaluable to me while writing this book. The simple truth is that I would not be who, what or where I am today without each and every one of you.

PREFACE

To Bill Phillips, winning means keeping your word and standing your ground.

As an entrepreneur, he sees success as coming from a person's overall character, attitude and approach to life. Where some notice obstacles, he views opportunities. When others give up, he refuses to back down. Where many take shortcuts, he finds solutions.

From growing up with next to nothing on his grandfather's farm in Arkansas to defending what was his on the inner-city streets of Detroit, Bill has maintained the same core principles that have come to define him as a leader and an individual: honesty, integrity and ingenuity.

Those are the values on which he first built Phillips Service Industries, which he has since turned into a multimillion-dollar corporation that gets the government contracts other companies can't handle.

As a world leader of aerospace technology and national defense, PSI has kept America's B-52 bombers in the air, outfitted its successor, the B-1 bomber with wing actuators, designed components for the space shuttle's robotic arm and sent products into space that have survived several Martian winters. Think that sounds tough? You should meet the man behind it all.

With Bill, what you see is what you get. He's a straight-shooting, straight-talking businessman who loves a good joke, knows how to tell a story and can fix the hydraulics system on an Air Force fighter plane yet will whip out the duct tape to repair his corporate jet. He's as comfortable at work in the nuclear missile silos of Utah as he is reading the books on *The New York Times'* bestseller list or sitting with Betty, his wife of over fifty-four years, in the front row at a Broadway play.

A family man and patriot, Bill holds on to old-fashioned American values as his company keeps America on the cutting edge.

His self-confidence and lack of limitations take him seamlessly from executing million-dollar corporate acquisitions in the boardroom to orchestrating hunting and fishing expeditions in the Alaskan wilderness with his family and friends, including heads of state, owners of NFL teams, bishops and industry leaders.

For Bill, it's all about making your own opportunities, taking risks, carving out your own path and living life to the fullest. Anything less means selling yourself short—something Bill, a consummate salesman, can't stomach.

Bill's entrepreneurial spirit, stubbornness, self-reliance and strong belief in never taking on a partner are what keep PSI a privately owned and run corporation among a world of IPOs. Yet, no matter how big his company becomes, it will always, at heart, be a family business, employing three generations of Phillips family members as well as hundreds of workers from surrounding communities.

Despite the complexities of twenty-first century global trade wars, international market shakeups and domestic business meltdowns, Bill's business motto—"winning means getting the other guy's money"—summarizes the hardscrabble determination of American entrepreneurship that will keep this country afloat and always moving ahead. PSI is the kind of company that will preserve the United States' status as an international leader in industry and technology far into the future.

But that is only part of Bill Phillips' legacy.

His type of entrepreneurship isn't about American muscle but

American know-how. Its focus isn't on American domination but American leadership. His success isn't measured by how much money he can hoard but how many lives he can better.

Though this is a book about an entrepreneur, these stories don't prescribe a secret formula for success or get-rich-quick business tips. After all, Bill is living proof that business doesn't happen in books. It takes place in the real world with real people, real opportunities and adventures—and real obstacles to overcome.

Instead, in the tradition of the biographies that Bill loves to read, this is a character study illustrating how one man achieved success by fighting for what he knows is right, seeing value in ideas that other people dismiss, refusing to compromise his code of ethics, and charging as much as the market will bear.

There is enough country wisdom, hard-earned experience and practical advice in Bill to fill at least another volume. Yet the portrait that emerges is complete: Bill Phillips is an icon of American business, a loving husband, father and grandfather, a legend among his colleagues and friends; a philanthropist; and a former military man who found a way to continue to serve his country long after his stint in the Air Force had ended.

He is more than an entrepreneur. He is an inspiration.

PART I

Portrait of the Entrepreneur as a Young Man

CHAPTER 1

Fresh From the Farm

The problem was the crop yield. Every farmer in the area had the same challenge: How could they get the maximum crop yield out of their land? Unlike today, there wasn't a bunch of technological devices and chemicals at the local feed store to increase their agricultural crops; in fact, the only place to pick up anything within a twenty-mile radius was the general store in the heart of town. Hard to believe there wasn't a Wal-Mart or a Home Depot on each corner, but that was the way life was in rural Arkansas in the 1940s. People had to rely on themselves—on their own innovation and creativity—for solutions.

I had just started grade school in Tuckerman, Arkansas—my hometown. For most boys my age, it wasn't uncommon to be working a farm already. Agriculture was the main industry in that tiny area of Jackson County, and my family cultivated cotton, corn, rice and a few other crops in order to earn a living. My job was to run the plough, which meant running a team of horses—usually two, but sometimes even four or six—which was quite a responsibility for a young boy.

Tractors and farm equipment were not common at that time, especially in Arkansas. Even automobiles were a rarity then. Conveniences that exist today hadn't even been conceptualized yet, so successful farming depended on manual labor mixed with a little ingenuity—and a lot of trial and error. Much of what I learned about being an entrepreneur, and a man overall, came from watching my grandfather manage the family farm.

———

I was born on October 4, 1933, in Jackson County, Arkansas, where Tuckerman is situated. Because the population in the South is more dispersed, a county might have two or more cities within it as well as large areas of unincorporated land. My hometown is about 100 miles north of Little Rock, just south of the Ozark Mountains, and the land that my grandfather farmed was in unincorporated Jackson County, a few miles away.

Times were tough during the early years of my childhood. The nation was still suffering a financial hangover from the 1920s and World War II had already begun overseas. But as a small boy in a small town, I was somewhat isolated from all of those events.

My mother came from a town called Yellville in the foothills of the Ozarks, and my father was a flatlander from Tuckerman. The populations of my parents' towns together totaled less than 4,000 people—and that number remains about the same today. Because of the towns' sizes, and because news traveled slowly then, most people in the area were less interested in what was happening around the world and more concerned about making a living here at home. Surviving day to day and making ends meet consumed most of their time and attention.

My paternal grandfather was a traditional farmer in many ways, but at the same time he was very unique. He toiled from sunrise to sunset and managed many acres of land, where he grew a variety of crops. In that way he was the traditional epitome of hard work and dedication. He was always trying to maximize his farm's production and provide the best he could for his family. But he was also always trying to invent or create a better way of farming that could get him a step ahead.

One day, as my grandfather and I were tending to the daily chores, he turned to me and scratched his head. He had a look on his weathered face that suggested he was searching for some new idea or solution. It was a look I had seen many times before.

"Bill," he said to me, "there has to be a way to get more crops out of this land."

"We could buy more land," I offered.

"That would be one solution, I suppose," he replied, without pointing out that it wasn't a financially feasible one.

He continued to scratch his head and rub his chin as if he were some complex thinking machine just starting to warm up. My grandfather was indeed a unique man. He had been involved with some of the earliest cotton gin machines in Arkansas and had helped improve the local saw mills, which were popular at that time. In that aspect he was an innovator willing to embrace new ideas and technologies—an inventor constantly trying to create original ways of completing a task more efficiently.

"You know, Bill," my grandfather said, thinking it over, "what if we could get better irrigation to the fields? That might improve our yield, especially when the droughts come."

"Sure," I said, going along with whatever he said.

"How 'bout you and I start digging some wells in the middle of the fields?"

I was happy to help and, before long, all of the fields had wells for irrigation. Whether or not a drought occurred, the increase in irrigation allowed the crops to produce more and the yields grew significantly over a short period of time, surpassing all the other farms in the area. My grandfather's innovation helped him out-produce all of the other farmers acre for acre and provided the answer he needed to achieve his goal.

When my grandfather died in 1951 his fellow farmers and the community of Jackson County recognized him for his developments in the farming industry. His obituary specifically mentioned his unique innovations and contributions in the area of field irrigation. What he had created eventually provided everyone with better crop yields because, in time, the other farmers had duplicated his irrigation technique. My grandfather was the first true entrepreneur I ever encountered.

Perhaps digging wells in a field doesn't seem like such a complex solution to a problem but sometimes solutions don't need to be complex. Solving a problem often just takes some common sense, a new perspective and a way of seeing something where others don't. The ability to be creative and the desire to find a solution are two key components of success and characteristics of an entrepreneur.

My grandfather was a tremendous influence on me in that regard. Perhaps he passed along his entrepreneurial genes and provided me with a basic foundation for my future. But simply being around him was enough to inspire anyone.

My farming days wouldn't last too long, since I would soon move to Detroit with my parents. But I have always carried with me the memory of how my grandfather approached his daily life. No matter what tasks he was doing or what problems arose he approached them with a sense of wonder and intrigue, and a different way of seeing things. He kept an open mind and kept things simple. That was what made him truly exceptional—and what first sowed the seeds of change in me.

Each small step—and even each misstep—along with every opportunity I've taken and every chance I've had to fail have brought me closer to where I am today. They say you reap what you sow. I say, even if you don't have much to sow to begin with, you can reap the rewards through hard work and the ability to come up with answers where others only see problems.

My company today takes on the big issues: among them how

to ensure safety and efficiency at nuclear-missile silos that have sat unchanged for over forty years and how to provide cutting-edge manufacturing technology to our military. We tackle the jobs that no one else wants. And we do it head-on, with the same kind of ingenuity and insight that was instilled in me nearly a lifetime ago on my grandfather's farm in Arkansas.

CHAPTER 2

Fighting for What's Mine

It's always been about the chocolate milk.

That's what I tell people who want to know how I managed to come from next to nothing and go on to build several multimillion-dollar corporations, working my way up to become one of the industry leaders in the world of hydraulic and electronic repair services and on the vanguard of nuclear-missile-silo design and the upgrading of systems of such powerful aircraft as the B-1 bomber and fighter jets.

Today I own large corporations that design and manufacture aerospace products, machinery used in the nuclear energy field, automated assembly machines and systems for our country's continued defense. For me, "business as usual" can mean anything from repairing electronics, servo valves and technical equipment in the automotive and mining industries to redesigning nuclear missile entry silos and state-of-the-art aircraft. And I do this on a daily basis.

My personal life has been just as successful. I have been married—happily, no less—for fifty-four years and have eight children with whom I share my life openly. I have also met many exciting people and enjoyed many different experiences and adventures along the way.

So what's the "secret" to this entrepreneur's success? Like I said, it's all about the chocolate milk.

In the fall of 1941, I had just turned eight years old and hadn't been living in Detroit for long. My father had taken a job with Cadillac and our family had left the hills of Arkansas to settle into a tiny, overcrowded apartment in a big, industrial city. It was quite a change from the small, Southern town I was used to—and being new to an area meant being put to the test early on.

The Great Depression had just ended and the nation was gearing up for war. Officially, World War II was already in progress but the bombing of Pearl Harbor wouldn't occur until December of that year. It wouldn't be long before the U.S. entered the battle but, for the time being, people were simply trying to get by. Many families had moved to Detroit because jobs were available there. As a result, there was a constant influx of new kids at school—and I was one of them.

So far, I'd been getting along alright on the school front. In those days, schools gave out pints of milk along with each student's report card. Resources were limited for many families and this was one way of making sure that kids got some decent nutrition occasionally. Every child received a pint of milk regardless of their marks but if your grades were particularly good you got a pint of chocolate milk instead of the regular kind. Now, I wasn't a consistently exceptional student, but the chocolate milk was a big incentive for me and I did get it on occasion. In fact, my first test as a new kid in the neighborhood came as a result of that simple reward.

As I was heading home from school on a particularly good report card day, I was met by one of the kids from my block who'd been living there much longer than I had. He eyed the chocolate milk I was holding, put down his books and squared off. Right then I knew I had a choice: I was going to have to either prove myself or lose my chocolate milk. My instincts told me to fight for it.

Without question, I was nervous as we prepared to do battle. The boy was taller and bigger than I was, but the instant our fists started flying it was as if my body were on autopilot. My fear evaporated and all I could think about was protecting what I'd earned.

I'm not sure if any eight-year-old ever really wins a fist fight but I think I landed a few more punches than the other kid, and he soon backed down. As we both stood there afterwards, panting and trying to catch our breath, I knew I had completed a rite of passage: I would get to keep what was rightfully mine, and the bully would have to find some other grade-schooler to mug or one who'd willingly hand over his milk—because it sure as heck wasn't going to be me.

This fight was my first life lesson in courage, and it felt good. More importantly, it taught me something. Families might not move around as much anymore, but proving your worth when entering a new field or environment hasn't changed a bit, especially in the business world. There will always be tests and rites of passage and to get through them, fortitude is just as important as being able to take a punch.

Over the years, I have run into many situations wherein I was faced with someone—whether it was an individual, another business or an agency—who was trying, essentially, to take away my chocolate milk. Fighting for it was the most natural thing in the world to me. After all, I had earned it. That didn't mean I wasn't nervous about some of the confrontations, but each time I walked away with what I consider most important: my self-respect. And, in most cases, I walked away with what I was fighting for as well.

If I hadn't stood my ground and fought for what was right, I never would have seen what could have been. Why let fear keep us from potential opportunities? You can always come up with some reason to be afraid. What you need is a stronger reason to overcome it.

Having been born during the Great Depression, my ideals and beliefs are characteristic of a generation that held character in high regard. Commitment and work ethic in what you're doing, getting to know people for who they are and treating them fairly, and being honest with yourself and others have always worked well for me.

Things aren't nearly as complex as people make them out to be. Sticking to your word, doing what's right and keeping a simple perspective will help you negotiate all of life's challenges—and come out the other side stronger and better for it. The focus on getting ahead at all costs forces us to lose sight of what makes a person truly successful—and I don't mean just financially.

Perhaps we all could benefit from going back to grade school and relearning some of those simple lessons: facing down bullies, standing up for yourself and fighting for what you've earned. Such basic beliefs will see us through the seemingly most difficult situations. After all, what's more difficult than getting through grade school on a daily basis?

I often wonder what would have happened if I had simply given in to that bully on my way home from school. I suspect I would have been picked on endlessly for lunch money or other items, and it would have continued for months if not years to come. Would that have changed my life's course? I'll never know the answer because I went with my instincts back then and I've been doing it ever since.

Of course, I'd hope the decisions we make when we're eight years old don't affect our lives that drastically. But I am thankful I chose to stand my ground, not because I was the winner or even because I got to keep my chocolate milk (which, in fact, spilled all over the ground during our scuffle!). I'm thankful because it taught me confidence and courage when fighting for the things I held important.

I am now seventy-six years old and have called Detroit my home for many years. During that time, I have witnessed a lot of changes and seen economic booms and busts. I sold newspapers as a boy and negotiated international business deals as an adult. I have had great business success stories and have also been burned by colleagues, employees and friends. In every instance, I have learned something and moved forward—with my self-respect intact and, hopefully, my chocolate milk in hand—ready to face whatever came next. Not knowing what lies around the corner is one of the most exciting things about life, especially as an entrepreneur. I wouldn't trade it for anything.

The fights I've had have helped me to forge ahead with a strong set of values and an honest, no-nonsense approach to whatever I was undertaking. In this age of rapid globalization, financial scandals and economic hardships, getting back to these basics might just be the remedy the world needs.

That, and a glass of cold chocolate milk.

CHAPTER 3

My First Wool Suit

You know how they say, "The suit makes the man"? Well, in my case, it wasn't so much the first suit I ever owned that made me, as an eight-year-old boy, feel like a man. It was the way I went about earning it by myself.

In 1941, my family moved to Detroit, a hot spot for employment. Many of the automotive plants involved in making tanks for the war effort were looking for extra workers—and it just so happened that my dad was looking for opportunities. So, in the blink of an eye, I found myself uprooted from the rural farmlands of my childhood and dropped into a strange, crowded, urban center.

Large buildings, busy streets and neighbors an arm's length away were quite a change from the familiar farm life I had known. We moved into a one-room apartment where my parents slept on a fold-down Murphy bed; I slept on a cot and my sister stayed in her bassinette, having just been born months before. "Cozy" would be a nice way of describing the situation, but "cramped" was more like it.

Fortunately, my father found work at the Cadillac factory and began almost immediately. My mother worked there as well for extra money. Though women's liberation had not yet become popular, many women worked in factories then to help earn enough for their families to get by, and their roles in the workforce became more prominent as men left to fight in the war. Even with both of my parents at work, however, wages were lean, to say the least.

I'm not saying that we had it the toughest by any means. Next to our apartment building were project developments where many of the factory workers and their families lived, and those homes were actually in worse condition than that tiny apartment of ours.

Still, it wasn't easy staying in an apartment building shared by dozens of other families. At times it was downright claustrophobic. One source of comfort was that many other families had moved from Arkansas to Detroit at the same time as us. I didn't know any of those other kids very well, but at least we were from the same place.

The migration to Detroit in the 1940s was similar to that from the East to the West in the early years of our nation. Opportunity and employment have always been magnets that pulled people away from their homes to explore new areas and possibilities. Sure, my family struggled to make ends meet, but it seemed like everyone was struggling together. Times were harder, but times were simpler, too. And the impending war created a sense that we all belonged together as Americans.

So, despite a few rough spots that came with being new to the area, I quickly adapted and made friends with the boys in my neighborhood. We'd often play war games, with one side being the Germans and the other side the Americans. Of course, everyone wanted to be the Americans, which made the teams a little uneven, but imagination and creativity kept us entertained. There weren't any video games or many organized sports leagues in those days. By necessity, we had to create our own fun.

While my parents were at the factory, a young girl in our apartment building watched my sister, which left me pretty much on my own most of the time after school. Fun and games with my friends were one thing, but by the time I turned eight years old, I was ready to go to work. I wanted to earn my own money. That was the start of my entrepreneurial spirit.

I began wracking my brain to come up with ways to earn some extra change—then, one day, I had an idea. With my parents' permission, I went to our landlady's apartment and introduced myself. I had a proposition for her that would hopefully be a win-win for both of us.

"What can I do for you?" she asked with a smile.

"There seems to be a bit of trash around the apartments," I stated matter-of-factly.

"Oh, really?" she asked, looking over my head at the grounds.

"I'd be happy to pick it up every day for a little money," I continued.

"Hmm. Are you dependable?"

"Yes, I am. And I would do a really nice job."

"I see. Well, I suppose I could let you do that for maybe five cents a week."

"Could you let me do it for ten cents?" I countered.

The landlady looked me up and down, studying me closely. She probably hadn't thought she would have to negotiate with an eight-year-old.

"Yes, I suppose I could," she consented.

That was all I needed to hear. I was in business! That same day, I began pulling my small, red wagon around to collect the trash, loading it up with cans and paper on the way to the dumpster. It wasn't exactly the cleanest work, but at least it was work—and though my earnings were almost nothing, they were better than having no money at all.

Like my grandfather, however, I would soon start thinking about ways to improve my situation. The thing about opportunities is that one will often lead to others. Failing to take advantage of a situation could close the door on dozens of others. Even at such a young age, I knew that every opportunity should be seen as the first step toward greater success.

For example, my school was always having paper and aluminum drives for the war effort, and kids would bring in these materials so the factories could make additional supplies and weaponry. By collecting trash for our landlady, I was able to contribute a lot to my school drive, too. One of the best sources of aluminum then were the pieces of foil inside cigarette packages, so I would take those from the trash, roll them into large balls and donate them to my school. It wasn't profitable but it was a chance to help out, which gave me a sense of pride and involvement and taught me that not all opportunities had to come with monetary rewards.

One day, however, my hard work really paid off. As I did my usual rounds in search of trash, I suddenly spotted a crumbled piece of dirty, green paper. I walked over to place it into my wagon but soon realized that it was no ordinary piece of garbage. It was a ten-dollar bill! Ten dollars then would be around $150 today, so you can imagine the thoughts a boy might have with such a find. A bicycle, a BB gun and a few other items immediately filled my mind.

I ran home to tell my mom all about it as soon as I had finished taking the trash to the dumpster.

"Mom, Mom!" I yelled, exploding through the apartment door. "I found ten dollars!"

"What? Where?" she replied, almost as amazed as I had been.

"I was picking up trash and there it was—just lying on the ground."

"Did somebody drop it, Bill?"

"Nobody was around. It wasn't even near anybody's trash cans or apartment."

Now, I realize that my mother could have done a lot of things with that money. She could have bought groceries for all of us; she could have used it to help pay for my sister's care; or she even could have put it away in case of an emergency. But she felt it was my reward for working hard. That simple gesture taught me a great deal about respect: She respected what I was doing and wanted me to benefit from it. Unfortunately for me, that didn't mean a bicycle or a BB gun. Instead, it meant my first new suit.

The next day, my mother, sister and I all went to purchase a wool suit for me. I still remember it well and have a picture of me wearing it when I was nine years old, sitting next to my sister. The suit was made from a dark gray tweed—the thickest and itchiest material ever invented.

I'm sure my mom wanted me to look nice and be warm, but a BB gun would have been a lot more fun. Still, I wore that wool suit on plenty of occasions, though only with my parents' encouragement. To this day, I cannot stand to wear anything with wool in it. But something more positive has stayed with me, too.

My mother's heart was in the right place; she wanted to support my initiative to earn money and take pride in myself for the hard work I had done. If I had never tried to earn extra money, I would never have found the ten dollars, so it was like a bonus for my creativity and innovation. That money also reinforced my willingness to work for what we couldn't afford.

My desire to be successful was forged in these early years but my motivation wasn't about buying this item or that. Personally, I could have lived without suits for the rest of my life. For me, success represented freedom.

Everyone I knew struggled so hard to live and had so few freedoms because of their limited incomes. More than anything, I wanted the freedom to make my own choices later in life, even if I had to work hard for that at the time.

My experience with picking up trash for the landlady fueled the fire within me to find other ways of earning extra money. What had begun as a simple idea for some pocket change had given me my first taste of success and had shown me the first steps to take on my way to becoming an entrepreneur. And that suited me just fine.

CHAPTER 4

The Wheels Are in Motion

In the summer of 1942, it might have been too hot to wear my scratchy wool suit but I was still itching for what every boy dreamt of: a bicycle and a BB gun. Despite my entrepreneurial efforts, I was no closer to either of them.

The government was spending money on the war and everyone was contributing as best they could. Though jobs were increasing, wages were not, and most people were living simply to make ends meet. My family was in no position to buy many things for my sister and me. Things were tight for us then, just as they were for everyone, but overall I remember those times as happy ones for me.

As luck would have it, my mom knew one of our neighbors, whose eighteen-year-old had a bicycle that was no longer needed. Mom knew I wanted a bike more than anything, and she was able to get one for me for free.

The catch?

That eighteen-year-old was a girl. So what I'd be getting was a girl's bike.

You can imagine the teasing I suffered on that account, but I wasn't about to give it up. It was still a bicycle, after all, and I was one of the few kids in the neighborhood who had one. In the 1940s, beggars really couldn't be choosers, so girl's bike or not, it was still something to be cherished.

Another highlight of that summer was going back to Tuckerman to see my grandfather again. My parents stayed in Detroit but arranged for me to go down by train with a family who was also from Arkansas. I couldn't wait to go! It had been almost a year since I had seen him.

I would be staying at my grandfather's for about a month and I really wanted to take my bicycle with me. I pleaded with my parents and they eventually agreed to send it along. Although it was placed in a freight car of a separate train and would be arriving a day later, I was still happy that my bike was making the trip. For me, it meant freedom.

Finally, the day came when I saw Grandpa Phillips. He stood on the wooden depot platform as I came off the train, looking just as I remembered him—tall and strong, with gentle eyes and a pleasant smile. After a hug and a few pats on the head from him, I collected my luggage and we headed toward the depot office to find out about my bike. After checking some list, the ticket person told us it was traveling on a train routed through St. Louis.

The next afternoon couldn't come fast enough, as far as I was concerned. My grandfather and I returned to collect my bicycle, which I somehow spotted at the far end of the depot's receiving platform. As I anxiously unearthed it from among the cargo boxes and freight, I could tell my grandfather was studying it closely.

"Bill," he finally said, breaking his silence, "that's a girl's bike"—as if that was the first time I had heard that bit of news.

"Yes, I know," I replied.

He could probably see the embarrassment on my face. "Why don't we see if we can take care of that?"

It always seemed like my grandfather had an endless number of resources and ways of envisioning things that no one else saw. So he and I took my two-wheeled transportation over to his friend, Carl, who ran the local blacksmith shop. The clanking of a blacksmith's hammer and the heat of the shop greeted us as we entered. It might have been as hot as hell, but it was like paradise to me.

"Carl," my grandfather announced, "can you take a look at this for me?"

"What do ya have there?" Carl asked. "Looks like a girl's bike."

"That it is," my grandfather replied. "But it belongs to my grandson."

"Oh, well, that *is* a problem," Carl stated plainly.

After much debate, conversation and strategizing, the two men mastered a plan to convert my girl's bike into a boy's. All it took was a curved pipe added across the frame and a new paint job—and my bicycle was instantly masculinized. It might not have been the best-looking in town but it was now a boy's bike nonetheless.

I was, of course, thrilled with the transformation, but what it showed me most of all was that my grandfather was always willing to go the extra mile not only to please his grandson but also to find a solution to a problem. Just like with his irrigation idea to help his fields produce better crops, he had figured out a simple answer to my bike issue. Sure, I could have continued to ride it as a girl's bike and take all the teasing, just as he could have survived on a lower crop yield with less irrigation. But by making the effort to search for a solution, my grandfather taught me that I didn't simply have to accept things as they were. If I didn't like something, I could always change it.

⸻

Even though I spent much of my childhood in Detroit, I have many fond memories of my grandfather. For instance, as the water rose up from the wells that he had dug on his farm, an irrigation pond would form and, from there, the water would slowly travel down the furrows of the fields, providing hydration to the crops. Coming from deep within the ground, the water was ice cold, so when we worked on the farm during the day, one of the first things we did was place a watermelon in the irrigation pond and let it sit there all morning. A little after midday, we'd return to share some delicious, chilled watermelon together.

My grandfather also made small boats and hats out of limestone paper, which is waterproof, allowing it to float. He would place a handmade boat in the irrigation pond early in the day and I would see it traveling down the furrows of the fields in different locations as we worked. Little things like that made the time fly by—and are what made my grandfather truly extraordinary. He never lost his ability to imagine and create.

It would have been very easy to become immersed in the toil of the day and not have taken the time or energy to make these small gestures. But my grandfather enjoyed simple pleasures and did the little things that made huge differences, like saving me from my friends' ridicule over a bike and making farm work more fun. The memories I have of a team of horses pulling a plough or helping with other hard chores are not nearly as vivid or as meaningful.

With his unique brand of creativity and simple values, my grandfather served as a great role model and instilled in me a strong foundation of what true value really was. He showed me that work was part of life and life was part of work—and that there was no reason to shortchange either one and every reason to make a change in something that fell short.

At the end of that summer spent with my grandfather, my bike wasn't the only thing that had been transformed.

CHAPTER 5

Learning a Life Lesson

It was time for another change of scenery—and, with it, another lesson in life.

Later that same year, my family moved back to Tuckerman. My father had gotten a job as a pipefitter at the recently built air base outside town and seemed pleased to be returning. Life in Detroit had been challenging but things were tough all over, and in times like those you wanted to get back to what you knew best. Both pipefitting and Arkansas provided that for my father, a social man who also liked the quiet life and had missed his friends back home.

Things hadn't changed much in Tuckerman while I was gone, but one thing *had* changed for sure: me. After being in a larger, urban school in Detroit, I was more aware of the world, even for an eight-year-old.

Still, the simple life of small-town Arkansas was familiar to me and I was able to fit back in rather easily to a slower pace of life. It also meant a lot to my family and me to be close to my grandparents again. So now, instead of playing between apartment buildings with the neighborhood kids in Detroit, I would keep busy exploring my grandfather's farm and playing with kids who were more gentle than those in Detroit—and both experiences taught me to appreciate all types of lifestyles. Between Detroit and Tuckerman, many things were different, but people were generally the same everywhere.

Each morning, after my mother helped me get ready, I walked to school—two miles away (I'd make the reverse trip in the afternoon). I generally walked the first mile from my grandfather's farm alone but by the time I made it to the center of town, I usually met up with some classmates and walked the second stretch with them. We walked down along the railroad tracks, wondering if we'd catch a glimpse of a train headed our way, and talked about the kinds of things kids talked about. Things were mostly simple and very straightforward then. Not everything, though.

Our school was an old, brick building built a long time before I had been born. It was the same one I had attended first grade in and I couldn't see that there had been any changes during my years-long absence. The same cracks in the mortar were still there, as were the same vinyl floors and chipped paint inside. Later that year, that school building burned to the ground and we had to relocate all of our classes to unoccupied buildings around the center of town. Some joker claiming to be a Japanese spy said he was responsible for the school's burning. There was fear that the Japanese were going to take over the world, and it didn't take much to alarm the town's residents. That story ran in the local newspaper and scared half the town to death for weeks, until we eventually found out it was a hoax.

Long before that, however, when the school year was new and everything was normal, I walked down the hallway to my fourth-grade classroom and placed my lunch and book bag away in my desk. We had assigned seats and everyone kept pretty quiet—there was no shouting or running around the room. Discipline was the order of the day back then.

I looked around the classroom and specifically noticed one girl who sat in the back. Lying next to her desk were two walking sticks, which were different from any canes I had seen before. They had metal extensions that went all the way to her upper arms, and there was one for each side of her body. I remembered her from when I had been at school previously, but I had never spoken to her before. She was different, and I didn't know what I should or shouldn't say.

Within a few minutes, the teacher came in and began our lessons. "Okay, class," Ms. Ledbetter stated, "please pass your homework up to the front."

Groans came from about half the room. We all dug into our desks and reluctantly handed papers to the people sitting in front of us. Mine was all crumpled as a result of its having to share bag space with my gym shoes and lunch. I just hoped the teacher didn't grade it according to smell.

As I turned to collect the papers from behind me, I glanced at the little girl once again. She was small and very thin. Her face was plain, with large brown eyes, and her light brown hair was combed back into a ponytail. Her legs were bent awkwardly in an unnatural position and were smaller than the rest of her body. She had been afflicted by something, and my guess was that it was polio.

At lunchtime, the students formed a line and headed outside. The day was beautiful, and Ms. Ledbetter was letting us eat on the playground. I noticed that the little girl stayed in her seat in the classroom and didn't line up with the rest of us. But about five minutes later I saw her come outside, walking on her crutches next to our teacher. She sat down alone on a bench and began to take her lunch from her brown paper bag. By then, I had nearly polished off my own lunch and was ready to get on with recess—the highlight of most every school day.

My school was the same as most: Some kids were in the popular crowd and some weren't. I happened to be one of those in the popular group and had plenty of friends to play with; if something was happening, I was usually in the mix. It wasn't like Detroit, where bullies seemed to be a dime a dozen, but that didn't mean the kids in Tuckerman didn't know how to tease.

"Bill, come here," one of my friends called from the other side of the playground.

I looked across and saw a group of kids all circled around the little girl with the crutches. When I walked closer, I could hear them teasing her.

"Why can't you walk right?" one boy asked.

"Why do your legs look like that?" asked another.

The little girl was still trying to finish her sandwich. She held her head low, gazing silently into the bag that lay in her lap, probably wishing she could crawl into it and hide. Meanwhile, the group of boys and girls gathered around her were still at it; they had called me over to join in on the fun.

For some reason, I just couldn't help myself. Maybe I was trying to blend back in. Maybe I was just being a boy. Anyway, I began walking around the girl as if conducting some examination and joined in the game.

"You look different," I said. "What's wrong with you?"

I saw the hurt on her face as soon as I had said it. She looked as if she had been stripped of everything she had. As if it were contagious, I felt her pain as I looked into her eyes. I sensed her loneliness and embarrassment, and that was a very powerful moment for me.

I'm well into my seventies now and that memory is still vivid in my mind. It troubles me every time I think about it. If I ever teased anyone again after that it was rare. Many other bullies would take their stabs at me through the years, as a child as well as an adult, but I would never allow myself to become a bully again. What I'd said made that little girl feel terrible, and I knew she had done absolutely nothing to deserve it.

Many things molded my character as I grew up, but I believe this event was one of the most intense. It taught me that standing up for what is right is more important than going along with the crowd—even if that means standing alone. Going against your ethics and what feels right in your heart is never worth it. I wish I hadn't said what I did to that girl, but since I couldn't retract it, I decided to learn from my mistake.

Injustices still bother me to this day, but now I have no problem speaking out against them. Because I harbor a keen sense of what is fair and right, I get upset when people intentionally try to take advantage of me or hurt others through cheating, lying or deception. I won't let that stop me from giving everyone the benefit of the doubt, though, unless they prove that they no longer deserve it.

Sometimes I wish that somebody had been there that day in school to set me straight, but in retrospect, I guess there was. That little girl and the look on her face were enough to teach me a lesson that I have carried with me through the rest of my life.

CHAPTER 6

Birth of a Salesman

The way we moved around when I was a child, you might have thought I came from a military family. Either that or my dad was a traveling salesman.

Well, one of us soon turned out to be a salesman, anyway.

After being back in Tuckerman for only a year, my father decided to move back to Detroit and take up his position at Cadillac once more. I never asked about his reason for returning but I figured he must have had a good one. My father wasn't the kind of person to make rash decisions. Although relocating back and forth between Michigan and Arkansas might suggest that he was spontaneous or indecisive, that was far from the truth. In fact, he ended up staying at General Motors for thirty-five years before he retired, so I think he made the right choice.

Upon our return to Detroit, we moved into a different neighborhood from where we had lived before—and this time we had a two-bedroom house rather than a one-room apartment. The only thing was that it wasn't in the best area. It was located in a housing project for migrant workers recruited for factories. Rows and rows of gray, cement-block homes lined narrow streets, welcoming the next wave of families. With the World War II effort in full swing, an even greater number of people were moving into Detroit for employment. But despite the less-than-desirable area where we lived, I was thankful to have more than a single room to accommodate all four of us.

We were all settled in at home. Then, there was just the issue of school to tackle.

———

In Arkansas, I had completed the fourth grade, so naturally I assumed I would be starting the fifth grade there in Michigan. But the school principal thought otherwise. When I walked into the school office to register by myself, I was escorted into the principal's office. Back then, your parents didn't necessarily go with you to handle your affairs at school. So there I sat alone, ready to plead my case.

The high, arched chair in the principal's office swallowed my ten-year-old frame. I doubt he would have even noticed me when he walked in had he not been forewarned of my presence. He was dressed in a short-sleeved shirt that could barely remain tucked into his pants because of his protruding belly. As he sat behind his desk, he adjusted his reading glasses to gaze at the papers in front of him.

"It says here on your form that you completed the fourth grade in Arkansas," he stated.

"Yes," I replied.

"Well, the problem is that schools in Arkansas are not as adept as those in Michigan," he continued. "You're going to need to complete the fourth grade here before you can move ahead."

"But I've already done the fourth grade," I exclaimed.

"Not in Michigan you haven't," he said with a sense of finality.

Needless to say, I wasn't very pleased. At that moment, I realized one of the things that I was unable to tolerate: I could not—and still cannot—stand to go backwards. I don't mind making mistakes; honestly, I have made plenty. But mistakes offer great opportunities for learning. Moving backwards serves no purpose whatsoever.

I wasn't going to repeat the fourth grade without a fight. I knew, even before I left the principal's office, that this was not over. So, the next day, I went back to the school with my mother, a strong and very fair woman who knew how frustrated I was over the situation. I figured that if I couldn't convince the principal by myself, she could possibly help me persuade him. Anyway, I had nothing to lose and everything to gain.

Once again, I sat in the principal's office and waited for him to arrive. He eventually walked in, wearing almost the identical outfit as the day before. After introducing himself briefly, he explained the situation to my mother just as he had to me.

"Mrs. Phillips, the curriculum in Arkansas just doesn't match that of our school," the principal announced. "William is simply going to have to repeat the fourth grade here."

"My name is Bill, not William," I interjected.

"Oh," he replied, "of course. *Bill* is going to need to repeat the fourth grade."

As I look back on this moment in my childhood, I realize this was my very first sales pitch. Of course, it would be one of many and certainly not my most eloquent, but it was still my first. I was ready to attempt the art of negotiation and to find out that an initial "no" can often be changed to a "yes." I was even willing to settle for a "we'll see."

"Mr. Sawgrass," I interjected. "If I can do fifth-grade work, will you let me stay in the fifth grade?"

The principal sat silently for a moment. He pondered what this young boy was proposing like he was considering the purchase of a new washing machine. Rubbing his chin, he weighed the risks and the benefits.

"William… I mean *Bill*… I just don't think that's a good idea."

"If I can't do the work, then I'll go back to fourth grade just like you said. But if I can, then I should be able to stay in the fifth grade, right?"

Again he paused and considered the proposition as I anxiously wondered what was going through his mind.

"Okay, Bill," he finally said. "I'll give you the first six-week term to see if you can handle the coursework. If you don't have passing marks, you will go back to fourth grade."

"But if I do pass, I can stay in fifth grade?"

"Yes."

I half expected him to shake my hand and sign a contract!

Needless to say, I handled the work and stayed in the fifth grade; I wasn't about to fail school after successfully completing the first sales job of my life. I also learned some things about myself in the process and some things about people in general. First, I realized that always striving to move ahead is important to me. You can call it pride or simply a dislike of inefficiency, but I've always liked to make progress in everything I do, even when I was in the fourth grade. Even mistakes and bad decisions can be considered progress, but going back to do the same thing all over again is nothing more than mere stagnation.

The other thing I learned was how to negotiate with people. Everyone needs to know their options—especially the one you want them to take. It was up to me to give the principal a fair solution that could have benefited both of us. He didn't really want to hold me back but had to follow the rules. His motivation was therefore to do what he thought was right.

But my motivation was to move ahead. So, I found a way for us to meet in the middle. Though I had negotiated once already with the landlady for my trash collection fee, I learned more about compromise, motivation and negotiation in talking with my school principal. Who says they don't teach anything practical in school?

If you never ask for something, you will never receive it—or, as my grandfather would say, "If you don't like something, change it." Either that or quit complaining.

Don't let fear or intimidation cause you to lose out on great opportunities. What if I hadn't stood up and pleaded my case to go into the fifth grade? The obvious answer is that I would have wasted time repeating the fourth grade. But, more importantly, I never would have known what might have happened if only I had *tried*.

For Mr. Sawgrass, our time in the office might have simply been another meeting with a student—hard-headed as that student was. For me, it was a wonderful achievement and a pivotal moment in becoming the salesperson I would eventually grow up to be.

CHAPTER 7

Opal's Flowers

If you just met me now—or after my stint in the Air Force—you might not take me as the type who went around selling flowers. But as a young boy, I had a fondness for pretty, green things. Particularly dollar bills.

One of the great things about living in Detroit was that we were close to my aunt Opal. She was married to my mother's brother and they had moved to the city around the same time we had. In fact, their house was next door to our duplex apartment, so I saw a lot of her and my cousins. Opal had four sons at the time, two of whom were already off fighting in the war. My other two cousins, who were still in school, were my companions while we were growing up.

One morning, Aunt Opal asked me to pick up some items for her at the dime store. That was nothing out of the ordinary for me. She usually had a list every week, which varied—but the requests were always interesting.

"Bill, here are the things I need," my aunt said, handing me a piece of paper.

"Okay," I answered, scanning the list. "But what's this stuff for?"

"You'll see soon enough," she replied. "Now run along."

This particular week she asked me to get some candles and four rolls of crepe paper in different colors. As far as I knew, it wasn't anybody's birthday, so I was excited to see what she would do with it all.

Aunt Opal hadn't received much formal education but she was an extremely bright and talented lady with amazing artistic abilities. Her home was decorated with so many beautiful paintings she had made that walking into it was like taking a trip to the local art museum. Maybe we should have charged admission.

So, off I went to the dime store—which in itself shows how dramatically times have changed. Today we have dollar stores, thanks to inflation, but the quality or degree of choices don't compare to the dime stores of old. In the 1940s, stores like Woolworth's were the only places to get most household items; though some things cost more than a dime, there was plenty to purchase for ten cents or less. About the only thing you couldn't get was groceries, which Aunt Opal didn't need for her art projects anyway.

I soon returned and handed Aunt Opal the supplies she had requested, then I sat and watched what she proceeded to create. She laid the supplies in front of her on the kitchen table and meticulously wove various colors of crepe paper into the shapes of different types of flowers; tulips, roses and other varieties came to life as she worked her magic. As the flowers were completed one by one, Aunt Opal arranged them into bouquets of a dozen or more.

She had already lit the candles, which were slowly melting. After the bouquets were done she collected the candle wax and placed it in a large pot over a low flame, keeping it hot. She then dipped her creations into the wax, which not only made the colors of the crepe paper really pop but also provided sturdiness to the bouquet. The end result was something spectacular, even to a ten-year-old boy who didn't have much use for flowers.

"Aunt Opal, I bet I could sell those," I piped up as I watched her make the bouquets. "I would split the profits with you."

"Do you really think people would buy them, Bill?" my aunt replied.

"I know they would! They're beautiful!" I said encouragingly.

"I don't know," Opal responded. "I like them, but I'm not sure anyone else would."

"Let me give it a try, Aunt Opal. What's it gonna hurt?"

"Well, alright. I suppose we can see what happens," she said.

I decided to sell each dozen flowers for forty-five cents, half of which I would give to Aunt Opal. My cousin, Fred, worked his way in to the profits as well. He and I went door to door all over the neighborhood, trying to sell Aunt Opal's wax bouquets. But, honestly, I did most of the selling. Fred usually just stood in the background silently, with a big grin on his face.

Fred hasn't changed a bit since he was a kid. He's the kind of guy who never had a great deal of ambition. That's no big secret, and Fred openly admits his tendency toward leisure. As long as I have known him, that is just who Fred has been.

A few years ago, after Fred's wife passed away, I gave him a call to see how he was doing.

"I'm doing alright, Bill," he told me.

"Well, what do you do all day?" I asked.

"In the morning, I sit in the back of my house in the shade, and then about noon, when the sun shifts, I move my chair around to the shade in the front."

"Sounds like you're getting your share of exercise," I joked.

"I don't want to overdo it, ya know," was his response.

That's Fred in a nutshell—a great sense of humor and a strong appreciation for the sedentary lifestyle.

So, I went around selling, with Fred tagging along, to see if Opal's bouquets would turn a profit. Believe it or not, we didn't just sell a few, but dozens! We sold so many that I had to start helping Aunt Opal make the bouquets. My artistic ability wasn't anything compared to hers, but I was willing to do whatever it took to keep our floral business thriving. That's the rule of supply and demand, and I was nothing if not a play-by-the-rules kind of kid (in that instance, anyway).

We might not have become wealthy peddling wax flowers but each of us received a little spare cash in our pockets. More importantly, I began to see opportunities where others didn't. I clearly saw that my aunt had incredible artistic talent, so taking advantage of the opportunity to sell her bouquets door to door made perfect sense to me. Seeing that kind of opportunity is a great asset for an entrepreneur. Many others don't—or won't—see what's right in front of their faces. Entrepreneurs not only see it; we find a way to sell it.

Maybe my aunt was too humble to recognize her own skills, but she took a chance on letting me sell her flowers. The market was out there and, as a result, we all enjoyed the sweet smell of success.

A few years ago, several of my family members and I got together for a reunion. Since my early days as a flower salesman, I have gone on to many larger successes and, as a result, travel often by corporate jet. While we were all sitting around, enjoying each other's company, my cousin Fred stood up to make a speech.

"Everyone, it's a pleasure to be here today and to see all of our family," he began. "And I am sure many of you have had the pleasure of seeing Bill's corporate jet. But what you may not realize is that Bill and I used to be in business together."

Everyone's attention was captured at this point. No one had any idea what my cousin was talking about—including me!

"Well, the truth is that Bill and I were partners in one of his first business ventures, and we split the profits," he continued. "Bill and I sold Opal's bouquets of waxed flowers around the neighborhood and made a nice little profit."

Fred paused for a brief second, then looked directly at me. "And, Bill, I've been thinking… It might be a good idea for us to start splitting the profits again!"

Fred got a good laugh from everyone—me, most of all—but to

be honest, he was right about one thing: Selling my aunt's flowers had been my first real sales business. I had many more through the course of my life but even at the age of eleven, I had learned how to deliver a sales pitch just as surely as other boys had learned to deliver baseball pitches.

Discovering your talents can often be half the battle. Making these talents obvious to others is the other half.

CHAPTER 8

Wagon Stories

Every kid loves clean, crisp snow in winter. Me—I also loved the dark, gray ash. Why? Because I was an eleven-year-old entrepreneur.

The winters in Detroit were frigid but, as a kid, I didn't care too much about the cold. I hoped for snow so I could get out of school sometimes and go play with my friends. If there was a blizzard, better still. Bring it on! Even without the snow, the cold wasn't a deterrent from going outside the house, especially for a boy with endless energy. Nothing out of the normal about that.

Here was the difference, though: Unlike most boys, who looked to have fun all the time, I often spent my days trying to figure out ways to make some extra money. One way or the other, I knew a young kid could earn a buck or two if he put his mind to it.

In my childhood, even a little bit of money seemed like a lot. There was no abundance, and part of my incentive to be successful was that I was driven by the hardships in life. Don't get me wrong—my family had everything we needed and I had a happy childhood. But my mom and dad worked hard so that we could enjoy even the basics—and by that I don't mean a TV or stereo. I'm talking about a roof over our heads, food on the table and transportation. You know, the real basics.

I think it's human nature to strive to have more for yourself and your family. I know my dad felt that way, and since we're all products of our environments to some extent, I grew up with the exact same values.

So, to do something about the situation, I came up with an idea. In our neighborhood, there were six homes per housing division, which meant six families. Each of these families had either a wood- or coal-burning stove that ran a minimum of seven months out of the year. As I mentioned, Detroit gets pretty cold.

The ashes that built up in these stoves required removal fairly often. They were placed in metal cans that had to be taken out to the curb. Every Thursday morning, a truck would come by and empty the cans; afterwards, they had to be collected again. Nobody liked going out into the cold more than absolutely necessary, which was where I saw a business opportunity.

For ten cents a container, I offered to take the ash cans from the other families' homes in our immediate neighborhood on Wednesday evening, then return them on Thursday evening after they had been emptied. I still had my wagon, which I would load the cans into to transport them through the ice and snow to the curb.

I made some money this way, and everyone seemed happy to let me handle this chore. Pretty soon I started doing it for other families outside the immediate housing division where we lived. Before long, I was even getting tips from people for my good service.

For most people in my shoes, getting paid per can with an occasional tip thrown in would have meant success. To me, it meant something else. If I was charging ten cents and people were giving me additional money on top of that, it meant I was undercharging everyone. I should have been able to get more money for the service I was providing. This made sense to me, so I began asking for twenty cents a can instead of ten.

This highlights one of my key principles in business even today: Always get what the traffic will bear. I hear about formulas for estimating prices where overhead is calculated and then an additional ten percent is added for standard profits. But what if your niche would support fifty-percent profits or more instead of just ten? I was never one to be afraid of asking for a higher price if I thought the market would support it and the service was worth it. If what you sell or provide is unique and nobody else is offering it, you don't need a formula for that. You just need to assess what people will pay and set your price. As in so many other areas in life, trial and error often works best. Simple, right?

When I later operated a repair business for heavy equipment hydraulics parts and servo valves, no one else was providing that kind of repair service. The companies that manufactured new equipment didn't have the time to repair broken parts. In fact, doing so would have cost them money since it would interrupt their assembly line processes. It was cheaper for them to make and sell new parts than to repair old ones.

But I could repair the old parts inexpensively. If a new piece of equipment was worth $500, how much would a repaired used part be worth to a company? Through trial and error, I realized that I could charge sixty percent of the price for a new part and do well because it didn't cost me anywhere near that much to do the repair. Plus, I was saving the customers the rest of the money it would have cost them for new parts, so they were more than happy to pay it.

If I had simply played it safe and priced my service at a small margin over cost, I would have severely undervalued it. Being unique lets you price your products and services according to what the market will pay. If there is little to no competition, better yet. Prices won't be driven down and you'll reap the benefits.

—————

None of my neighbors had problems with the increase in the price to collect their ash cans. I didn't lose any customers, and I doubled my earnings as a result.

Some people have asked if I ever felt shy or embarrassed about charging a higher price, but that honestly never crossed my mind, even as a boy. I guess it was simply a matter of supply and demand. No one else was collecting those cans and braving the cold weather, so for most people twenty cents was still a bargain.

That mindset worked well then and it works well today. Some things don't change.

And, yes, I still sometimes wish for snow days.

CHAPTER 9

Cleaning Up in Business

By twelve, I was a seasoned pro. My sales pitch was improving—as were my revenues.

One idea evolved into another and I began to see opportunities where others didn't. I also saw a lot of dust and crumbs, thanks to my new business venture.

Knocking on a neighbor's door one Saturday afternoon, I tried out my recently perfected sales pitch. "Hi," I said when he answered. "I'm going around the neighborhood cleaning everyone's couches and chairs."

"Cleaning couches and chairs?" he repeated with a puzzled look on his face.

"Yes. I have a vacuum cleaner that can get all the old dust out of your cushions," I continued.

"Well, I'm not sure they need cleaning." He was still in his dingy robe, looking like he hadn't shaved in a few days. I was pretty sure his furniture wouldn't be in much better condition than he was.

"You'd be surprised how much dust and soot collects over the winter," I told him, undismayed. "I'd be happy to check if you like."

As he ushered me into his living room, I knew I was halfway there. Getting in the door was the first vital step. I'd already learned that from cleaning quite a few couches and chairs by then.

I walked over to my neighbor's couch and slapped my hand on

the cushion. A big puff of dust rose up into the air, which almost always did the trick.

"Wow… I suppose it does need a little cleaning," he said.

I knew then that I had another customer.

World War II had just ended, and many companies had begun making products for private use. One of the latest to hit the market was the vacuum cleaner. My father had bought my mother a brand new Rex-Air and, after she used it to clean our living room, it was obvious to me that we couldn't be the only household with dirty upholstery. With coal and wood burning more than half the year, the dust in the air from the smoke and exhaust buildup gradually seeped into the furniture. Other than taking the cushions outside and beating them with a broom, there was really no other way to clean them well.

Vacuum cleaners were the more modern alternative, though they didn't have bags on them to collect the grime then. Instead, each one had a little bowl filled with water at its base. As the particles of dust and dirt were sucked through the machine, they would get trapped in the water, which had to be emptied intermittently. I don't remember how many bowls it took to clean our furniture, but I'm sure it was several—enough to impress me and give me a good idea.

Fortunately for me, no one else in the neighborhood had a vacuum cleaner and that meant another chance to make some extra money. My mom was getting accustomed to my asking to do odd jobs for other people, so when I asked if I could take the vacuum cleaner around the neighborhood, it came as no big surprise to her. I think she was kind of expecting it since I'd hung around to watch her do the housework instead of disappearing with my friends, like most kids did the second there were chores to be done. So, with my mom's permission—and her vacuum cleaner—I was on my way.

In the 1940s, many homes had formal living rooms or sitting rooms for entertaining guests. Often this was where the nicer furniture was kept, and many families wanted me to clean those couches and chairs first. The family room was usually separate, and sometimes they'd want me to clean the furniture in there as well.

My standard charge was one dollar for every two pieces of furniture. A dollar was a good bit of money then, but the wear and tear on the vacuum cleaner—not to mention the time it took me—made this a fair price. Plus, no one else was doing it.

When I quoted the price to my neighbor with the five o'clock shadow, I could have sworn his face went a little white underneath all the stubble. In fact, from the moment he'd first opened the door, I could tell he was going to be a difficult customer.

"You're charging a dollar for cleaning two pieces of furniture?" he balked.

"Yes. I'm sure you'll be happy when it's all nice and clean. It'll look a hundred percent better—like new furniture, but for only a dollar," I said.

"I see. Well, how about you do it for seventy-five cents?"

"I've been charging a dollar all day. You can ask some of the other neighbors. I'm sure they'll tell you it was worth it."

"Yeah? I'll tell you what," he countered. "If you can do it for seventy-five cents, I'll let you clean my couch and one of my chairs. Otherwise, I'll pass."

I thought it over, then agreed to do it for the discounted price— that was how badly I wanted the job. Big mistake.

He led me into his sitting room, with its three-seat, upholstered couch and high-back chair, which were by far the filthiest pieces of furniture I had ever seen. At one time—maybe the end of the First

World War—their fabric might have been light beige with a floral print, but now the overall color was gray with wilted weeds. I wanted to turn around and leave as soon as I saw them.

"Okay, these are the ones I want cleaned," he announced. "I'll be in the living room."

I was at the man's house for nearly four hours before I had gotten all the soot and dust out of his furniture and restored them to something you'd actually want to sit on. As I left with my hard-earned seventy-five cents, I vowed never to undersell my services again—and I still don't to this day. It would have been better for me had I walked away from that job rather than spending half the day cleaning for the reduced rate.

I had already figured out what the market would bear for cleaning two pieces of furniture; plenty of people had paid a dollar and were very pleased with the results. There was absolutely no reason to take a lower price—it wasn't fair to me.

To make matters worse, on my way home with the vacuum cleaner, while I was thinking over my bad decision, two older boys approached me. One was tall and lanky, the other a bit shorter and chunky. It was like coming face to face with an ostrich and a bulldog.

"Hey, kid, we hear you've been making a little extra money cleaning furniture," the ostrich announced.

"What's it to you?" I replied.

"Plenty, 'cause you're gonna hand over your money to us," he responded.

"No, I'm not."

"We'll see about that," the bulldog chimed in.

Before I knew it they were throwing punches at me, and I felt anger like never before. I was like a trapped tiger, fighting with all my might to break free. I kept swinging and swinging well after they had given up. There was no way I would part with even seventy-five cents, especially after the misery I'd gone through to get it. And there was no way a bird and a dog were any match for a tiger.

The two boys finally retreated, shouting threats to try to save face. As with most bullies, they didn't turn out to be as tough as they thought they were.

I left with my profits still in my pocket, never having had any problem fighting for what was right. That went more so for anyone who tried to mess with my money. Every dollar I'd earned was through honest labor and ingenuity—and still is. If someone decided to try to take that from me, they'd have a serious battle on their hands. Those two boys found out the hard way, as have several other people throughout my career.

Being fair and honest gives you the freedom to fight for what's just without having to worry about hypocrisy. You never need to compromise your values, whether it comes to standing up for yourself or sticking to your price for cleaning furniture. I might have learned that last part a little too late, but it's a lesson that has served me well through the years.

It's the same in business as it is with vacuum cleaners: Sometimes, when you make a mistake, you've just got to suck it up and push on.

CHAPTER 10

Baseball and Legends

I wasn't just a tiger in business. I was a tiger, too, when it came to baseball—well, at least, I was an avid fan of the Detroit Tigers. As a teen, I also played in the city's Bill Rogell League, which was the forerunner of Little League.

Bill Rogell was a great short stop who played for the Tigers. After his career in the majors he dedicated himself to civic duties in Detroit, which taught me a lot about giving back. He formed a youth baseball league in which teams from different neighborhoods would play against one another; large enough neighborhoods might even have had two teams.

We only had one team representing our area and my goal was to play third base. I liked the position well enough, but I had a bigger reason for wanting it: Third base was where you could find my favorite player of all time, George Kell.

Kell had grown up in Swifton, Arkansas—less than ten miles from where I'd been born. He learned the basics of the sport from his father, the town barber, and, from that humble beginning, went on to become a ten-time Major League all-star with a career batting average over .300. Later, he became larger than life as a Detroit Tigers' broadcast announcer. Everything Kell ever did turned to gold.

I first learned of George Kell in 1947, when my then-favorite player, Barney McClosky, was traded for him. The news first shocked and depressed me, but my father fixed that problem by informing me of Kell's Arkansas roots. That was all it took for me to feel a bond with the team's newest player, and before long I dreamed of playing third base as well as he did.

My neighborhood team in the Bill Rogell League was like all the other teams—our managers and coaches were volunteers, and we relied on local gas stations and pub owners to sponsor us in order to get jerseys and equipment. Our team had only enough money for nine jerseys, one for each of those lucky enough to play during the game. If you got hurt or lost your position, you had to give up your jersey. Those were the breaks.

Now, our jerseys were green and yellow and just plain ugly, but wearing one made me stand out—and not in a bad way. I had earned that uniform and a position at third, but it didn't take long for me to lose both.

During one of the early season games, I watched in agony—and seeming slow motion—as a ground ball snuck beneath my glove and through my legs, allowing the other team to score. When I looked over at my team manager, the stern expression on his face said everything I needed to know about getting my act together in the infield. That expression got even worse when the next ground ball did the same exact thing.

"Phillips," he announced, when the inning was over, "you're not playing third anymore."

After taking off my jersey and handing it to my replacement, I went into the dugout and sat on the bench. We finished the game, and I walked home in a plain old T-shirt.

As I entered my house, my mother was cooking dinner. She glanced in my direction when she heard the door open and close.

"How was your game?" she asked.

"Okay," I answered.

"Where's your jersey?"

"I lost it."

"How'd that happen?"

"I let two ground balls go past me," I flatly replied.

"That's too bad."

That acknowledgement and a pat on the head were my only consolation, and from there, life moved on. There was no dwelling on the loss of the jersey—or on my embarrassment. My parents didn't call the coach to complain and I knew whining wouldn't get me anywhere; it simply was what it was.

During my childhood, people focused on putting food on the table and having enough to get by. A few hurt feelings were nothing to be concerned about. Toughness was what counted. It wasn't only expected—it was required.

Despite my disappointment over losing my jersey, my love of baseball remained as strong as ever, as did my interest in George Kell. I learned that he spent the off season near his hometown of Swifton, and he became involved in automotive dealerships after his career as a short stop was over.

As luck would have it, my cousin James became close with George's family and even managed a car dealership with him in Newport, Arkansas. James was my mother's sister's son, and he and I always had a great relationship.

In 1984, he invited me to meet George Kell, and I was honored, to say the least. I made the trip to Newport to shake the hand of the man who had been one of my childhood heroes. Kell had just been inducted into the National Baseball Hall of Fame and had written an autobiography. The visit was brief, but he was humble and a gentleman, and I left with my own personally signed copy of his book, as well as a great memory.

George Kell passed away on March 24, 2009. James invited me to the funeral in Swifton, but the huge attendance would have made it nearly impossible for me to gain any personal meaning from the occasion. As far as I was concerned, meeting him years before had been special enough. His humility and generosity taught me a great deal about how success should be handled.

Kell portrayed himself as an average guy despite his accomplishments and, in fact, he was. No matter how great his batting average or how many broadcasting awards he received, he was just a man doing what he loved and doing it well. Success is a great thing, but keeping it in perspective is important, as is not losing sight of what got you there in the first place.

I don't follow baseball as closely as I once did, but I still love the sport—despite the many changes in its management and marketing. The history of the game is incredibly rich and I'm sure that players like George Kell still exist among today's teams, unaffected by steroid scandals and contract negotiations.

Hopefully, kids today can learn the same thing from them that a ballplayer from Swifton, Arkansas, showed me: The potential for greatness can be found in every single one of us. All it takes to achieve it is working hard at what we love—and always keeping our eyes on the ball.

CHAPTER 11

The Wrong Route

By the time I was fifteen years old, I was a newspaperman. Okay, a newspaper delivery boy, if you want to get technical. But it was still a start in media sales.

At that point in my life, odd jobs around the neighborhood weren't steady or lucrative enough for my liking. Getting a job with one of the newspaper companies around town seemed like a more reliable way to earn some money.

Newspaper routes were pretty common afterschool jobs for boys my age, and my buddy's father worked for the *Detroit News*, which gave me the opportunity to start peddling papers on a street corner in addition to still doing odd jobs here and there. I also sold the *Detroit Free Press* wherever I could and had a regular route for the *Detroit Times*. I was responsible for delivering so much news that I felt like Edward R. Murrow, only with ink-stained hands.

I ran my regular newspaper route on foot or bicycle, delivering the papers as well as collecting money from my customers on a weekly basis. The *Detroit Times* cost forty-five cents a week for daily delivery and the majority of my customers paid without any difficulty, but occasionally some couldn't afford it or would try to finagle their way out of paying the bill. Unfortunately for me, that meant I was out the money—the *Times* wouldn't reimburse me for deliveries I couldn't collect. But they wanted a good customer base, so they had a vested interest in keeping their customers happy.

On my normal route, there was one customer who was always trouble—isn't there one in every crowd? He either would be late in his payments or would purposefully avoid me when it came time to collect. At first I didn't think much of it, assuming he was just having a rough spell, but pretty soon I began to get irritated by not getting paid for my work.

One day, as I was delivering newspapers, I caught him just as he was about to take off in his Chevrolet. The sound of my voice startled him, and the look on his face suggested he was less than thrilled to see me coming.

"Mr. Hancock, I need to collect the last two weeks' payments for the newspaper," I announced as I came up his front walkway.

"Not today," he replied. "I'll pay next week."

"I'm sorry but I need to collect the money for the paper today," I insisted.

"Well, I can't pay today. It will just have to wait 'til next week."

"Then I'll just hold delivery until you can catch up."

"I'll catch up, but don't go holding any delivery," he snapped. "Just bring me my paper and I'll pay when I can."

"Sorry, I can't do that. I'd be happy to deliver it again once you pay."

"What's your name?" he asked, narrowing his eyes.

"Bill Phillips."

"I'll have a talk with your manager and see what he thinks about you refusing to give me my paper."

"That's fine. I'm sure he won't want to give you one, either, until you pay for it."

"We'll just see about that."

It never fails: The customers who can't pay or who refuse to stick to agreements are always the most vocal. So, I wasn't surprised that when I got back to the newspaper office, my manager was waiting to speak with me. Of course, the guy had called and complained about my not delivering his newspaper, to which he felt entitled whether he paid or not. But I had pretty strong feelings to the contrary. After all, it was my paycheck he was messing with.

"Bill, let me have a word with you," my manager said as I dropped off my newspaper bag for the evening.

"Yes, Mr. Ryan," I replied, knowing exactly where this was going.

"I heard you refused to deliver the newspaper to one of our customers today," he began.

"The guy refused to pay for it, plus he still owes me for two weeks."

"Well, I want you to deliver his newspaper to him tomorrow and let me worry about his bill."

"No, I don't think so," I said.

"What do you mean you don't think so?"

"I'm the one picking up the papers and delivering them to his house. If he doesn't pay for me to do that, then I'm not gonna deliver his paper."

"Well, I'm *telling* you to deliver it to him, Bill."

"I'm sorry, but I'm not going to," I stated simply.

My manager was absolutely dumbfounded. In front of him was a fifteen-year-old boy refusing—on principle—to do what he was told. I don't think he'd ever been presented with such a dilemma. I was a good delivery boy, always punctual and reliable, and I did my job well. It must have seemed out of character for me to be so resistant all of sudden, but to me it was perfectly consistent with who I was: someone who always stood up for what he thought was right.

This customer expected to get something for nothing—and while that something was a newspaper printed by the *Detroit Times,* part of the money he paid went to me for delivering it. If the manager wanted to give him a paper for free, that was his business. But I wasn't about to bring it to him. That, I felt, was *my* decision. The guy could go get his own paper at the newsstand if he really wanted it that badly.

My manager leaned back in his chair, took off his glasses and laid them on the desk in front of him.

"Bill, either make the deliveries or I'm gonna have to give your route to someone else," he said.

"I'm not delivering to him until he pays his bill."

I suppose my manager had no choice but to let me go; even so, I think he respected me for taking a stand.

The saying that "the customer is always right" is important in providing good service, but there's a point when customers may demand more than what's fair. Being in the newspaper business, I saw the issue as black and white.

After that, I began working for the *Detroit Free Press,* a much smaller newspaper with morning and evening editions and a much smaller client base. My regular customers paid four cents per home delivery—and the best part was that they paid as each paper was delivered, so I never had to deal with a payment problem again.

Perhaps it was the natural salesman and entrepreneur in me taking the initiative, but before long I saw an opportunity to earn a little extra money by carrying five extra copies of the evening edition with me on my normal route each day. As I delivered to my regular customers, I'd yell, "*Free Press!* Get today's copy of the *Free Press!*" along the way. I'd charge five cents to anyone who wanted to buy one—and I usually sold out of those extra copies. Just goes to show that there's opportunity everywhere, even in our normal routes and routines.

In addition to my newspaper routes, I had another part-time job working as a pinsetter in the local bowling alley. Automatic pinsetters had yet to be invented, so my job was to collect and replace the pins after they fell and send the bowling balls back down the alleys to the customers. If I worked extremely fast, the manager gave me two lanes instead of one (we'll call it a "spare"), which meant double the money for the same amount of time. As you might guess, I handled the two lanes, making the most of the opportunity.

Thankfully, as a boy and as an adult, I have always had a great deal of energy. I did my schoolwork, took on extra jobs and have never been afraid of working hard—but I also believed in being treated fairly. You get what you give.

Having many diverse jobs early in life gave me a hands-on education in good business practices and how to deal with even the toughest of customers. While books and formal education are important, nothing is as powerful as experience.

From my early neighborhood jobs to selling newspapers and setting up pins, each opportunity took me a little farther down the path toward becoming an entrepreneur, which I guess you could say was "right down my alley."

CHAPTER 12

A Father of Invention

It used to be that commercials regularly interrupted your television shows; now, it seems that the programs are what interrupt the advertisements. If you go to any professional sporting event, sponsorships saturate every square inch of the arena or stadium, to the point that you wonder whether the guy on first is thinking about stealing second or switching his auto insurance.

In the late 1940s, however, none of these techniques were common. But door-to-door salesmen were.

After the war, veterans flocked to these positions and sold a variety of items in different neighborhoods. I'd see them quite often, so I easily picked up some sales techniques by paying attention to their pitches. And, believe me, I put them to good use.

My grandfather must have passed down some of his ingenuity through his genes, since Dad was quite an inventor as well, with some impressive ideas of his own.

When I was sixteen, he designed and created a lawn sprinkler. Those weren't common in 1949—and the one he invented was even more unique. Depending on the volume of water that was pumped through the sprinkler, it could cover a radius of eighteen inches to fifteen feet, plus it ran smoothly, in contrast to many of the other devices on the market. His secret was the addition of ball bearings that allowed the sprinkler head to rotate evenly.

My dad and I produced and manufactured these lawn sprinklers in our garage, and we even had the design officially patented. Everything was done professionally before we ever set out to make our first sale. That was a great thing about my father: He paid attention to details and wasn't afraid of working hard. With his plumbing knowledge from being a pipefitter and my newly honed sales technique, his lawn sprinkler was sure to be a success.

My father and I began driving around the neighborhood, selling our product door to door. Each of us carried a sprinkler in hand for demonstration purposes and had plenty of others in the car if we were successful in a sale.

When we came upon an appealing street, Dad would take one side and I would take the other. House by house, we rang doorbells and tried to get homeowners to let us demonstrate the sprinklers on their lawns, knowing that if we could show their ability, the likelihood of sales was much greater. It was a similar strategy to the one I'd used while cleaning furniture: Seeing really was believing—especially when it came to customers seeing benefits and results.

Despite the age difference, I actually had more experience in sales than my father did. His background had been mostly in factories, but I had already been out selling flowers, cleaning services and newspapers—and had become pretty savvy about getting my foot in the door and marketing a product. So, it was no surprise to either of us that I sold more sprinklers than my dad did on any given day.

"Hello, my name is Bill Phillips," I announced one afternoon to a typical customer as he opened the door of his home. "How are you today?"

"I'm doing alright," the man answered. "Can I help you?"

"I noticed you keep your lawn in really good shape."

"I do. I like working in the yard," he replied. "What can I do for you?"

"With all this dry weather, I have something that can help you keep your lawn looking great."

"What's that?"

"It's the latest in lawn sprinkler design. It lets you water your lawn at whatever radius you want all the way up to fifteen feet."

"Well, I don't know. I do pretty well with my hose."

"Which hose? That one over there?" I said, pointing to it nearby.

"Yes."

"Could I just give you a look at what this sprinkler can do as opposed to just an ordinary hose?"

"Sure," he said, excitedly.

Of course, this was my sales pitch, but it was an honest one. The man's lawn *was* nicely kept, and I promoted the product accurately—as I have throughout my life. I learned early that when conducting sales, sincerity and honesty work much better than trying to trick someone into buying a product or service. If you can't deliver on what you say, you will lose a customer for life. But if you honor your word and give it to them straight, they keep coming back and buying more.

As I began to show this man how well my father's sprinkler design worked, his neighbor's balding head popped up over the fence. I suspect that he had been watching me go door to door and had finally gotten his chance to heckle the salesman. I also suspect that he didn't want to be outdone by his neighbor, who was already considering purchasing the sprinkler.

I went about my business, connecting the lawn sprinkler to the hose, and gradually adjusted the volume of the water to show how it spread evenly and smoothly across the lawn in an increased radius. Without question, my customer was interested, and he began to ask more about the product's ability.

"That's pretty nifty," he said, impressed. "Is it guaranteed to last?"

"Yes," I replied. "We guarantee it for a year after purchase."

"I don't know, Sam," the neighbor said, still peering over the fence. "I know a guy at work who bought a sprinkler and it never worked right."

My customer turned and looked at his neighbor, then back at me.

"You'll replace it if it doesn't work correctly, right?" he asked, seeming to want to appease his neighbor.

"Yes," I assured him. "If anything doesn't work properly, I'll be happy to make it right."

"How much is it?" my customer asked.

"Two dollars and fifty cents," I stated.

"I wouldn't pay that much," the neighbor interrupted. "I saw one at the hardware store last week for half that price."

"I'm sure you won't find anything like this for less money," I said. "In fact, you won't find anything quite like this at all."

"Sam, it ain't worth it," the neighbor stated.

My customer hesitated. "Maybe I'll think it over," he finally said.

Man, was that neighbor lucky a fence was there to separate us! Steaming mad, but trying to stay professional, I picked up my sprinkler and put the hose back in its place. As I did, my customer leaned over and whispered, "Come back tomorrow." He wanted to buy the sprinkler but didn't want to do it in front of his nosy neighbor.

I was happy to make the sale the next day, but for the life of me couldn't figure out why my customer didn't have the guts to stand up to his neighbor and tell him to mind his own business, especially since the neighbor was getting in the way of his best interests. He could've missed out on this opportunity—and many more in life.

My father and I, on the other hand, made the most of our opportunities. By the end of the summer we'd sold many lawn sprinklers, and I'd even arranged a deal to sell half a dozen to the local hardware store for a nice profit.

My experience selling lawn sprinklers helped me to become a

better salesperson overall and taught me a lot about personalities and people. It also showed me that sales involves more than a sprinkling of sociology and psychology.

CHAPTER 13

Pots, Pans and Wallpaper

"I think I've heard enough," the man stated bluntly as he opened his front door, showing us the way out. "I've changed my mind about buying the pans. I'm not interested."

Obviously, things hadn't gone so well, but only a day earlier, the sale had been as good as guaranteed. How could it all have gone so wrong?

I had just graduated high school and hadn't yet decided what I was going to do with my life. But I knew I liked sales and business, so I decided to improve my skills by working for a company that sold pots and pans, as well as some other kitchenware, door to door. Given my experience and enthusiasm, I thought I would be a perfect fit for the job and that I'd gain some valuable tricks of the trade along the way.

Turned out the first trick was on me.

I'd been working for this company for several weeks and still hadn't made a single sale. Every evening I walked around neighborhoods, knocking on doors until I wasn't sure which hurt worse, my feet or my knuckles. I'd go into my sales pitch, marketing my pots and pans, hoping for that elusive first sale.

I always went in the evenings because that was when both the husband and wife were most likely home. I'd make the sales pitch to the wife, since she'd be the one using the products, but the husband usually made the decision on whether or not to purchase them. Despite these carefully thought out strategies and my best efforts, I had been unsuccessful so far.

One evening, I came to the home of a nice man who opened the door and allowed me to come inside to present my wares. I sat down at his kitchen table with my demonstration bag, and he took the seat across from me, listening intently as I showed him the pots and pans and answered his questions.

"You know, I might like to buy a set of those as a gift for my daughter," he said. "But I'd like to think about it some more. Would you mind coming back tomorrow night?"

"Of course," I replied, thrilled to make my potential first sale. "I'll bring the entire collection so you can choose exactly what you'd like."

We agreed on a time and I left.

The next morning, as luck would have it, I attended a seminar at the local branch office of my company; its title was "Better Techniques in Sales." The district manager was traveling around to all the branch offices, offering guidance on how to make the best sales pitch possible. He was supposedly an expert, and my branch was hoping to improve its figures by educating its force. For me, it was a win-win: I was all for making more sales *and* learning more about the business.

The district manager looked to be only in his late twenties. With his jet-black hair slicked back onto his scalp, he stood up in front of about a dozen of us salespeople and gave his speech. He spoke with confidence and sounded quite knowledgeable. At the end of his talk, he held a question-and-answer session, and I mentioned that I had a pending sale with a customer that evening. He offered to come along to demonstrate the "finer" skills of sales to me. What could it have hurt, right?

When we arrived at the appointment, I introduced him to my

customer, who invited us inside. What I failed to mention—what I didn't think *needed* to be mentioned—to this expert salesman/district manager of mine was that the inside of this man's home had an interesting style of wallpaper for that era: one of the earliest varieties of brown burlap paperweave grasscloth. Very few people even knew about this particular wall covering, and even fewer had it in their homes. It wasn't inexpensive, either.

Apparently, my district sales manager had never seen anything like it, and his opinion was less than enthusiastic. "Where did you get that wallpaper?" he asked in a tone that clearly inferred distaste.

The customer paused. Feeling a bit of tension, I quickly interjected my own question as a diversion. "Would you like to see the other products that I brought?"

"Sure," the man responded as we all sat down in the living room.

"I don't think I've ever seen anything like it," the district manager continued, still looking around distractedly at the décor. He hadn't seemed to notice that we'd moved on. "Did the house come this way?"

"No," the customer replied, notably irritated by my manager's lack of sensitivity.

"These are the pots you were most interested in," I interrupted again, trying to refocus the conversation on business.

By that time, it was too late. If the customer had had any interest in making a purchase, it evaporated once my manager opened his mouth.

One of the important rules of sales is that in order to create a sense of satisfaction with a purchase, you must make the customer feel appreciated. By voicing his dissatisfaction with the customer's décor, my manager had done the exact opposite, making him feel disrespected and unappreciated. Creating a good feeling about buying the products was nearly impossible once the mood had been altered as drastically as that.

It came down to this: My manager either was purposefully trying to sabotage my sale or was the worst salesperson I had ever met in my life. Either way, I lost the sale. We weren't in that man's home more than five minutes before he kicked us to the curb. It was one of the most horrible sales calls I'd ever had. And to think this guy was supposed to be some kind of expert brought in to teach the entire company's sales force! With an education like that, we'd be bankrupt in no time.

The next morning, I turned in all my pots and pans and left the company. The position had done little to improve my sales skills—at most, it taught me a thing or two about what *not* to do.

In this case, as in so many others, appearances were extremely deceiving. This company was one of the largest kitchenware manufacturers but had terrible sales techniques and marketing campaigns. Just because it was the biggest definitely did not make it the best. And its expert district "manager" had managed to destroy my sale. I'd have been stunned if he'd ever improved anyone's ability—much less be invited into many people's homes.

Though I was only eighteen, I knew more about sales than he did. My approach was to assess how a customer reacted to a product and then provide them with the information they needed to make a decision—and that usually worked well.

I wasn't dishonest and never used false information to make a sale, but I could put on many different faces and be somewhat of a chameleon, which helped in understanding potential customers and their needs. The district manager had not yet learned this basic rule.

I knew this job wasn't going to make me a better salesperson, so I had no qualms about walking away. I would have been offered better opportunities anywhere else—possibly even on the unemployment line!

Trusting that the district manager was indeed a sales expert was initially an honest mistake, but continuing to believe it after that first experience would have been foolish on my part and against my better instincts.

Sometimes, you just have to see the writing on the grasscloth-covered wall.

CHAPTER 14

Dairy Indulgences

Of course, life wasn't all work. I was probably a little more interested in earning a buck or two than many other teenagers, but I had my fair share of fun as well.

After my experience with selling pots and pans, I got a summer job working with my friend Hugh at a local dairy plant, where I had worked after school during my senior year.

The owner had four stores, all of which sold bottled milk, ice cream and other dairy products. The main store also had a plant to bottle the milk and a drive-in restaurant for hamburgers, cheeseburgers, milkshakes and more. Hugh and I spent most of our time at the main store but traveled to all of the locations, making deliveries and picking up empty bottles. But that wasn't all we were trying to pick up.

Bottling milk and working at a dairy plant might not sound like that much fun, but you have to consider the environment. First of all, there were ice cream and milkshakes around, which was always nice, but, more importantly, all the stores—especially the main one—employed attractive girls to wait on the customers. Being the only two young guys amidst so many pretty women wasn't a bad way to spend the summer. Let's just say it was all the motivation Hugh and I needed to get up in the morning and go to work.

One of our tasks was to drive the dairy truck to the satellite stores, where we delivered full bottles of milk and other products and collected the empties to take back to the main plant. Both of us took turns driving the truck while we talked about life, goals and girls. Okay, mostly girls.

Hugh was one of my best friends from high school and working with him made the summer fun, despite all the hard work we did. But the highlight was pulling up in front of the girls when we were driving the big box truck, which we thought made us look pretty important.

"I hope Michelle's working today," I said to Hugh as we approached one of the stores. "I'm gonna ask her out for this Saturday if she is."

"She isn't gonna go out with you," he replied.

"Why not?"

"Because I'm gonna ask her first," he stated with a grin.

Hugh was only joking, but the fact was that we did manage to fill our date schedules when we made our rounds.

We weren't under much pressure about time as we unloaded the milk bottles from the truck and placed them in the refrigerators, so we'd take a few short breaks to have conversations with the girls. Sometimes we even got lucky and spent a little bit of time making out in a refrigerator room—which definitely made the deliveries worth it. What's better than kissing a hot girl in a cool room on a warm, summer day?

Once, I got an unexpected surprise in the refrigerator room at one of the remote stores. Rachel, a girl I had been out with a few times, was working that day. I thought she might want to take a break with me for a moment or two.

"Hi, Rachel," I said with a smile as I walked in with a crate of milk. "Wanna help me load this into the cooler?"

"Hmm. I don't know, Bill," she replied flirtatiously.

"I thought maybe you could help me with the door," I coaxed.

"Oh, is that what you thought?" she said with a grin.

"What else would I be thinking?"

Despite my best lines, Rachel decided not to help me with the refrigerator door that day—which was fortunate because as I went into the back of the store and opened the cooler, I saw that someone else had beaten me to the punch. It seemed that Hugh and I weren't the only ones who used the refrigerator for some extracurricular activity.

"Excuse me," I stammered, setting the milk crate on the floor and turning to make a quick exit.

"We were just taking inventory," the store manager replied, wiping lipstick off his face.

"Sure," I said, walking out.

I could barely keep from laughing as I made my way to the truck. I had just caught the store manager with one of the waitresses—and I was sure his wife wouldn't have appreciated that very much. I wasn't even married and I knew not to treat women that way. You didn't cheat in business and you didn't cheat on commitments. It was that simple.

Hugh and I packed up quickly that day, talking about it the whole way back to the main store. We never told anyone else at the dairy plant about what I'd seen, but from that day on, we always checked the coolers first before we invited anyone in with us.

What I took away from that job—other than a few phone numbers—was the lesson that no matter what you do in life, people make experiences richer. It's important to get to know those you work with; whether it's a colleague, an employee or a consultant, everyone has a great deal to offer, sometimes even friendship. You should give people respect until they stop earning it, and you should never cheat them no matter what.

In the end, you'll remember those people you meet more than

you remember how much money you make or how many hours you put in. And if you're lucky like I was, the people around you will help make work a little "cooler."

PART II

For Love and Country

CHAPTER 15

Joining the Air Force

The sky's the limit!

That was how I always felt about the opportunities that the Air Force provided, so, that summer after graduating high school, I decided to join. In fact, Hugh and I ended up joining the military together, enlisting for the Korean War.

Many of my friends chose to work on factory assembly lines instead, but for the life of me I couldn't understand why. Factories offered security but few opportunities for the future. Why would a young man with the world ahead of him ever choose security over opportunity?

Many years later, I saw one of my high-school friends who had made that choice and dedicated his life to factory work. He was two years away from retirement and couldn't wait for that day to arrive. But when I asked him what he would do once retired, he didn't have any plans.

"I think I'll just relax and lie around the house," he replied.

That might have sounded good to him, but I've always known that type of lifestyle just isn't for me. I'll take opportunity and action over security and lying around any day of the week.

By early 1952, I was ready for a change.

The Korean War began in 1950 as North Korea pushed into South Korea in what was, in theory, a civil war. But being that the Cold War was in full throttle, allies of both of the Korean sides expanded it into a much larger conflict. The Soviet Union and eventually China sided with North Korea while the United Nations, including U.S. forces, went to the aid of South Korea.

Open enlistment had been approved, and I made the choice to serve my country. It was a decision that would significantly shape the rest of my life.

My first stop was Lackland Air Force Base in San Antonio, Texas. Known as the gateway to the Air Force, Lackland was the main basic training center for all new recruits and had been established as part of Kelly Fields in 1942, during World War II. When the U.S. Air Force was recognized as a distinct branch of the military in 1947, the base was renamed after General Frank Lackland, who first conceptualized an aviation training center for cadets.

After three months of basic training at Lackland, I was enrolled in airplane mechanics training at Sheppard Air Force Base in northwest Texas. I thoroughly enjoyed being at Sheppard; working with aircraft at that time was like working with the space shuttle today. It was one of the coolest jobs around.

After I learned about airplane systems in general, the training center administered an exam to assess my understanding of the mechanical concepts. As a result of my high marks, I was ordered to go to Chanute Field in southern Illinois to become a hydraulics specialist.

Learning hydraulics would turn out to be the cornerstone of much of my success in business, but well before that I was interested in the technical aspects of mechanical systems. With my background predominantly in sales, I would have expected topics like hydraulics systems to be less than exciting, but both my father and grandfather had been inventors, and I naturally had a strong interest in how things worked.

I remember how, early in high school, many boys—including me—had taken shop class; we'd worked with metal and wood, learning the basics of various trades. Repeatedly, someone in the class stole the tools. Because theft was such a serious issue and a cost to the school, the punishment was that everyone in the class had to study "shop math" for an entire week, which school officials hoped would prompt the culprit to confess—or prompt his classmates to tell on him. I don't recall that either of those scenarios ever came to pass, so for quite a few weeks, while the machines didn't operate, we'd learn shop math, and I received a healthy dose of basic engineering mathematics because of it.

As strange as it sounds, that high school punishment was a good educational foundation for my time at Chanute Field, which was the technical training center for the Air Force, located about 100 miles south of Chicago. As enlisted men, when we were granted holidays, we could travel only within seventy-five miles of base, which intentionally kept us out of Chicago and kept our minds on our training.

At Chanute, we were taught a variety of skills concerning aircraft repair; life-support specialists and firefighters underwent training there as well. Named after Octave Chanute, a late-nineteenth-century aeronautical pioneer, the center was well known for being technically savvy, and some of the best technical mechanics and specialists trained there.

As I learned to repair hydraulics on several aircraft, including those made by Douglas, Boeing, Grumman and more, little did I realize that this knowledge would change the course of my life. It was the beginning of my career in both hydraulics and aerospace.

When my specialty training was completed, I received my next assignment and found out where I would be stationed.

"Airman Phillips," my technical sergeant called out.

"Yes, sir," I said, stepping forward.

"You will be in the Northeast Air Command. Your assignment is Pepperrell Air Force Base in Newfoundland."

"Yes, sir."

I only had a rough idea where Newfoundland was. Other than Arkansas, Michigan, Texas and Illinois, I had never traveled anywhere—let alone ventured out of the country. Newfoundland could have been on the opposite side of the world for all I knew. But I had a thirty-day leave before my three-year term of duty began, so that gave me plenty of time to buy a map and figure it out.

It turned out that Newfoundland occupied the easternmost part of Canada—so, needless to say, it was a bit cold when I arrived, and remained that way for most of the year. The U.S. had built bases there during the latter part of World War II to ensure the safety of Atlantic Ocean supply ships, and Newfoundland actually had two Air Force stations.

<hr />

Though we weren't near the actual combat of the Korean War, our activities were anything but safe. My assignment had me traveling to other bases in the Northeast Air Command, including one in Labrador, one in Iceland, three in Greenland and one close to the North Pole. While flying through Greenland, which we often did, the planes had to travel up a long, narrow *fjord,* tightly squeezed between two steep mountains, in order to reach two of the bases.

Our landing strip wasn't exactly a welcoming sight upon arrival: There was only one approach path and if we overshot the runway, we'd head off a mountain. More than one plane was lost that way during my tour of duty.

One time, a buddy of mine and I were traveling on a flight through Greenland when the plane lost one of its four engines, which became completely engulfed in flames.

"Pull the fire extinguisher on engine number two!" the pilot yelled out.

My friend John quickly pulled the lever that released the nitrogen foam to extinguish the fire in the second engine.

"There's still a fire, sir," John yelled back.

"Pull it again, Airman!"

The second time, the fire was extinguished and John sat back down with the rest of us. But the relief was short-lived.

"Put your life jackets on, boys," the pilot announced.

"What for?" one of the other airmen asked.

There was no response. I'm not sure that he was really expecting one, either.

We all knew that if the other engine went out, we'd be falling directly into the ocean. With or without life jackets, we would all freeze to death instantly—that was, if we somehow survived the crash. But this was the military, so we did as we were told and secured our life jackets in place.

We made it safely to our target base. Still, there I was, not even twenty years old, flying in the most extreme conditions, with temperatures at that altitude dropping to sixty below zero. Despite the rugged terrain, however, I was happy to be there and wouldn't have traded it for the world.

Servicing the hydraulics systems on aircraft throughout the Northeast Air Command was a challenge, which I've always liked, and I became intrigued by aeronautical technologies and the engineering of hydraulics, and learned as much about them as I could. I truly believe that everything happens for a reason, and my stint in the Air Force was one of the best decisions I ever made. It molded the rest of my life in many ways.

I had finally discovered something besides sales and business that started a fire in me—and all it took was a tour of duty in freezing Newfoundland to light it.

CHAPTER 16

One in Every Crowd

There's an old Air Force joke that goes like this: An Air Force commander was waiting to depart from Pepperell Air Base in Newfoundland. He was in a hurry to leave but couldn't until his aircraft's holding tank had been pumped out. The airman assigned to the job came late, then was slow in performing his duties.

With each minute that the commander was stuck on the ground, he became angrier, berating the airman and threatening strict punishment if he didn't get the task done immediately. The airman responded, "Sir, I have no stripes, it's twenty below zero, I'm stationed in Newfoundland and I'm pumping sewage out of airplanes. What could you possibly do to punish me more?"

This joke goes to show two things: One, military life isn't easy; it's hardcore and often mentally and physically punishing. Two, it helps to have a sense of humor, even under intense pressure and stressful conditions. In fact, that's often when we need it most of all.

⁓

While stationed in Newfoundland, I witnessed a wide range of talents among my fellow enlisted men: There were gifted musicians, natural athletes and some with skills that were completely unpredictable. My friend Butler was one of the latter. His specialty was seeing the lighter side of life and drawing cartoons—particularly caricatures of officers and enlisted men. Unfortunately, our colonel wasn't much of an art lover and didn't appreciate Butler's unique talents or sense of humor.

In many ways, Butler reminded me of Corporal Klinger from the TV show *M*A*S*H*—minus the women's clothing. He was always pulling some stunt and getting into trouble just for the sake of stirring things up. One day he'd gain a stripe and the next day he'd lose it. But Butler didn't really care about the stripes. He was more interested in keeping up morale and having a little fun at the expense of some of the officers.

He enjoyed antagonizing one of our colonels in particular—a short man who was constantly in a bad mood. Butler took great pleasure in provoking him, and we all got a kick out of it, too, since no one really liked this colonel. I suppose a built-in audience made it that much more fun for Butler—and judging by how often he got in trouble, the punishments and reprimands must have been worth it for the laughs he got.

I'll give you an example of his brand of humor. On the air base, both the officers and the enlisted men would relax in a coffee shop located in the hangar. In between flights or assignments, we'd congregate to enjoy some company and some hot coffee, sharing jokes and stories, discussing the news and getting to know each other a little better.

Coffee mugs hung from hooks on the walls, and everyone—officers and enlisted men alike—had his own cup for easy access. We all knew whose mug was whose depending on the name, nickname or design that labeled it.

As part of his normal routine, Butler would snag the colonel's coffee mug whenever he was off base and drink out of it in joking defiance. He did that almost every day—until the colonel happened to walk in on him one time.

"Butler!" the colonel yelled. "I assume you know that's my coffee mug you're drinking out of."

"Oh?" Butler replied innocently. "I didn't realize, sir."

"I'm sure you didn't," the colonel responded sarcastically. "Get over there and wash it out for me…now!"

"Yes, sir, Colonel," Butler replied, casually getting out of his chair. "Would you like me to pour your coffee as well, sir?"

The colonel glared at him, trying to figure out if he was being patronizing or exactly what he was up to.

"Butler," the colonel finally drawled, "what is your problem?"

"My mother dropped me on my head once, sir, and…" He left the sentence hanging, as if that explained everything. Besides, I think Butler felt that the *colonel* was the one with the problem.

"That's it, Butler," the colonel yelled. "In my office, pronto!"

Once again, Butler was going to lose a stripe. But he wasn't hung up on things like rank or status; he was more interested in having a good time, no matter where he was. Even on an Air Force base in Newfoundland.

I liked Butler's attitude. He had confidence, always pulled his own weight, and loved making people laugh. He never really hurt anybody with his jokes and lived life to the fullest. As a result, we all enjoyed our time there more when he was around.

Sure, Butler could have used a more serious perspective at times, but he did his job and never let his buddies down. He just wasn't one for the formalities and discipline of military life.

Somehow, Butler made it through his term of service with the Air Force—just as we all did eventually. I liked Newfoundland and didn't mind my assignment there; in fact, it turned out that I would extend my tour in order to get married and, with one year left to go on my enlistment, I asked to finish it in Newfoundland.

But the climate was harsh (particularly during the winter when daylight was brief), the terrain was rough and the work was no joke.

Having guys like Butler around made the experience a lot more tolerable and showed me that there was humor in almost every situation if I was willing to look hard enough or see things from a positive perspective.

In contrast, people like the colonel, who couldn't see the humor in anything, created a more sullen environment and could make even the most exciting experiences seem dull.

Many of the other commanders who rotated through the Northeast Air Command to teach us aeronautical skills and techniques were World War II veterans, and they respectfully treated us as real people rather than subordinates. Not many felt the need to be condescending or exert their ranks in order to establish positions of power. They had nothing to prove and they knew it.

Without question, I learned more from those veterans who treated me with respect than I ever did from guys like the colonel, who measured self-importance by how many oak leaf clusters he had on his uniforms. Eventually, the uniforms come off and you're left with what's underneath. In the military, as in business, how you treat people is more important than how high a position you attain.

And that's no joke.

CHAPTER 17

Why Newfoundland?

A lot of military men hold special memories of women they met overseas or girls waiting for them back home. Some of mine are of Moscow Molly. I couldn't tell you what she looked like, and though she spoke to me on countless evenings, I never really wanted to hear what she had to say. Sound like a bad relationship? It was.

But Moscow Molly wasn't my ex. She was my enemy.

"This is a broadcast from the Soviet Union with a special hello to those airmen stationed at Thule Air Force Base."

The voice belonged to "Moscow Molly," a nickname given to a female radio personality who used to spread pro-Soviet propaganda and try to make U.S. troops feel unsafe. Most of the Canadian bases and those in the Northeast Air Command received the radio signal for her transoceanic broadcasts from Moscow. She might have sounded seductive, but that didn't make her messages any less unsettling.

Her personal greetings were meant as reminders that she—and the enemy—knew exactly where we were stationed. Sometimes they even knew the specific names of men arriving at the base, or if a light was burnt out along a runway.

Moscow Molly's real name was Annette Teshlich. She was the daughter of an American defector and had lived in the USSR as a

Soviet citizen since 1935. As a host on Radio Moscow, she often broadcasted information about various American, European and Canadian air bases. Even the CIA admitted that her reports were amazingly detailed and factual. On occasion, she'd even refer to some of the men's wives or girlfriends by name to make them lose focus on their duties and worry about how things were back home.

Moscow Molly's broadcasts were not only indicative of the technology at the time; they also reflected the concern of that era over espionage and defectors. This is probably one of the reasons why I've held on to her memory. She certainly knew how to make an impression on us—we didn't like what she said, but we listened anyway. Why? Because living in Newfoundland was like living in a vacuum. Even bad news was better than no news at all.

Most of the men serving with me didn't understand the purpose of being stationed in Newfoundland. We had enlisted for the Korean War, after all, but weren't anywhere near North or South Korea.

The reason for it was pretty clear to me, though. The bases of the Northeast Air Command were established by the United States during World War II and were located along a line from Europe through Canada all the way to Alaska. Because of natural geography, it was shorter for a Soviet plane to fly over the northern border of the USSR and toward the United States than all the way across Europe. Of course, our West Coast defense had been increased since the attack on Pearl Harbor, and the sole purpose of our air base in Newfoundland was to serve as a defense line across the northern borders, to intercept any foreign intruders. If a break in the line of defense occurred, the Air Force would be alerted and mobilized immediately.

Since it was my responsibility to keep the hydraulic systems on the aircrafts in proper, functioning order, I periodically traveled to all of the bases within the Northeast Air Command, and I became very knowledgeable about many different aircraft and about hydraulics in general. When you're isolated like we were, and you're responsible for just one discipline, it's amazing how adept you become at it. Your focus and attention are automatically increased—especially if there are few distractions in the immediate area. To that end, Newfoundland made perfect sense.

Try as she might have, Moscow Molly couldn't rattle me enough to distract me from my duties. And, to this day, I keep my mind on the mission before me. I've maintained the same accuracy and precision in navigating all matters of business that I did when working on Air Force planes. The stakes in both cases are extremely high—and without focus, there's a long way to fall.

My company is currently redesigning the silo entry systems for nuclear missiles, which were the reason my air base and others near it were closed after the Korean War. With such precise, long-range weapons at their disposal, defense bases were no longer necessary there. The U.S. no longer needed the Northeast Air Command because of the development of nuclear missile technology. From the plains of the Midwest and from the western United States, we could now target any country necessary if a breach of territory occurred. It was no longer vital to have extensive Air Force personnel located around our country's perimeter. The nuclear era, with its concomitant radar abilities, made these air bases essentially obsolete.

But the fact that I was still involved in defending our nation's borders—even though I had been out of the military for more than fifty years—was really astounding to me. Through my career in aeronautical technologies, which had started in Newfoundland so many years earlier, I was still able to take part in protecting my country.

The missile silos on which my company was working were

just a little more than forty years old, which meant they had been constructed right around the time the Korean War ended. It's like I picked up where I had left off!

Newfoundland might not have been the front line, but, all these decades later, I'm still on the cutting edge of our country's defense.

CHAPTER 18

Valentine's Day

"C'mon, Bill," my buddy pleaded. "You should come. It'll be fun."

"I'm exhausted," I replied. "I think I'm just gonna call it a night."

Generally, I'm not one to be talked into things. I'm immune to sales pitches unless *I'm* the one doing the selling, and I usually have a pretty good idea of what I want. However, this was one time when I was glad I allowed myself to be persuaded.

I had been stationed in Newfoundland for about a year. After a ten-hour service call to one of the other air bases, I arrived back at our base dead to the world. The weather had been brutal and, between the repairs and the flight, sleep sounded like the only activity in which I wanted to participate. But, fortunately, my friends were relentless in their attempts to convince me otherwise.

"Bill, it's a Valentine's Day party," another guy told me. "There'll be plenty of girls there." Those were the magic words that brought me back to life.

After a game of pool and some continued persuasion, I changed my mind and decided to go to the party. After all, parties didn't occur all the time. And I certainly wouldn't have had access to girls if I stayed on the base. Regardless of how tired I was, I didn't want to miss an opportunity like that! My buddies waited while I changed into some civilian clothes and then we went out to enjoy ourselves.

The party was being held in a private home and the place looked great, with a lot of beautiful girls in equally beautiful dresses. Most were Irish Catholic—the predominant religion in Newfoundland. One of the local girls was hosting the party and her parents served as chaperones, which was customary in those days.

My buddies and I entered the room and began to fall into conversation with a few of the prettier guests. I was having a good time—that was until I spotted one particularly attractive young lady across the room. That turned a good evening into a great one!

She stood about ten feet away from me, and I couldn't take my eyes off her. She had beautiful, dark brown hair and her smile was electric. I finished part of my drink and tried to stay focused on the conversation with my friends but really, my attention was solely on her. Something about her—or was it everything about her?—drew my eyes like a magnet. I couldn't tear myself away. Unfortunately, she was talking to one of the other guys in my squadron, so I had to wait for a chance to introduce myself.

I waited and waited. I knew she noticed me admiring her from afar—my staring wasn't exactly subtle—but her conversation with the other guy seemed like it was going to last all night. Maybe even longer than my tour of duty.

I would have had to eventually reenlist or interrupt their discussion because there wasn't any way I was going to leave the party without talking to her. But my patience was rewarded when I saw her standing alone.

"I suppose you know I've been watching you?" I asked when I walked up to her.

"Yes," she replied.

"You're a very pretty girl," I continued. "I'd really like to take you out sometime."

It might not have been the most original line, but it was all that would come out of my mouth at the time. Besides, that was sincerely how I felt, and I think she could tell I was being honest and respectful.

I decided not to wait to ask her on a date. "Can I walk you home?" I blurted out right then.

"Someone else has already asked to walk me home," she responded.

"Who?"

"That guy over there." She pointed to someone in my squadron.

"Him? I know him. He's no good," I said with a smile.

She smiled back, amused.

"Then can I at least have your phone number?" I persisted.

She paused—I think just to make me sweat it out—before she finally consented. I wrote down her number and double checked to be sure I had it correct. There was no way I was going to get that wrong. I said "good night" and thanked her for her number. Then, of course, I called her the very next day.

Her name was Bridget, and the rest was history. Within a year we were married and for over fifty-four years, I have had the pleasure of calling her my wife. The only problem is I've been calling her by the wrong name.

The nickname for Bridget was "Biddy," but I misunderstood and thought everyone was saying "Betty." I didn't find out the truth until two days before our wedding, when she said she had something important to tell me.

Believe it or not, Betty was actually worried that I wouldn't want to marry her because of the miscommunication. But after she told me the whole story, I laughed out loud and went through with the wedding anyway! I had already introduced her to my entire family as "Betty," however, so the name stuck and she still goes by it to this day.

Meeting and spending my life with this amazing woman has been one of the most-natural things I have ever done. I followed my instincts once again and they did not let me down.

That doesn't mean that married life has always been a bed of roses; all relationships, whether business or personal, have their own ups and downs. But anything worth having is worth working at.

From the moment I first saw Betty we shared a connection that was simply meant to be. She has made me a better person all the while and is the reason why I've been able to achieve—and enjoy— the level of success I have today. Simply put, my life would have been incomplete without her.

Every choice in life has its own set of consequences. What if I had gone to bed that night instead of going to the Valentine's Day party? Or what if I hadn't had the courage—or patience—to intro- duce myself to her and ask for her phone number? Perhaps Betty and I would have met another time during my stay in Newfoundland (in fact, I'd like to think it was our destiny to be together). But if the opportunity to meet her would have come along only that one time, I am very happy I took advantage of it.

You have to be ready to act upon your intuition when moments like that appear, or a door may close that can never reopen. Is the fear of change or rejection or the unknown really worth that risk? Personally, I don't think anything is.

To this day, Valentine's Day is my wife's favorite holiday. I could probably get away with forgetting our anniversary, but if I ever forgot Valentine's Day, I'd be in a heap of trouble. Fortunately, that's never happened. How could I forget?

Betty has been my rock and my life's companion from that very first Valentine's Day party. Ever since, she has enriched my life in countless ways. We now have eight children and twenty grandchil- dren; the key to her amazing job as a mother is that she has always shown up for our kids in any capacity. She has always shown up. You can't say that about a lot of people.

She has also been there with me through all of my successes and failures in both business and in life. More than anything else, she has truly made me a wealthy man.

CHAPTER 19

An Infidel

Once I know something is right, I don't waste my time struggling over the decision. The decision at that point has already been made. It's just a matter of having the guts to go through with it. You think I'm talking about business? I'm also talking about a merger of a different kind.

Betty and I dated for several months, but it was clear that she was the one for me from the beginning. Before long, I proposed and she accepted. We set a date to be married in late January, nearly a year from our first meeting. But before we could proceed with our wedding plans, I had to receive permission from my commander. Getting married in the military isn't necessarily the easiest task.

Unfortunately, my acting commander happened to be the same colonel who my friend Butler loved to tease, and his demeanor hadn't much improved through the course of my tenure in Newfoundland. If anything, the stick that had been stuck up his butt must have gotten shoved further up.

Without hesitation, he flatly denied my request to marry Betty. He said that he couldn't allow any of the local girls to take advantage of the enlisted men. Well, it was nice that he worried about defending my honor like that, but I think it would have been more accurate for him to say that he was a miserable excuse of a man and wasn't going to be happy unless everyone else was miserable.

Needless to say, Betty and I were upset about this, but I wasn't one to let a little thing like a roadblock get in the way of my life's course. Though my immediate commander had denied my request to get married, I knew that a commander of higher rank could override his denial. As luck would have it, I knew just the person. His name was Colonel Bower.

Colonel Bower was one of the World War II veterans who were still enlisted in the military during the Korean War. He was also a hero, decorated for his acts of bravery during combat against the Japanese during the previous war. Everyone respected Colonel Bower; his reputation preceded him. Despite that, he wore his high standing with great humility.

When I had first arrived at Pepperrell Air Force Base, I had seen Colonel Bower walking around the hangars and thought he looked familiar.

"John, who's that commander over there?" I asked my buddy.

"Him? That's Colonel Bower—a World War II vet."

"But where do I know him from?" I continued.

"He's pretty famous," John replied. "He flew with Jimmy Doolittle. Maybe that's how you know him."

Of course. I had recognized Colonel Bower because he was one of the famous Doolittle Raiders. One of the sixteen pilots involved in the Doolittle Raid in 1942, Colonel Bower had flown the number-twelve B-25B Mitchell bomber, named *Fickle Finger of Fate,* as a member of the thirty-seventh bomb squadron. Despite not having any previous experience in taking off from an aircraft carrier, Colonel Bower and the other pilots did so successfully from the *USS Hornet* deep in enemy waters off the coast of Japan.

The *USS Hornet* had been spotted earlier than expected by Japanese surveillance aircraft, so the Doolittle Raiders had to fly ten hours earlier than planned. All sixteen planes left the carrier en route to their target. Traveling over 2,000 miles, each plane dropped bombs over key areas in Japan. However, the earlier departure resulted in all of the planes running out of fuel prior to making their planned escape into China. All of the planes were lost because of this, with most crashing along the eastern coast of China or into the Pacific Ocean.

Amazingly, most of the pilots survived, and Colonel Bower was among those who made it. He crashed in northeast Chuckow, located in northern China, and survived to continue on with a long and distinguished career in the military.

Shortly before the time I proposed to Betty, Colonel Bower had been promoted to group commander over our entire squadron, so he naturally outranked my immediate commander, who had denied my request to get married. It was time to go over his head.

When I saw Colonel Bower around the air base the next time, I asked his permission to marry Betty. He congratulated me and enthusiastically granted the request without a second thought. Betty and I were able to proceed with our plans.

Afterwards, Colonel Bower and I gradually got to know one another. He was not only a brilliant commander but also one of the nicest people I had ever met. The colonel is now ninety years old and lives in Boulder, Colorado; he's one of the last nine surviving Doolittle Raiders. I still visit him on occasion and have always been proud to call him my friend and commander. He has particularly enjoyed Betty's company over the years and was very fond of the Newfoundland culture and its people.

Colonel Bower is not only a decorated veteran but also a hero and a gentleman. They don't make many like that anymore.

———

I thought that getting permission from the military was going to be the biggest hurdle to getting married. I was wrong.

The next step was getting the priest's approval. Betty and her family were devout Catholics, and they had attended St. John's Cathedral in Newfoundland for most of their lives.

St. John's was a magnificent work of architecture. Originally built in 1699, the first chapel was a wooden structure, as were the others that followed, but battles between the French and British resulted in their being destroyed repeatedly. In 1843, the first stone cathedral was built, and its foundations still form the central structure of the church today.

Getting married in such surroundings would have been incredible. But in order for that to happen, I had to complete Catholicism classes under the supervision of Father Murphy, a serious but kind man. He was shorter than I was and had a sort of grandfatherly appearance. Betty had known him since she was a little girl, but this was my first time ever meeting him.

Now, I'm not really one to get nervous about meeting anyone, ever, but the cathedral itself was awe-inspiring and I couldn't help but feel humbled as we entered and proceeded toward Father Murphy's office.

"So, Bill," the priest began, "you wish to marry Betty and learn Catholicism."

"Yes, Father," I replied.

"I see. Let me gather some basic information from you before we set up your classes."

I couldn't imagine what else he needed to know; he already had my name, address and military background—and I hadn't thought to bring along my dental records or grade school report cards to Newfoundland.

"What religious denomination are you, Bill?" Father Murphy asked.

"None," I responded.

"I beg your pardon?" he asked in surprise.

"I'm not of any denomination."

"But surely you grew up going to some type of church."

"No."

"You mean to tell me you have no experience at all with any form of religion?

"No."

"Were you baptized—splashed with water?" The father was starting to sound a little desperate now.

But the truth was that I hadn't really been exposed to religion previously, so I'd never had much of a chance to explore my spiritual side. My family hadn't attended church when I was growing up and I guess I had always been busy with other things on Sundays. Let's just say there was hardly ever a day of rest for me.

"Well, I have to write *something* on your form," Father Murphy stated, somewhat perplexed.

I was sorry I couldn't be of more help.

He sat in thought for a few seconds, then said, "I suppose I'll just write *infidel.*"

Infidel? Was that really what he said? I wondered.

It was.

"I've never met anyone like you," he stated, while writing my new status on the form.

"Father, I have two hundred people in my squadron. We're all in the same boat," I responded.

Still, I was beginning my married life as a Catholic infidel, which didn't sound too good. I was going to ask Betty what kind of girl in her right mind would want to marry an infidel, but then I thought better of it.

Turned out, I wasn't the only one singled out in that way by Father Murphy and given such a distinct honor. One of my good buddies in the Air Force, John Cross, had married a girl from Newfoundland also. Unlike Betty and me, they decided to get married in a non-Catholic ceremony, and I was the best man at his wedding.

So, after Betty had accepted my marriage proposal, I wanted to reciprocate. John and I had been sitting in the cockpit of one of the aircraft one afternoon and I asked if he'd be willing to be my best man. John was happy to oblige, but there was only one problem: He wasn't Catholic, either, and Father Murphy wouldn't allow him to be my best man because of it. I guess that would have been one too many infidels and he was worried we'd overthrow something or start a coup.

Not too long ago, I called John, who's living in New Mexico, to see how he was doing, and after all these years, he still remembers Father Murphy refusing to let him be in my wedding. Being labeled an "infidel" is more powerful than you might think—especially to a military man.

Anyway, I made it through the Catholicism classes, became a Catholic and was added to the church's head count. I was also married to Betty in St. John's Cathedral in a beautiful ceremony. Because I was a converted infidel, we had to be married at the side altar of the cathedral instead of in the main church. Though that might sound harsh, the side altar at St. John's was actually more impressive than most entire churches that I have visited since. Besides, standing next to Betty, I had the best view in the house.

Today, I'm still a Catholic and have served as chairman of the board of a Catholic college in Detroit. I have even met the Pope in Rome face to face! For someone who, in 1955, was considered a religious infidel, these are incredible experiences and confirm my belief that truly anything is possible.

<hr>

I still laugh about my experience at St. John's every time I think about it. From Father Murphy's perspective, if I wasn't Catholic, then I wasn't part of the team. He certainly meant well, but the concept of pigeonholing people doesn't really sit right with me, and I'm not sure spirituality is meant to be so well defined and categorized, either.

Take other aspects of my life, for example. My background is that of an Arkansas farm boy, but I went on to be a top player in industry. I believe in old-fashioned values but remain on the cutting edge of technology, welcoming and embracing change. I've got eclectic tastes and will read the entire list of *New York Times*' bestsellers along with comedy books written by Woody Allen. I'm a successful businessman who hasn't screwed anybody over in the process but won't back down from a punch. And as much as I love financial freedom, I believe it isn't about the money or the things it buys, but the living itself.

As far as my religious affiliation, I know that if I believe in God, I have difficulties. But if I don't believe in God, I have more difficulties. And that, to me, is a successful relationship.

CHAPTER 20

Duty and Domestic Life

Before I married Betty, I had been married once already—to the military.

So, after only a brief, three-day pass for a honeymoon, Betty and I settled into marriage while I continued my tour of duty at Pepperrell Air Force Base. We began our life together as newlyweds in a small apartment in St. John's, Newfoundland. But, shortly afterwards, we rented the third floor of a large home across town, where we stayed with Betty's sister and her husband.

I had originally signed up for a two-year term of duty, but after getting married I wanted to stay in St. John's a bit longer so that I could become better acquainted with Betty's family. I also enjoyed being stationed in Newfoundland and working on military aircraft, so I asked my commander for permission to extend my tour of military service for another year; unlike my request to get married, this one was immediately granted.

So, what was life like for a married couple at Pepperrell Air Force Base? Actually, it wasn't all that different than typical civilian life. Because of the structured nature of military service, Betty and I became domesticated fairly quickly. I got up every morning and went to work at the base, and most evenings I returned home to spend time with my new wife and have dinner. We would occasionally go out with some friends or her family, but mostly we stayed at home with her sister and brother-in-law. It was domestic bliss amidst military duty.

Life and its routines were simple. Betty and I were in love, and we had great times both by ourselves and with her family. St. John's was a great place to spend the first few years of our married life. It was quiet and peaceful, and neither of us wanted anything else. Sometimes the most peaceful times in your life pass you by without your realizing how satisfied you were at that moment. But I realized how lucky I was even then.

Perhaps life on a military base isn't for every newlywed couple, but my wife and I made the most of our time there. Betty is not only beautiful; she's also tough as nails. During my military stint, she rolled with the punches and never complained about much of anything.

On occasion, I received surprise orders to fly to another Air Force base for a couple of days, leaving Betty alone. But she handled the changes quite well. She worked as a secretary for the Newfoundland government, so she had a clear understanding of and respect for how public service and the military operated. None of those inconveniences mattered much to us at the time.

Before my service with the Northeast Air Command was completed, Betty and I were blessed with our first child. Our oldest daughter, Lynn, was born a few months before my tour ended in 1955. During Betty's pregnancy, she was under the care of the Air Force obstetrician, who resided on the base and was responsible for all the expectant mothers married to the men in the Northeast Air Command. Being pregnant on a military base in Newfoundland certainly had its challenges. Not only was the climate rough, but the chances of receiving pampered care or special attention were nonexistent. That point was driven home the day after my daughter's delivery.

"You can go down to the chow hall and get some dinner if you like," the nurse told Betty.

"You mean I have to stand in the chow line for food?" Betty asked.

"I'm afraid so," the nurse replied.

"But I just had a baby yesterday."

"I know. But that's the rule."

Betty begrudgingly got in the chow line with the other women receiving postnatal care, as well as some of the other hospital patients. If she had any complaint during our honeymoon year in Newfoundland, it was the lack of tender loving care in the military hospital. But she was strong; she sucked it up and stood in line.

Regardless, the happy times and experiences outweighed the bad by far. We met incredible people like Colonel Bower and spent valuable time with Betty's parents and family, which would be hard to come by as the years went by. I also learned many skills during that time period that would serve me for the rest of my life and career. Life was basic but rich, and those times taught me to appreciate the simple pleasures. Even today, I don't consider a private jet to be a status symbol, but a way to bring my grandchildren to visit us in Michigan.

In 1956, the whole world was changing. The Strategic Air Command was getting ready to activate the 704th Strategic Missile Wing. The KC-135 Stratotanker had recently been introduced into military service, making in-air refueling—which had long been an Air Force dream—a reality and giving our aircraft almost-unlimited range. The Cold War was heating up, and Betty and I were scheduled to return to the U.S. in February when my tour with the Air Force came to an end.

We were assigned to fly back on one of my squadron's airplanes along with several other families. Betty and I, along with our baby, Lynn, reported at 2:00 a.m. to the terminal, where we boarded the plane. Our first stop was New Jersey; from there we took a taxi to visit Betty's sister, Fran, and her family on Staten Island. For a week, I commuted daily to the discharge center in Brooklyn, where I had to go to be formally discharged from the Air Force.

I had mixed feelings about ending my military duty—but I didn't know then that I'd be returning to my relationship with the Air Force and other branches of the armed services throughout the course of my career. Instead, I was focusing on the present and the opportunities that awaited.

My discharge was completed after a few days, during which we stayed with Betty's sister, and soon it was time to board another plane. Before I knew it, I was back in Detroit—and we were home.

For several months, we'd be living with my parents—and the next phase of our young married and family life was about to begin.

⎯⎯⎯

Perhaps it was the newness of my marriage or the simplicity of our life, but I remember our days in Newfoundland as some of the best I'd ever had. I still believe that the simple things are some of the most precious.

I had now left the familiarity of military life behind to explore civilian life and the business world once again, and it would be a while before Betty and I would experience the peacefulness we had come to know in Newfoundland. The war might have been over, but the battle had just begun.

CHAPTER 21

Re-Exploring Entrepreneurship

Like many military personnel returning to the States after the Korean War, I was finding solid employment hard to come by. Betty and I had already started our family and had few resources of our own, and we didn't want to count on the support of our families forever.

So, within a few weeks, I was able to land a position installing acoustic ceilings. It wasn't exactly my dream job but at least it allowed us to get up on our feet before too long. No matter the political or economic climate, I always had confidence that I could make a living in the Detroit area. I'd done it after the Depression and I could do it now. All it took was ingenuity and self-reliance. It was just that with Lynn's arrival, I felt additional pressures that I hadn't experienced before.

After about nine months of installing acoustic ceilings, my entrepreneurial spirit began to get the better of me. Sure, my current job was secure, but I wasn't one to settle for mediocrity. After all, how far could you get by just settling for the easiest or quickest or next thing that came along? I'd tell you—only I wasn't about to stick around and find out.

I wanted to take a chance on paving my own career path. I wanted to bust through that ceiling that I'd reached by working for someone else. I knew enough about the installation process at that point to run my own business, so I began to plan how I would finance my startup company and acquire the staff to help me.

After putting out some feelers, I found two other guys who were willing to start my business with me. Together we scraped up $3,000 to fund the initial costs, and soon I was installing acoustic ceilings for my own company. I was twenty-two years old then and officially owned my first business.

I had been working as a salesperson and a businessman since I was eight, but running my own company was a little different from simply selling my services around the neighborhood. I was well equipped to make sales and perform the installations, but there were also overhead to be managed, bills to be paid, bookkeeping to be organized and employees to supervise. But none of that was overwhelming to me. What ended up being the most frustrating part of the business was the customers.

You might find that fact surprising since I had already been dealing with customers for a large portion of my young life—some of them pretty difficult, too. But just like my neighbor who'd wanted to whittle down my price for cleaning his filthy furniture, customers who constantly renegotiated their expenses drove me crazy. In fact, they still do today. I will keep up my part of the deal with good products and service, and I expect them to do the same with payment and respect for my work. Doing business together is entering into a contract, whether it's on paper or simply your word. You don't go back on it, and you don't try to bargain it down.

If my earliest customers had been reasonable, my experience in the ceiling installation business might have turned out to be completely different. I could have been dealing with ceiling tiles instead of servo valve technology, but it wasn't meant to be.

One of my first customers was the brother of a close friend, which seemed like a safe bet. But personal relationships don't mean much to most people in business. This guy was in real estate and when he heard that I was starting my own business installing acoustic ceilings, he was eager to be my client—probably hoping for a relative-of-a-friend discount. I gave him a fair bid for the materials and installation, and he accepted. But after the project began, it was obvious that it was going to be a hassle.

"Hey, Bill," he began, "is this ceiling really as good as you say it is?"

"Of course," I replied. "I wouldn't tell you otherwise. That's a sure way to lose customers and recommendations. Plus, it's not my style."

"Well, it just looks like the quality isn't that good."

"It's one of the best acoustic ceilings around, Jim," I assured him.

"It seems a bit pricey," he added.

"Jim," I said, breathing deeply to control my temper, "I promise you're getting a good deal."

I managed to appease his concerns that afternoon, but the following day the two men who were working with me told me that he had again complained about the quality and price of the ceiling. Because he was a friend's brother—and so I could be assured of getting the job, since I was trying to get my new business off the ground—I had already given him a low bid. His insistence on trying to weasel his way out of the agreed upon price was starting to irritate me, especially since we'd already started the job.

I went to Jim's house the following day to finish the project. By that point, we had prepared the ceiling for the acoustic tile installation and invested a great deal of time in the work. This was the last day, and I wanted everything to go smoothly. But as I stood on top of the scaffolding, gluing the ceiling pieces into place, Jim walked in again.

"Bill, how's it coming?" he asked.

"It's going well," I replied. "We should be able to finish up real soon."

"I've been meaning to talk to you about that. I'm a little disappointed in the way the ceiling looks. I think we should adjust the price some."

I stopped what I was doing and turned to look at him from my scaffolding.

"Jim, you knew what this ceiling looked like when you accepted the price," I said. "You've already got a nice discount."

"Yeah, but it's not what I expected. Maybe if the price was a little lower I'd be okay with it."

I jumped down off the scaffolding with a loud *thud,* walked over to Jim and got up right in his face.

"Ever since I took this job you've been trying to nickel and dime me, even though you agreed to the bid," I stated. "I'll tell you what… I'm gonna take this ceiling off your hands."

I got back up on the scaffolding and, along with my employees, began taking down the ceiling pieces that we had already installed, trying to salvage as much as we could. I was so sick of the customer's constant badgering to lower my price that I decided to walk away from the job altogether. He was trying to mess with my money, and I wasn't having it.

"You can't do that!" Jim exclaimed.

"Watch me," I replied.

"I'm calling my attorney!"

"Go right ahead."

Piece by piece, I took the ceiling out and loaded it into my truck. There was nothing he could do about it but watch.

It was my product, and the customer had broken our contract. He was not at all happy about having a ceiling half installed and then taken out, but he had only himself to blame. He'd taken a risk in trying to get a cheaper price, and it had blown up in his face. He had messed with the wrong guy.

Jim's expression when I pulled away from his house was priceless—it was almost worth all of the time and energy that I'd wasted. He couldn't believe that I had called his bluff, and I considered his shock and speechlessness to be my payment.

I closed my acoustic ceiling business after that encounter, and it would be many years before I would give in to my entrepreneurial desires again. I would not put up with people trying to get out of paying me what I was due—and I won't to this day. I will always fight for what's right and what's mine.

You can't be afraid to stand up for yourself in any situation. People will try to take advantage of you, and you're the only one who can let them—or stop them. If you are truthful and honest in your dealings, then you should have all the confidence in the world to say it, stand your ground and get what you deserve.

Even though I lost my investment in my company, I didn't compromise my principles by yielding to Jim's persistent requests to lower my price. In the end, I walked away richer in character, even though I was a little less rich in the bank.

PART III

Finding My Footing and Paving My Way

CHAPTER 22

Right Back Where I Started

After my adventures in independence, I returned to selling and installing acoustic ceilings for the same company I had worked for previously. I'd had it up to here with ceilings by then, but my feet were firmly planted on the ground. I had to do something to earn a living.

I had never been a dreamer to begin with. I was a realist and an optimist—and definitely an opportunist (and I mean that in the good way). I saw what was in front of me, then found ways to improve upon it or make a profit. I didn't just dream; I went out and did something about it.

But acoustic ceilings didn't interest or inspire me a whole lot, though selling was always something I enjoyed. My experiences in the Air Force had opened my eyes to something else and left me with significant expertise in engineering and hydraulics. It had given me education, training, skills and knowledge in those subjects—and it had also stimulated my interest. It was hard for me to just go back to selling other people's products when I had something of value to offer. The field of hydraulics was starting to become very popular in the country—and I was at the forefront.

You might be wondering right about now what a hydraulic system is. Hydraulics, in the truest sense, has been around since ancient times, when hydraulic systems used fluids to generate or transfer power for various undertakings, such as building the Great Pyramids. Fluid displacement allowed large stones to be moved upward with less manpower and, thus, monuments were created that have withstood the test of centuries.

Today, a hydraulic system commonly uses a pump to apply pressure to fluids (usually some type of oil). The pressure stored in the fluid can then be used in another part of the machine to create force or power.

Hydraulic systems in the 1950s, however, and into the next decade, had more to do with mechanical machinery. Many traditional machines that operated on simple mechanics were being redesigned to include hydraulic pumps. Doing so gave the machines greater power and efficiency. It was a hot field, rife with possibilities, and I'd have been damned if I was just going to let that all pass me by.

So, while I was working hard at installing ceilings, I kept one eye open to other opportunities. Then, one afternoon, a coworker and I were putting up acoustic tiles on the upper floor of an office building at Selfridge Air Force Base, northeast of Detroit. As we went about our job, I glanced through the window toward the ground below and was surprised by what I saw: A man in civilian clothes was draining the hydraulic brakes on a military jet.

I knew exactly what he was doing since I had done the same thing many times during my years in the service. But I couldn't understand why a civilian was doing it. Typically, only enlisted personnel would be allowed to work on military equipment. When my colleague and I finished up our job, I made my way downstairs to investigate.

As I walked out onto the platform, the man was studying the underbelly of the aircraft. He must have been pretty focused because he nearly jumped out of his skin when I introduced myself.

"It looks like you're working on the hydraulic brakes," I remarked.

"Yeah, that's right," he responded. "You know a little about aircraft?"

"I was trained as a hydraulics specialist in the Air Force for three years."

"No kidding? My boss would sure like to talk to you," he stated.

"Why's that?"

"'Cause he's looking for hydraulics specialists to work up at Willow Run."

"I'd be more than happy to talk to him. How come you're in civilian garb?"

"Oh, I work for the base but it's kinda like a reserve position. I'm not enlisted anymore. Most of the specialists working here are civilians. We just contract with the Air Force."

Talk about being at the right place at the right time! During World War II, Willow Run had been an airplane bomber plant. But after the war, it had been converted into a public airfield with some commercial flights; a few of the flights at Detroit City Airport were relocated there. Even though it was located fairly west of the city in Ypsilanti, Michigan, Willow Run was one of Detroit's main airports through the mid-1950s. It wasn't until the late '60s that Metro became the major airport for the greater Detroit area.

When I went to speak with the new commander of Willow Run, some of its hangars were again being used for military purposes for a new squadron. The commander desperately needed personnel with hydraulics experience, and I was clearly qualified for the job.

Within a week or two, I was traveling from my home in Melvindale to a hangar at Willow Run. Not only did I serve as a hydraulics specialist but I also got to fly in the jets with some of the trainers from time to time. I was only a year out of the Air Force and I happily found myself right back in it again. This wasn't like being stuck in the rut and security of installing ceilings. It was more like finding myself again and facing challenges.

Technically, I was a civilian, but I was playing by the same set of military rules and operating among a hierarchy of officers. It reminded me of what I liked and didn't like about the military—I enjoyed the hydraulic systems, engineering and sales, but the formality and restrictions were too confining for someone with a free spirit.

The opportunity to leave my job as an acoustic ceiling salesperson and get reacquainted with the aeronautical industry was just what I needed—and I didn't hesitate to jump at the chance. Henry David Thoreau said, "Most men lead lives of quiet desperation and go to the grave with the song still in them." That isn't me. I'm neither quiet nor desperate. I'm loud and assertive when I'm going after what I want. I don't step on anyone's toes, but I don't cower in the corner, either.

Whether it's a lack of confidence or an overabundance of fear, I believe that most people are unwilling to take chances on opportunities or to act on hunches. But that can make all the difference between success and complacency. Yes, I was at the right place at the right time at that air base, but I didn't blow it. Instead, I chose to act.

I don't like going backwards, and returning to work for the Air Force wasn't exactly the same thing I had done before. Willow Run allowed me to return to a field I liked and explore my options in more depth. Because it was a civilian job, I could leave at any time, but while I was there, I could hone my skills and find out more about what my interests truly were—which would ultimately lead me in another direction.

Making the most of that moment and seizing the opportunity was what opened the door. But I was the one who took the steps to walk through it.

CHAPTER 23

Dancing to Harry Belafonte

They say the Army is the toughest job you'll ever love. I say the Air Force is the toughest education you'll ever get.

The Air Force made sure we stayed on top of all the latest technologies—from new ways to design hydraulic systems to learning about each part on brand-new aircraft. It kept its staff, both civilian and military, up to date and looking toward the future, which was a huge benefit for me.

Not too long after I started working at Willow Run, my squadron leader wanted me to travel to Dallas to get educated about a new airplane and all of its intricacies. The teaching course would last four weeks, and my squadron leader arranged for me to catch a ride there with one of the base pilots. At the time, Betty and I were living with my parents, so although I was going to be gone for a quite while, I knew she had some help and wouldn't be alone.

I was scheduled to leave early on a Sunday morning but the night before, I stayed out a little too late and had a few too many drinks. When the alarm went off at five-thirty in the morning, it felt as if I had just laid my head on the pillow.

Somehow, through a slight whiskey haze, I managed to get myself to the Air Force base on time to meet the pilot, and I couldn't wait to get to Dallas so I could rest and recuperate.

We would be flying on a training jet, which sat two passengers in a central cockpit. It looked like it would be plenty fast. As dawn broke we climbed inside and prepared for takeoff. The pilot sat in the front of the cockpit, where a student normally sat, and I took the seat in the rear. My head was swimming before we ever made it to the runway. I knew the moment I sat down in the plane that the flight was going to be a long one.

We could have easily made the entire flight from Detroit to Dallas that day, but the pilot had friends in St. Louis and he'd made plans to visit them on the way down; we would spend the night there before going on to Dallas the next morning. I had nowhere to be until Monday morning, so the stopover in St. Louis sounded fine. The flight there would take less than an hour, which meant that I would be back on land sooner than I'd originally thought. In my condition, the sooner was definitely the better.

As long as I made it to my first class in Dallas, I didn't really care how or when we got there, and the pilot was pretty excited about seeing his friends, so I went along with the plan.

Within minutes, I found myself cruising toward St. Louis. The sky was crystal blue, and it was a beautiful morning for a flight. I tried to concentrate on taking some slow, deep breaths and ignoring the pounding rhythm of the pain in my head. But soon, the pounding was replaced by a different type of rhythm: In my earphones, I began to hear music playing progressively louder and louder.

"Day-oh… Day-ay-ay-oh. Daylight come and me wanna go home."

I looked in front of me and could see the pilot bouncing his head in time with the music. He certainly was enjoying himself—and I was glad that at least *someone* was having a good time. So, it looked like the pilot, Harry Belafonte and I would be traveling to St. Louis together.

"Six foot, seven foot, eight foot, bunch! Daylight come and me wanna go home."

At that point, "home" sounded like a good idea. "Bed" sounded even better! The music was blaring in my ears but the volume soon became the least of my worries. It wasn't enough for the pilot to listen to Mr. Belafonte; he had to dance to the music as well. And I don't mean that thing he was doing with his head or that he actually got up and danced with his feet. Instead, he began rocking the jet back and forth, from side to side, swaying with the tempo of the song. My headache suddenly took a backseat so that my stomach could voice its own complaints. I was beginning to be really thankful we weren't traveling all the way down to Dallas.

Fortunately, I managed to keep myself together for the remainder of the flight. In the distance, I could see the runway of the St. Louis airport where we would be landing. The ground had never looked so good to me before, but I still had to suffer through the landing.

The weather was perfect, but the pilot was feeling like quite a daredevil on this particular day. I wonder if he had seen how green my face was when we'd embarked on our journey, or if he was just pumped up from the music. Either way, he dove fast and hard toward the runway, deciding only at the last possible moment to level off the plane for landing. The wheels hit the pavement with a *thud* and the subsequent jolt was the finale to what had been a pretty uncomfortable flight for me.

At that time, in the late 1950s, entertainment options didn't exactly abound, as they do today. So, for kicks, some families would go to the local air field on Sunday mornings and watch the jets land and take off. All along the runway at Scott Air Force Base in St. Louis, nicely dressed families stood along a chain-link fence, watching the planes come and go.

As our jet landed, I was hoping they didn't have a clear view into the cockpit, or they would've seen more than they bargained for that day. From the moment we touched down until the jet came to a complete stop, I was throwing up in my oxygen mask before finally ripping it from my face.

My pilot turned and looked back at me with a straight face. "You know Air Force rules?" he asked.

It was all I could do to respond, but I slowly looked up from my mask to meet his gaze. "You throw it up, you clean it up," I replied, none too thrilled.

"That's right," he responded with a big grin.

I spent the next hour cleaning up my mess, but even so, I was happy to be stationary and on the ground. By the time we went over to his friends' house for dinner, I was feeling much better and ended up having a good time. We left as scheduled the next morning for Dallas, where I learned a hell of a lot about hydraulics, despite a few bumps along the way.

To this day, I still can't help but remember my trip to St. Louis when I hear Harry Belafonte's "The Banana Boat Song." Daylight came a little too early for me that day.

CHAPTER 24

Training, Planes and Automobiles

"Wanted: Hydraulics Lab Technician in Chrysler Research Division."

That was the advertisement in the classified section of the *Detroit Times*. When I came across it I had been working at Willow Run for about a year, and the frequent travel and the formality of the military were becoming tiresome. I was seeking something with greater creativity and room to implement ideas. Working on different aircraft was exciting and interesting, but the military structure was not. There were endless regulations and time-consuming procedures, which simply did not foster the environment of individuality and independence that always brought out the best in me.

The want ad for the job at Chrysler immediately grabbed my attention. Not only did the position involve hydraulic systems but it was in the research division, which meant being involved with new engineering designs (specifically, in this case, the development of hydraulic systems for the power steering in Chrysler vehicles). With my background and experience, I knew I would be perfect for the position. So, I typed up a résumé, dressed in my best (non-wool) suit and went for an interview. I got the job! Within a few weeks, I left Willow Run and began working as a hydraulics lab technician.

Though I knew a tremendous amount about hydraulics, I had worked almost exclusively on airplanes during my jobs in the Air

Force and at Willow Run. I didn't know at first whether or not making the transition to automobiles would be difficult. But the concepts and mechanics between the two were the same and, through focus and attention to detail, I naturally adapted to different types of hydraulic components in the automobile setting.

My technical skills within the hydraulics arena continued to improve at Chrysler, and I became very knowledgeable about power-steering designs and their operations. But hydraulics and power steering weren't all that I learned there. As a lab technician, I test drove the latest-model cars as they were released and collected engineering data about the way they functioned. A colleague and I would take the newly designed cars into the city at night or out on a test track to assess their performance. (That was a pretty good job perk, if you ask me!) We then reported our findings back to the division's manager so that design alterations or improvements could be made.

I wore many hats in my new job: I was a mechanic, a researcher, an engineer, a professional driver (not NASCAR, but a cool thing to tell people nonetheless) and, of course, a hydraulics specialist. I found the increased responsibility, diversity and greater involvement more interesting, and soon I knew as much about automobiles as I did about aircraft.

Despite all my responsibilities, my key role was to help design an effective power-steering system for Chrysler cars. Power steering was new to most vehicles in the late 1950s and early '60s and some manufacturers still had a few kinks to work out. Even Chrysler had run into its own set of challenges regarding its power-steering system.

The problem was that many of the power-steering columns were failing to return to neutral after the steering wheel turned. In other words, if someone turned to the right at an intersection, the steering wheel would stay turned to the right, causing the car to go up onto the curb. Alright, it was more than a small kink. Accidents involving people hitting poles, trees and other objects while driving Chrysler automobiles were occurring way too often, and something needed to be done quickly. Reportedly, three percent of Chrysler vehicles had faulty power-steering systems that could result in these dysfunctions, which made life on the road—as well as the sidewalk—a lot more dangerous.

I wasn't the only lab technician trying to solve the problem, but so far no one had identified the cause or the solution. Late one evening, I sat in the Chrysler plant, staring at one of the failed power-steering units. I was trying to determine why the steering mechanism would suddenly lock in place. But the longer I stared, the more questions I had. For starters, what was inside the apparatus that would prevent it from returning to neutral? I decided to place the failed steering unit in a vise so I could examine its mechanisms more clearly.

The steering mechanism consisted of a threaded rod from the steering wheel. As the steering wheel was turned to the left or right, these threads would cause a metal block to move up or down and direct the tires accordingly. In order to make this process smooth, the threads were filled with ball bearings aided by a hydraulic pump for power. As I sat and watched the mechanism in action, I slowly turned the wheel and applied torque. Then, suddenly, I noticed something strange.

The ball bearings became bouncy as I began to turn the steering column; as a result, they weren't evenly entering the threads of the steering rod. The ball bearing guide that directed their entry into the threads was unable to function well with the increased torque. After a few more hours of investigation, I found that placing a bit of pressure on the ball bearing guide prevented this instability. It took less than a pound of pressure on the ball guide to solve the problem.

The next morning, I showed my lab manager and colleagues the results of my discovery.

"I think you've found it, Bill," my manager stated. "Let's make a trip to Indianapolis in the morning and see if we can put this thing to rest."

Indianapolis was where many of Chrysler's parts were made and also where many of the faulty steering mechanisms had been sent previously. With the help of the other technicians, I designed a conical spring that placed a small amount of pressure on the ball bearing guide, providing the stability needed. Then, we went to test it in Indianapolis.

Putting the spring in place corrected ninety-seven percent of the previously faulty steering mechanisms. The problem had been solved, and I was deemed a hero for finding the solution. I had saved Chrysler a ton of money and bad press—and I had saved some drivers from potentially serious accidents—all by doing the same thing I had always done: finding a different way to look at things. It was what Henry Ford had done well before me when he'd invented the automobile and what Lee Iacocca, the president and CEO of Chrysler, had done in the '80s when he revived the failing company.

When I got back to Detroit, several of the executives came down to our department to shake my hand and show their appreciation of my efforts. But over the course of the next week, the attention shifted from me to our entire lab then to another lab technician who had been groomed to be the rising star of our department. This guy was eventually given sole credit for solving the steering dilemma. He had been at Chrysler longer than I had and it appeared that the higher-ups had bigger and better plans for him within the company. Giving him the credit made it seem as if they had backed the right horse all along. But you can imagine how that sat with me.

I didn't need the pat on the back from the company executives because I knew I had done my job well. However, the corporate politics taught me some good lessons about how to treat people. There are always people who are out to steal the glory from those who actually put in the time and do the work. I've seen it in all sorts of people, regardless of their positions. The bottom line is that everyone wants to be treated fairly and appreciated for their efforts. Chrysler couldn't see that because the executives didn't know me at all and didn't really bother getting to know their workers, and my own lab manager wasn't willing to go against the grain and stand up for me. As a result, I didn't feel appreciated, which didn't give me much encouragement to work harder for the company.

In every company I have ever owned and operated, I have made the effort to get to know personally the people who work for me. Those who do stellar jobs are going to hear about it directly from me, with great sincerity and appreciation. Sure, all employees gets salaries to compensate them for their time and labor. But those who really expend the effort have the biggest effects on my bottom line—and will always have places within my company.

By the same token, if workers do their jobs poorly, they will, without question, hear about it from me as well. I don't care if you've worked with me for twenty years or twenty days—I tell it like it is, and I believe in everyone pulling their own weight.

I am both forthright and honest, and I treat people fairly. I don't view my employees as pieces on an assembly line, but I don't want to see anyone holding up production, either. That's something I learned from the auto industry: You do not ever want to see those assembly lines stop, not even for a second. If there's a problem, you think fast on your feet and fix it. And whoever's responsible for messing up the works will have to be replaced. That's the only way to keep company standards high—as well as the quality of our country's products.

I appreciate a job well done. I also expect nothing less.

CHAPTER 25

Put to the Test

"Bernie, tomorrow night we have a test drive," I said.

"Yeah, that's a cryin' shame, huh?" he replied with a big grin.

One of the pluses of working in research and development at Chrysler was taking out new cars even before they reached the production lines. The up-and-coming models would need to be tested repeatedly, not only in the lab but also on the road, before final approval was awarded. One of my responsibilities was examining our products' road performance. It was something I didn't take lightly. But that didn't mean I forgot to have fun along the way.

Bernie was one of my good friends and colleagues at Chrysler, and he would often go out to test drive cars with me. There were several remote areas we went to that allowed good conditions for our technical assessments. Because the cars hadn't been seen by the public yet, we only went to unpopulated places, usually at night. Some of the cars never made it to production, so we tried to keep a low profile and be as discrete as possible. Chrysler didn't need any advertisements for the ones that didn't work.

One of the best times at my job was the fall of each year. Unlike today, when new automotive models are introduced throughout the year, new cars in the 1960s were only introduced in the autumn. For example, the 1960 New Yorker would be introduced in the fall of 1959. Therefore, each summer, the technicians in research and development were responsible for assessing the new Chrysler models before they went out on the market.

Chrysler wasn't the only company releasing their new models then. General Motors and Ford also introduced their new cars at the same time. Of course, each company wanted to examine the competition's product beforehand, and the "Big Three" automakers were all in the same predicament. So, out of professional courtesy, the companies exchanged their new models with one another. The level of competition was so high that they were willing to share their own secrets in order to see what the others were doing.

In the summer of 1959, it was my responsibility to test three new models that would be introduced to the public in a couple of months. They were the Chrysler Valiant, the Ford Falcon and the General Motors Corvair. I had to stack them against each other and see how Chrysler measured up.

These models were some of the very first small cars introduced by American automakers, so testing them was a unique opportunity, especially since they handled differently than their larger predecessors.

We received the GM Corvair and the Ford Falcon for testing, and I made arrangements to examine each of the three cars under the cover of darkness so I could make my report without any spectators present to make independent comparisons. After all, who knew where Chrysler would rank?

For the first test, on a nice, clear, moonlit evening, I took the Chrysler Valiant to a remote area in Michigan where I had tested many other cars. It was a perfect night to open the Valiant up and see what she could do.

The course I chose had a great, S-shaped curve that wasn't banked. This S-curve and other maneuvers were part of the standard assessment and, during the drive, several instruments would be applied to the vehicle to test its performance and stability. As part of the routine, I accelerated the car to at least forty-five miles per hour through the curve to see how it handled, and I wrote up a report about my findings at the end of the evening. The Valiant performed very well without difficulty and received a better-than-satisfactory report.

The next evening I took the Ford Falcon out for a test drive and made the same assessments. The conditions were similar, and I chose the same course on which to test it. I couldn't wait to take on that S-curve again! The Falcon also performed very well and I found little to criticize regarding its design and performance. I completed my report and called it a night.

On the third evening, it was time to test the Corvair. The weather cooperated, and a bright moon shone overhead as I went to the same course once again. I drove the Corvair to the testing area and everything seemed fine so far. It handled well, the instruments responded appropriately and the initial feel was solid. It looked like it was going to be another uneventful night.

However, as I began to negotiate the curve, something strange happened. It felt as if the rear end of the car was sliding out from under me. I took the curve a couple more times at forty-five miles per hour, and each time I had to back off the acceleration because the car felt unstable. Once I dropped the speed under forty, I was finally able to gain control and handle the curve comfortably.

I knew something was wrong with the rear axle. So, the next morning, I made my report to Chrysler's team of engineers.

"This car isn't well designed," I told them. "The rear feels as if it's skidding on ice."

"What do you mean?" one of them asked.

"I mean the rear axle is unstable, as if it's causing the car to oversteer when it hits a curve."

My responsibilities regarding the assessment of the Corvair were done, and it was then up to the engineers to determine if the car's rear axle and design were flawed. I don't know the end result of their findings or whether they reported anything to General Motors. They certainly had no contractual or business obligation to do so—but ethical concerns are another question altogether. What I do know is that the Corvairs were released that year and many people suffered serious injuries from accidents while driving them.

In fact, *Time* magazine reported that in 1965, as many as eighty-five lawsuits were filed against General Motors over accidents involving Corvairs and their rear axles. I was left to wonder whether or not GM knew about the problem before that model went into production. Even if Chrysler hadn't said anything, they certainly did their own assessments.

In today's climate, regarding U.S. automakers, public opinion has been strongly affected by the corporations' failure to be honest with the American people. Why am I not surprised?

The need for more economical cars has been obvious since the 1970s, and technologies that would allow greater fuel efficiency or alternative fuel usage have been available for at least a decade. So, why haven't we heard about these before? I blame a business-as-usual mentality, a corporate aversion to change—as well as the costs and retraining that comes with it—and a healthy dose of arrogance on the part of American automakers. Combined, they are running one of the country's most important industries into the ground.

I look back on my experience with the Corvair and see the same problems in the business policy of automakers then that we have now. Lying to your customers—and yourself—is one of the worst things you can do in business. When problems arise, I tackle them head on. They don't go away or get better by themselves. You've got to rise to the challenge, take responsibility and fix the issue. Otherwise, you'll have violated the trust of your customers.

From the time when I was selling cleaning services around my neighborhood, I figured out and always tried to follow these lessons: Provide a good service, be honest with your customers and charge the highest price that the market will bear (it's worth it to satisfied consumers). I hadn't changed those rules once by the time I'd worked my way up to designing hydraulic systems in cars. Over and over, those strategies provided me with solid success.

Hopefully, before it's too late, American automakers will learn the same lessons that a young boy from Arkansas did. Those were the values that the U.S. automotive industry was built upon—way before it went into a tailspin.

CHAPTER 26

The Hudson

Layoffs are never good news. They're even worse when they happen in the dead of winter, when heating costs are up. And they're the absolute worst when you have a family to support. But those were the tough breaks I was about to face.

It was February of 1961. I had served in Newfoundland. I'd been to Greenland. I thought I knew what cold was. I was wrong.

That winter in Detroit was one of the coldest I have ever experienced. It was absolutely frigid, freeze-through-your-parka, frostbite-from-stepping-out-the-front-door cold.

I was still working for Chrysler and arrived at my job as usual one morning: frozen stiff but not a second late. I was called into the manager's office unexpectedly.

"Have a seat, Bill," my manager said—rarely a good sign. "I'm afraid I have some bad news for you. We have to lay off a lot of our technicians in research and development. Unfortunately, you're among that group."

"Why me?" I asked, aware of the excellent work I had done for that company.

"It's all about tenure. There are other techs who have been here longer, you understand. That's just the way it goes. Hopefully, the layoffs won't last too long."

"When do they start?"

"You can work the rest of the week."

The cold air from outside had just made its way into the building and I felt a chill run through me as I realized the awesome responsibility I had to my family. Still, I can't say that I was exactly worried. I knew I would find something else. I had made a habit of landing on my feet. I had no choice.

I also knew I wasn't alone, for better or worse. Many other technicians were being laid off, including my friend Bernie Thompson. He and I had been through a lot together since we'd first started at Chrysler at about the same time. So, for those last five days, Bernie and I commiserated as we finished our duties for the research and development division.

We walked into the plant together on Friday morning, our final day. Both of us had entered that building every morning for three years, but this would be the last time. Although I didn't want to lose my job, the thought of moving on didn't scare me. Somehow, I knew I would find another position. And I was more than ready for whatever was next.

Bernie and I went about our normal activities that day, then packed up our belongings before the five o'clock bell rang. With a box of my personal items in hand and my coat securely fastened, I walked out of the Chrysler plant for good. You'd think my mind would have been on the future, but all I could think about was how damn cold it was just then. Bernie must have been thinking the same thing.

"Bill, is it me, or is it colder now than it was this morning?" he asked.

"It's always colder without a job," I replied with a smile.

Since Bernie and I both were in limbo, we were looking for any odd jobs to make ends meet. I knew a lady who needed some repair work on an old, 1948 Hudson. In its day, the Hudson had been the epitome of luxury and performance. But her particular car was more than thirteen years old and had seen better days. Its power steering didn't operate any longer, and the lady wanted to know if I could fix it. I gladly took the job and asked Bernie if he wanted to help; he was more than happy to pick up some extra cash.

As a bonus, he knew a mechanic who would let us use his hydraulic lift. We could place the Hudson on the lift and get everything done much more efficiently. The only problem was that the garage was about five miles away from the lady's home.

Bernie and I woke up early one morning and rode to her house in Bernie's DeSoto. Once we arrived, I got into the Hudson, which I would drive over to the mechanic's garage while Bernie led the way in his DeSoto. He knew the directions, and we thought it wouldn't be a bad idea to have another car just in case. It was a good plan.

As I would soon find out, though, the power steering wasn't the only thing that didn't work on the Hudson.

By the time we left the lady's house, snow had begun falling and was accumulating quickly. The air was so frigid that the snow stuck to everything instantly—windshields, streets, you name it. The roads were already covered with a coat of snow when I started the drive.

The further we drove, the worse the visibility became. We were both proceeding cautiously on the snowy, icy roads, slowly making our way closer to the garage. When we were only a couple of blocks from it, I saw a busy intersection up ahead—the first one I'd come upon since leaving the lady's house. As we approached the intersection, the light turned red.

Bernie brought his car to a slow halt without any trouble at all. As I tried to slow down the Hudson, however, I realized that not only did the power steering not work—neither did the brakes!

At first, I thought it was the icy road, but I pumped the brakes a few times and nothing happened. Not even a small skid. I knew I had two choices: I could either smash into the rear end of Bernie's DeSoto or take my chances going through the intersection. I chose the latter.

As if in slow motion, I went rolling by Bernie's car and through the intersection. He looked at me and I looked at him through our cars' windows as I slid past. His expression seemed to convey some type of parting farewell, as if he were saying, "See ya on the other side, buddy." And I'm sure my face showed complete surprise.

Miraculously, I somehow made it all the way through the traffic to the opposite corner, where I hiked up onto the curb without incident. As I got out of the Hudson and looked back at my tire tracks through the snowy intersection, all I could do was laugh. What else was there to do? What a way to earn a dollar!

With a bit of effort, Bernie and I freed the old Hudson from its temporary resting place on the curb and managed to get it safely to the garage. Once it was up on the hydraulic lift, we repaired the brakes first—which was my first priority. Then, we fixed the power steering as well, which was very similar to what we had worked on at Chrysler.

By the end of the day, we successfully delivered the Hudson back to its owner in exchange for $100, which we split evenly. The job had turned out to be a pretty good deal, even though it had hit the skids earlier on. If I had glided through that intersection a second earlier or later, who knows what I would have hit or how it might have ended? Like always, however, I was willing to do whatever it took to bring home an income.

Bernie and I took on some more extra work together, and then within a week or so I found another full-time job. But that wasn't the last time I was involved in layoffs. Only next time, I was on the other side of the desk.

Like I said, layoffs are never good news, and at any stage of my career, I didn't like having to let people go. But even in the midst of my company's financial crisis there were some employees I wouldn't lay off because they'd worked too hard for me and I felt I owed them something. I've had some workers stay with me for over thirty-five years.

Of course, that's not always the case. There were employees I had to fire for not carrying their own weight. When it came to executives, I took a page from Henry Ford's book and would go down to their offices and fire them face to face. That way I didn't have to worry about getting them out of *my* office. I'd tell them their services weren't needed anymore, thank them for their time, turn around and get them the hell out of my sight.

Firings are personal—a result of not having done your job. Layoffs are circumstantial, often unavoidable. But work? It's always there somewhere. And I was always willing to go after it, or to create it myself.

In life and in business, you have no choice but to roll with the tough breaks.

CHAPTER 27

The Steps Back Into Sales

Post-military, I've never been out of work for more than a week. Some would say I've been very lucky. Others would realize that luck had little to do with it.

———

Shortly after Chrysler, I took a job repairing hydraulic machinery at a local bakery. There was one major drawback: I had to work the nightshift.

By then, Betty and I had already expanded our family to five children. You can imagine how difficult it was to sleep during the day in our household. From midnight to 8:00 a.m., I would repair the machines at the bakery while they weren't in operation. Then, I tried to catch whatever sleep I could before returning for my shift the next evening. It didn't take me very long to begin looking for employment elsewhere.

———

Following the bakery, I took a position at Massey Ferguson, working with tractors and hydraulic machinery. After having worked on jets and automobiles, I just didn't find tractors as exciting, and the job didn't pay quite as well, either. But going to Massey Ferguson was a good move for me. For one, it kept me in the field of hydraulics and engineering. And, secondly, I made contacts within that industry that would help me for years to come. I met some of my closest friends while working at Massey Ferguson, one of whom ended up working with me for more than twenty-eight years.

So, while there were a lot of benefits to my position at Massey Ferguson, I also wanted to be more than just a technician working with hydraulics. I was interested in systems designs, engineering concepts and, most of all, sales. My options to expand into those areas at Massey Ferguson were limited. So, I left the tractors and took another track.

The next opportunity I took led me to Southfield, Michigan, just outside of Detroit. I got a position in the Bendix Corporation, which developed and designed components for commercial vehicles. Their product lines included system controls, braking systems and different types of safety technologies. My job was in the controls division, where I designed controls and hydraulics for a variety of machine tools.

Numerically controlled machines were being upgraded to contain hydraulic controls, the benefits of which were catching on, especially within the aerospace and oil industries. My department was responsible for providing these controls to all Bendix customers.

You might wonder how a hydraulics specialist and airplane mechanic suddenly had the skills to design control systems for machines without any formal education in engineering. The truth is, I actually did have some formal education. At the time, I was actively enrolled in a mechanical engineering curriculum at one of the local community colleges and, as a result, had learned a great deal about engineering design and systems.

I had enrolled in the college toward the end of my tenure at

Chrysler in order to obtain an engineering degree on the GI Bill, and I was still plugging away at my studies while working at Bendix. To me, it was the ideal situation: I was able to apply my night-school lessons to my subsequent design projects, which meant combining book learning and hands-on experience. Between the two, I was developing my engineering skills rapidly and my learning curve was extremely steep.

So steep, in fact, that I was ready to climb up to the next rung on the ladder.

After I had been working at Bendix for several weeks, I came to know a regional salesman who periodically called upon our division. He sold hydraulic equipment parts and his name was Josh Shay. As a company that designed and manufactured hydraulic controls, we had a pretty steady need for his products, and I could tell immediately that not only did he know their technical aspects thoroughly but he was also an excellent salesman.

It was great to meet someone so experienced in sales who had a background much like my own. Josh and I had many detailed conversations about hydraulics during the months I worked at Bendix. But, one day, he called for another reason.

"Hello, Bill," Josh said in what started as a routine call.

"Hey, Josh," I replied. "How are things?"

"Going pretty well, I suppose," he continued. "You got a minute? I'd like to talk to you about a little proposition."

I always kept my eyes and ears open to new prospects. "Yeah, what's that?" I replied.

"How would you like to come work for my company?"

Opportunity was knocking again. Josh's business sold hydraulic equipment to corporations that either handled their own machinery repairs in-house or provided services to larger vendors. But Josh didn't manufacture the parts himself. He was simply the middleman, selling products for a variety of manufacturers.

He was a sales distributor, and his business was small; in fact, his entire staff consisted of him and a bookkeeper. Not even enough players to have a proper hand of poker after work.

Regardless, Josh was busy and he found that he couldn't handle the sales meetings and technical phone calls in the office by himself. He needed someone who could not only address the detailed questions about the equipment but also handle office sales—and he thought I would be a good fit for the job.

"Well, I don't know, Josh," I said. "What's the pay?"

"I can offer one hundred and sixty dollars a week," he answered. "And we have good health insurance."

"Not bad. But let me think about it."

"You should know something, Bill," he interjected. "Because we're small, I don't have any unemployment benefits. I know you have a family to think about."

Josh was right about that. Betty and I had quite a few mouths to feed. As in enough for a basketball team, once they got taller. But the chance to get back into sales was very appealing to me and the salary he was offering was significantly better than what I was currently making. Besides, I wasn't that worried about unemployment. I knew I'd always find a way to land on my feet.

The division head at Bendix knew Josh well and also knew that he had asked me to join his company. He was one of those bosses with whom I could speak freely, without any concern that he would use it against me. We shared a mutual respect, and that week he called me into his office to talk openly about my decision.

"I hear Josh Shay asked you to go work for him," he announced as soon as I took a seat.

"Yes, he did," I replied.

"Have you made any decisions?" he asked.

"Not yet."

"Bill, you know I like you and I'm gonna shoot straight. I don't want to lose you here, but I also think it's a bad move for your sake. You have a solid position at Bendix and you can't beat the benefits."

"You're right, but the chance for me to both get back into sales and work in hydraulics is certainly worth considering."

"Maybe, but it's a pretty big risk. Here, you've got a sure thing."

Like most everyone else I knew, my boss valued security more than the pursuit of something better. Given the choice between a stable living with solid benefits and a job that is interesting but has some risk, most people will choose security every time. But I've never been one to buy in to that mindset. To me, that meant taking the middle ground and never really knowing what might have been.

Call it confidence, but I always believed that things would work out if I followed my instincts and took a chance on something that felt right. Choosing the secure route—simply for the sake of security—sounded boring and limiting, like living in a protective bubble all the time. Sure, nothing bad is going to happen, but at the same time you're missing out on all that life has to offer. Life is made up of risks. So is success.

I talked it over with Betty and decided to take the position with Josh Shay. It turned out to be one of the best decisions of my life. That pivotal step brought me back to something I had always loved: sales.

If I had taken the sure way, I would probably still be sitting in a lab somewhere, designing engineering plans for someone else's company. Playing it safe like that would have restricted my entrepreneurial potential. Instead, I took the chance and never looked back.

That's the only sure way to keep moving forward.

CHAPTER 28

Salesman and Shrink

Sales may be known as the "art of the deal" but it also includes the science of psychology.

Josh Shay knew this. He was one of the best salesmen I had ever met in my life. Not only did he have the ability to promote a product, but he was also clearly a student of the profession and of psychology. He had an innate sense of how to read people and determine what they wanted to know or hear—without tricking them into buying his products. In that way, we were the same, although I was only twenty-eight and Josh was about forty when I joined his company.

Josh always told it like it was. That was how he gained customers' trust; they knew they would get an honest assessment from him. But that didn't mean he didn't know how to present his products properly to potential buyers. By understanding other people, Josh could direct the conversation to address those aspects most important to them to both ease their minds and gain their trust.

The psychology behind a sale is far more important than knowledge of the product or the ability to present it well. If a salesman doesn't know the customer he's dealing with, the chances of making a sale go down significantly. Sometimes right down the drain.

Through example, Josh reinforced what I already knew intuitively about sales but had never thoroughly examined: I needed to learn more about *who I was selling to* before I could truly succeed in selling them the product.

"Bill, the key is to find out what's troubling your customer," Josh stated. "Everyone is looking for some type of solution."

"Even if things are running smoothly?" I responded.

"Even if things are running smoothly," he repeated. "If things are going well, people are at least looking to find a way to maintain the status quo if not improve the situation."

He was right. After all, I was always looking for ways to improve things. Why wouldn't my customers?

<hr>

As much as Josh was a student of his clients, he was also quite a teacher, ready to share with me everything he had learned about salesmanship and people through his long career in sales. As we rode from sales call to sales call together, he'd instruct me on the finer points of selling. It was like attending a mobile seminar on customer relations—and then I'd be able to go out and immediately put it into action.

Josh's wife was a teacher, and together they made a great couple. Every time I saw her she would ask how my children were doing in school and what their academic plans for the future were. For both Josh and his wife, education was clearly first and foremost.

Josh was happy to hear that I was enrolled in night courses to learn mechanical engineering. The day after each class, while we drove from place to place, we'd discuss some of the recent material I'd learned.

"So, what are they teaching you these days?" he would typically ask.

"We're covering thermodynamics and how they're used in design," I'd reply.

"Thermodynamics! That's a great subject."

From there, Josh would expound on several real-life examples of how thermodynamics were used in his engineering designs. He even described how he might explain the concept to his clients so they could have a better understanding of the products. Josh and I made a strong team back then—I was enthusiastic about learning all I could and he was a dedicated teacher. In the evenings, Josh taught a hydraulics course at one of the local colleges. He had been teaching for many years, reasoning that it kept his engineering skills sharp. He would tell me acronyms he used to help him remember different lists of information, and on a daily basis we would tackle math problems and design dilemmas for many of our customers. Both of us enjoyed the challenge of solving complicated problems, whether they involved hydraulics or basic engineering concepts. And being able to solve problems never hurts in sales, either!

Josh was one of the first people who showed me how to bridge the gap between my more technical areas of expertise and my sales ability. Being well liked and naturally personable, he had little trouble meeting customers and engaging them in conversation. But, more importantly, his level of technical knowledge awarded him respect from everyone to whom he spoke. He was a smart engineer and through his conversations with customers, he'd routinely help them solve their engineering problems. He provided a service above and beyond what his products provided.

That was perhaps the most important thing I learned from Josh, and I continue to do the same thing with my own companies to this day: I figure out solutions and design products to fill those needs.

Because Josh was able to demonstrate a sound knowledge of his products and their uses, he easily gained people's trust. That, plus his social skills, ultimately made him a great salesperson.

In sales, nothing is more important than trust because it reduces the risk a customer feels when purchasing a product or service. Once trust is established the sale becomes much easier. People aren't so hesitant to hand over their money to someone they know they can trust.

That kind of trust is what allowed me to establish some of my very first clients after joining Josh's company. I contacted my previous managers and colleagues at Massey Ferguson; I had worked there for nearly a year and left on a good note. They knew they could trust me, and I was able to make several new sales for Josh's business as a result.

"I'm working with Josh Shay now, selling hydraulic equipment parts," I told Roger, my former manager at Massey Fergusen, over the phone one day.

"No kidding?" he said. "Sounds like a good fit for you."

"Yeah, I think so," I agreed.

"So, what can I do for you?" he asked.

"I was looking at Josh's product line and there's some equipment that might make a lot of sense for you—help out with some of the issues we were having when I was there."

"Well, as you know, we're usually in need of something. One machine or another always needs repair."

"How about I set up a meeting with you next week?"

"Sounds good. I'd like to catch up with you, anyway—and we might just help my business in the process."

The people at Massey Ferguson knew me well and trusted me—and they realized that I had a good understanding of what they needed. I didn't have to prove to them that I was honest and selling a good product. They knew I wouldn't have taken the job otherwise.

Josh taught me how to accomplish this sense of trust not only with people I already knew but with customers I had just met. By assessing people's needs and providing them with solutions I could form a strong sales relationship with just about anyone.

I was happy to be working in sales again, especially with Josh there as an example. He made me see more clearly how I could combine my engineering knowledge with my natural selling abilities to create a pretty unstoppable sales technique. Most salesmen were dealing in smoke and mirrors. Josh and I knew our products inside-out and could deliver on our promises. We were the real deal.

Working with Josh, I was gaining experience and education, and he was gaining an enthusiastic colleague who was able to increase his company's sales and business revenues.

It was great to be using my sales skills again—it felt natural somehow. I knew I was finally on the right track. And that I'd be in it for the long run.

CHAPTER 29

Worth Its Weight in Salt

Most days, I was very thankful that my interests and talent lay in sales rather than, say, tourism and hospitality. This was one of those days.

Michigan in the midst of winter can be a dismal place; the sky is often overcast and gray, and the temperature is bitterly cold. Those were the conditions as I walked along the icy sidewalk to our single-story office building to start my morning.

By then, I had been working with Josh Shay for a while. Sometimes we'd still make sales calls together, and other times I'd stay in the office, handling customers' questions. I enjoyed both—discussing hydraulics and engineering—and, of course, making sales.

At nine o'clock in the morning, Josh walked into the office. He was covered from head to toe, wearing a thick, wool overcoat, heavy gloves, a hat and earmuffs. It was almost impossible to identify him until he began to take off some layers within the heated sanctuary of our office. I had only arrived a few minutes earlier but was already comfortably seated at my desk.

He greeted me, then placed his winter garb onto a chair and methodically proceeded to check his to-do list for the day. That was when the phone rang. Josh picked it up.

"Mr. Shay," the caller began. "I understand you design hydraulic systems."

"Depends on what you have in mind," Josh replied. "We do handle a lot of hydraulic systems."

"This is Michael Murphy from the Michigan Highway Department. I'd like to talk to you about designing a salt spreader for our plow trucks."

"I see. When are you available to meet?" Josh asked.

"Is today too early? How about two o'clock downtown at our main office?"

"Sounds fine. I'll be there."

Today wasn't too early by any means. Not if it meant the possibility of landing a state contract. Hell, we would've tunneled our way through the snow for that. For any small business, a large contract with the state could mean financial stability for a good, long while—and that kind of opportunity didn't come very often.

For the rest of the morning, we tried to keep our minds on the business in front of us. But as it got closer to two, we were pretty excited about the prospect of working for the state. We drove Josh's car and parked in front of the municipal building in Detroit, then made our way along the icy sidewalks to the front steps.

Like most municipal buildings, it was dark and gray with old, vinyl flooring—somewhere between a schoolhouse and a state prison. It begged for a renovation to bring it into modern times. Our footsteps echoed in the long, cold hallway as we approached Mr. Murphy's office door.

"Good afternoon," Josh said to the secretary once we'd stepped in. "We have a two o'clock appointment with Mr. Murphy. I'm Josh Shay and this is Bill Phillips."

"Very well," she replied. "Please have a seat."

With military precision, Mr. Murphy stepped out from the back office at exactly two o'clock, not one second early or late for our scheduled appointment. He must have been watching the clock and waiting for that precise moment to appear, figuring his accuracy would impress us. It did. Josh and I both stood as he entered the room.

Murphy was a tall, stout man who held an unlit cigar in the corner of his mouth. Being that we were the only ones in the waiting room, he directed his attention to us immediately.

"Hi, there," he said in a booming voice. "I'm Michael Murphy. I presume one of you is Josh Shay?"

"Yes, nice to meet you," Josh responded while shaking his hand. "This is my associate, Bill Phillips."

"Come in the office and have a seat," he said, leading the way. "How 'bout some coffee?"

"Sure," Josh replied. He still hadn't warmed up after the short walk from the car.

"Bill, would you like some?" Murphy offered.

I accepted the coffee and we sat down across from an oversized desk in Murphy's office. The desk took up more than half of the room; piles of what appeared to be unorganized papers were scattered across the top of it, leaving little room for any open workspace. Several half-filled Styrofoam cups of coffee peppered the desktop as well. It made sense that he needed such a huge desk. Where else would he keep his garbage?

"Gentleman, we have a problem," Murphy began after taking a seat. "As you most likely already know, the highway department handles all the sand spreaders during the snow and ice storms for the major highways and roads throughout Michigan."

"Yes," Josh acknowledged.

"Well, the problem is that the sand keeps clogging up the spreaders and we're having to backtrack over and over the same roads."

"I see," Josh said.

"What we're looking to do is design a better spreader that doesn't get clogged," Murphy continued. "And we want to use salt instead of sand."

"And you thought hydraulics might work better for that?" Josh asked.

"Indeed. I've seen some of our other construction vehicles use hydraulic systems and that seems like the way to go."

I took a sip of my bitter coffee as I listened to Murphy explain the intricacies of their current machine. It seemed that a highway truck carried a load of sand in the back, which was then pulled into a spinner by an auger. The spinner consisted of a rotating wheel that threw the sand out onto the highway. But, once the sand combined with rain, ice and snow, the mixture would clog the auger and spinner, rendering them ineffective.

By using hydraulics to assist the motor-powered apparatus, greater power would be generated to spread the material. This would help prevent it from becoming clogged. Likewise, by using soluble salt instead of sand, the degree of clogging would be reduced.

Josh and I discussed the possibilities of how we might have gone about designing a better salt spreader for their trucks; as we threw around ideas, Murphy tilted back in his chair, moving his cigar from one side of his mouth to the other. That was his "tell" to show that he liked what he heard.

After some back-and-forth considerations, Murphy stood up and we all shook hands, agreeing to proceed with the project. Josh and I would put together some design drawings with specifications and, if they were approved, the spreaders would be manufactured for all the trucks.

I finished the last of my coffee, which no longer tasted quite so bitter, and headed with Josh back to the office. Neither of us could wait to get started on the project as soon as possible.

At that point in my career, I knew a great deal about hydraulics and their repair but was still learning mechanical engineering concepts at night school. Josh usually drew up most of the engineering designs back then, with me as an assistant, but he had never designed anything similar to a salt spreader before. Neither of us had any idea how much salt should be spread over the given surface area of a road. Too much and the expense of operations would be costly. Too little and the effectiveness of the apparatus would be poor.

"How do we figure out how much salt to spread?" I asked Josh as we were going over some design proposals.

"I'm not exactly sure, but there's one way to find out," he replied. On the day we decided to determine the details of our new design, the temperature dipped down further than before and the sky had an orangey tint, signaling that a snowstorm was on its way. I had gone home for dinner, to have some of Betty's pot roast and potatoes, which were guaranteed to stick to my ribs and help keep me warm throughout the evening's experiment.

When I arrived at the highway department's central headquarters, Josh had just pulled up as well. We were both bundled in as much winter clothing as possible and we each grabbed a shovel. It might have looked like we were two guys getting ready to shovel out people's driveways for a few dollars, but we were actually embarking on a research and development project: We were going to find out exactly how much salt our machines needed to spread to melt the ice and snow. It would take hours, but we were going to get that information firsthand.

That, and maybe frostbite.

One of the things I admired most about Josh was his ability to keep things simple. Most people make situations and solutions too complex and in the process lose sight of the obvious. That wasn't the case with Josh. Despite his detailed technical knowledge, his solution for determining how much salt was needed and how far to spread it didn't involve a bunch of calculations and formulas drawn on paper. It was going to be handled the old-fashioned way—in the field.

He and I stood in the back of one of the moving municipal trucks and tossed out salt, shovel by shovel, until we figured out exactly how much was required per traveled mile and how far it needed to be dispersed. It might not have seemed too technically savvy, but it was simple—and, most importantly, accurate.

Of course, "simple" doesn't mean it was easy. By the end of the night, our fingers were numb and the muscles in our shoulders and backs were knotted. But, neither Josh nor I complained, or even noticed very much. There is something peaceful and satisfying about tackling a project head on and finding a solution to a problem. We were so focused on the task at hand that it didn't faze us much when we could no longer feel our own hands.

The following day, we used the information we had gathered on that cold and snowy evening to calculate exactly how to spread the salt most effectively. Shortly afterward, our design was approved by the state and the spreader units were manufactured and put into place on roads throughout Michigan.

Through our willingness to take on any problem, we'd found a solution, gotten a state contract and made driving conditions safer for everyone—and I even cut down on my salt intake after that.

We were able to land this big job because we came up with the simplest, most direct method and put in the hardest effort to find the answer. Those are what you call "the basics" in business. They are the essentials and always will be. Any get-rich-quick, how-to-succeed, self-help business book that tells you otherwise isn't worth its salt.

CHAPTER 30

An Early Sales Engineer

I had fallen asleep in my chair again.
The problem? Well, the chair was in the middle of a college classroom.
I had tried to fight off the fatigue, but sleep won out despite my attempts to ward it off. Perhaps I had been out for several minutes or only a few seconds—I had no way of knowing. Either way, my brief nap was rudely interrupted by the noise of everyone around me rustling as they got ready to leave.

Startled, I opened my eyes and realized that class had ended. The other students had packed up their materials and were heading out of the room. I quickly stood, gathered my own things and followed suit.

The cool night air was refreshing as I walked to my car outside of the community college. Every Monday, Wednesday and Friday after work, I diligently attended class in the engineering building to learn about mechanical engineering and its related fields. But despite my interest in the subjects, life commitments were causing me to fall behind in my coursework. I worked all day with Josh Shay, attended school at night on the GI Bill and took care of my duties as a husband and father at home.

Though I always had plenty of energy, the hours in the day were simply becoming too few for me to keep up with everything. Something had to give.

The following week, I drove to work as usual, ready to settle in to my normal routine. But when I got to my desk, I found an envelope with my name on it. I opened it up and took out the commission check inside. It was from Josh, for one of the large sales I had made the previous month.

I sat back at my desk and studied the amount on the check, intuitively calculating how long it would have taken me to make that same amount of money while I was working at Bendix. The answer came along with the realization that engineering alone would never have the same financial potential as sales. As I thought about that, Josh came in.

"Bill," he said, tossing his coat into his office. "Did you find the check?"

"I did," I replied. "That was a nice surprise."

"So was the sale," Josh responded.

A few hours later, I took a walk to one of the local diners for lunch. I knew I should have been doing class work as usual during my lunch hour in order to keep up on my engineering assignments, but I kept walking anyway. I felt a little like celebrating.

Besides, the more I thought about engineering school, the less enthused I became about it. It was beginning to make more sense to dedicate my efforts to sales rather than to trying to balance all my responsibilities between work and school. I was spreading myself a little thin rather than concentrating my energy on what I already knew I wanted to do.

I enjoyed sales as much as engineering, but I didn't know of anyone except Josh who managed to do both. I didn't necessarily want to sacrifice one for the other and felt I could have the best of both worlds by staying with this company, learning everything I could, getting real-world experience and letting the school responsibilities go.

At my current position, I was already getting a firsthand education on the psychology of sales as well as on engineering design. I mean, how many of my classmates had already designed machines for the state? I had an advantage and I knew that if I focused even more of my time and energy on my job, my ability to earn a better living would be beyond question.

I returned to the office without even bothering to stop at the diner. I had just walked around and thought about my choices the entire time—but once I had made the decision, I was ready to put it into effect. I opened the glass door to the office and saw Josh sitting at his desk, making some notations in his daily planner. He briefly looked up to see that it was me before returning to his writing.

"Josh," I interrupted. "I've made a decision."

The confident tone in my voice made him put down his pen and give me his full attention.

"I'm going to quit college and dedicate my time to sales," I stated.

Josh paused and rubbed his chin with his hand. I knew what he was thinking. He believed in education more than anything and was trying to figure out how to talk me out of my decision.

"Bill," he began. "I'm not sure that's the best thing."

"I thought you might say that," I responded. "But keeping up with school and work is nearly impossible."

"Maybe you could cut your work hours a bit. Would that help?"

"It might, but I like sales and I don't want to cut my hours here. To be honest, I'm learning as much engineering on the job as I am in class. More, even. And I can make better money in sales."

Josh paused again and rubbed his face. He understood what I was saying, but he still didn't like the fact that I was quitting school.

"It's your decision, Bill. But think it over. An education is important."

"I'm getting an education either way," I told him. But I knew where I was getting it quicker.

I left it at that and went home in the evening to discuss it with Betty—though I had already made up my mind. I'm a strong advocate for education, and all of my children have received college and even graduate-level degrees. But education can be gained in many different ways. The amount of knowledge and skills I learned in the Air Force was substantial, and what I had already learned from working with Josh was significant. The question for me wasn't whether or not to continue my education but *how* I was going to continue it.

In the Air Force, I'd learned about aircraft by working on them, not by studying pictures in books. I took them apart, put them together and learned it all as I did it, piece by piece. For me, educating myself while on the job would be similar. I already had the basics and the theory; what I wanted was the practical application, the details and the doing. That kind of education would improve not only my abilities but also my bank account.

In the 1960s, there was no such position as a sales engineer—but that was the path I chose, determined to blaze the way. Such a dual career separated me from the crowd and gave me unique skills. I poured all my energies into becoming the best salesperson and hydraulics engineer possible—and, in time, this certainly proved to be rewarding.

Josh never said anything else about my decision. What was there to say? Before long, I was designing plans and calculating engineering formulas as well as he was. He knew I'd made the right choice for me and he could see how much I was learning day to day.

I didn't need the security of a college education or the sure path to a degree. I knew all along which road was best for me. It just hadn't been paved before.

CHAPTER 31

The End of the Ride

Science often outpaces ethics. Sometimes the strides we make with technical and medical discoveries cause us, as a society, to arrive at a crossroads prematurely. We have the scientific capability before we even know what we should use it for—or *if* we should use it at all, for that matter. Nuclear fission was like that. So is stem cell research. But hydraulics? Sadly, the story was the same.

———

It was a Saturday in the summer of 1964—a beautiful day for a shopping center to hold its grand opening, which was a pretty big event back then. The sun was bright in the sky and all the neighborhood kids were outside, riding their bikes or playing tag and baseball—including mine.

I, on the other hand, was on my way to work. Not the office, but going downtown to check on our handiwork. Josh and I had spent months designing a hydraulics system for an amusement ride that was going to be unveiled later that day. The ride was one of the highlights of the shopping center's grand opening.

Back then, outdoor shopping malls were the norm (indoor mega-malls had not yet been conceptualized) and new ones were often introduced with fanfare and festivities. Amusement park rides, as well as giveaways and other entertainment, created an almost carnival-like atmosphere to attract customers. The rides were always a big hit with the kids. And, of course, where kids went, parents with shopping lists followed close by.

Josh and I had been working together for a few years by then, and we had expanded our services to accommodate many new and unexpected types of clients. Hydraulic motors were becoming the standard in many areas of industry, and we were being contacted by all sorts of companies to assist in the hydraulic conversions of their existing equipment. Concrete suppliers, contractors, roofing specialists and various other mechanical companies had heard good things about our services from our other clients. As a result, Josh and I had become progressively busier throughout the local area.

Hydraulic motors were typically smaller, eliminated much hardware and were simpler in design compared to traditional motors. Additionally, they were often more powerful and efficient. All of these factors made hydraulic systems more attractive—and us even busier. Our clientele had become so diverse that we never knew who might contact us next with what type of project. But we never expected to be called for a ride.

That was the climate when Josh and I had begun our project with the amusement park ride. Out of the blue, the owner of some amusement park equipment contacted us to see if we'd be onboard.

"My name is John Summers," he began, "and I heard good things about your company. I'm interested in converting some of my amusement rides to hydraulic systems."

That was something Josh and I had never even considered. Tackling a project of that magnitude required serious engineering designs and implementation. After all, kids' safety was riding on it.

The specific machine in question was a type of merry-go-round but instead of horses, passengers rode in small cars that rotated around a central hub, rising and dropping as they circled. The current system operated through a series of chains and belts powered by a standard motor. Summers wanted to replace all that with a hydraulic apparatus that was more powerful and efficient.

Well, I had plenty of experience with all kinds of automobiles—but this was something new. So, Josh and I spent many months working on the ride, putting together a prototype and completing various tests. Through trial and error, we eventually found an effective design and submitted it to Mr. Summers. I have to admit, the amusement ride was pretty spectacular. An array of colorful, two-passenger cars attached to spider-like arms spun around and around, taking riders up and down repeatedly for a five-minute duration. All of the motion was facilitated by a hydraulic system that used an array of tubes carrying oil from the motor to the working machinery. Josh and I were proud of our efforts—and we wanted to give the kids the rides of their lives.

So, when the day finally came to showcase our work and put our new hydraulic system to the test, I went to run one final check on the equipment before the grand opening began. Everything seemed to be in good working order.

Satisfied, I came back home and walked over to my neighbor's house to offer him some tickets for the ride.

"Jim, the new shopping center down in Melvindale is opening today," I said. "I thought you might want to take your kids down for some free amusement rides."

"You finally got it done," Jim said, knowing how long I had been working on the project.

"Finally," I responded with a smile.

"Thanks. I'll take the kids down there this afternoon. I'm sure they'll love it."

I went inside my house, feeling content, and proceeded to enjoy the rest of my Saturday...at least until I heard a knock about three hours later. When I opened my front door, there stood my neighbor, looking a little different from usual. His salt-and-pepper hair was slicked back and completely black, and his previously white shirt was about the furthest color from the original as possible. He looked like Elvis in a black jumpsuit.

Before I could speak, he asked, "What kind of ride are you running over there?"

"What do you mean?" I asked. "What happened?"

"My sons and I were waiting to go on the merry-go-round with the free tickets you gave us and right in the middle of the ride, everyone standing on line got soaked in black oil."

"Jim, I'm so sorry!" I said, shocked.

I hopped in my car and went straight to the shopping center to see what had gone wrong. When I got there, the merry-go-round had already been stopped because one of the hoses from the hydraulics system had become disconnected. Oil was everywhere. It was anything but merry.

As I began to examine the ride, the owner arrived and was less than pleased. I told him we needed the weekend to work it out.

By Monday, Josh and I had replaced all the hoses on the ride and retested every component. Everything seemed to be fine again, but once the machine started operating, it shut down almost immediately. According to our calculations and assessment, everything should have been working properly. But, clearly, that wasn't the case.

Josh and I literally went back to the drawing board. We went over every single piece of the design and every possible calculation. The only thing we could figure was that the specifications for the hydraulic cylinders were somehow inaccurate. These numbers were supposed to describe the capability of the hydraulic parts. But, according to our estimations, the only reason why the machine wouldn't operate correctly was that these manufacturing specifications were wrong. If their reported capacity to handle a certain load was inaccurate, that would have caused the hose to disconnect and the machine to shut down.

Despite double and triple checking everything, nothing else made sense to us.

The next day, we called the manufacturer of the hydraulic cylinders. After reviewing all our data, he agreed to come and examine the machine, but, despite our detailing every aspect of our design and showing him the amusement ride itself, he refused to admit that anything was wrong with his hydraulic cylinders or their specifications.

In short, Josh and I had hit a roadblock. We were still confident in our findings, but we couldn't come up with a satisfactory way to get the ride back up and running safely without repurchasing all new equipment. Our only option was to tell Mr. Summers what we had found.

We went to his office, armed with all of our drawings and the calculations to explain our findings.

"Mr. Summers," I began. "I'm afraid the problems with the amusement ride are bigger than we thought."

"What do you mean?" he asked, sitting up in his chair.

"We've gone over our designs repeatedly, and the only thing that makes sense is that the hydraulic cylinders can't handle the load of the machine," Josh stated.

"Then why did you order them?" Summers asked.

"We ordered them according to what their specifications said they could handle," I replied. "But we don't believe they can handle the load the manufacturer says they can."

"Then the manufacturer needs to replace them," he asserted.

"We tried that, but he refused," Josh said.

"So, what are you suggesting?"

"We're suggesting you don't run the ride again until the cylinders can be replaced with more powerful ones," I concluded. "It's just not safe."

"Hmmm, let me think about it and I'll get back to you," Mr. Summers responded.

"You understand we can't guarantee its safety if you run it," I said.

"I understand. I'll let you know what I decide."

To me, there was no decision. But, most people, at some point or another, are confronted with whether or not to do the right thing. Josh and I clearly stated our position to Mr. Summers about the safety of the ride—and we stood behind our opinion, regardless of whether it would cost more money or effort to fix it. We didn't feel it was safe in its current state.

We had little to lose by sharing our opinion since we'd been compensated for our time and effort already. On the other hand, Mr. Summers was faced with an ethical decision. Was he going to heed our warning about the machine's safety and purchase new equipment? Was he simply going to stop running the ride? Or was he going to take a chance and continue to operate it despite what we'd told him? It was the kind of decision that could affect the rest of someone's life.

When Josh and I returned to the office, we drafted a letter and mailed it, certified, to Summers' office, restating the facts that we had just explained to him. That was how strongly we felt about the issue. But that meeting was the last time we spoke to Mr. Summers in person.

A few months later, on a Friday afternoon, another shopping center was having its grand opening in a town not too far away. Crowds gathered for the event and hundreds of people were present to enjoy the festivities.

It was another sunny day, just like when we'd introduced our amusement ride. But that wasn't the only similarity.

Tragically, this grand opening was scarred by a ride malfunction as well—but this time, three children died as a result. To make matters worse, it was the same amusement ride, owned by Mr. Summers, that Josh and I had designed.

As I read about the terrible event in the newspaper, I replayed our last meeting with Mr. Summers in my head. Josh and I had thoroughly expressed how unsafe we'd thought the machine was, but the bottom line was that we hadn't been in control of the ultimate decision about whether to fix it or operate it the way it was. It had been completely out of our hands.

This kind of story can keep you awake at night, wondering if the world is ready for new technology. My neighbors' kids could have been on that ride. My own kids could have. Josh and I had brought hydraulics technology to a field where the equipment manufacturers and owners weren't yet ready to make the tough decisions.

In the end, you have to do your very best not only in designing your products but also in educating the people you design them for, though all you can do is hope they will take your words—and their responsibilities—seriously. I am sure Mr. Summers wishes he had made a different decision about that amusement park ride, just as I'm sure we all hope ethical answers will keep pace with our technological abilities.

Otherwise, we're making progress. But at what price?

CHAPTER 32

Professor Phillips

It was time for me to go back to school. Only this time I wouldn't in my chair, sleeping my way through evening classes. I'd be standing in front instead. Teaching.

But would anyone be learning?

<hr/>

Josh and I had been incredibly busy for months. We were traveling from project to project not only in Michigan but also throughout Ohio. We had secured jobs with automated factories as well as many other smaller, private companies that wanted to have hydraulics systems designed for their machinery.

By then, we had adopted a philosophy: "Physics is physics." With that, we felt there was nothing we couldn't design. We would take a stab at just about any hydraulic system for any need—and we'd overwhelmingly succeed.

As our skills and clients became more sophisticated, our product lines also became more technically savvy. We found that our competition diminished as we qualitatively separated ourselves from the rest of the pack. Yet, despite our success and growth, we always kept trying to improve our abilities.

That was where teaching came in.

Josh had been an instructor of courses in hydraulic systems at this particular college for a number of years, and he suggested I give it a try myself. He believed that teaching others allowed you to understand engineering concepts from more than one perspective. Different people naturally had different ways of comprehending and also different ways of learning. In teaching, you had to experiment with various ways of getting the message across to the students; in the process, you couldn't help but develop a more thorough knowledge of the subject yourself.

Through my Air Force training and my day-to-day job—which had me designing all sorts of machinery—I had learned a great deal about mechanical design and engineering. Along with my formal education, that made me well equipped to pass on my knowledge to an eager group of students.

I arrived at the two-story, red-brick building about thirty minutes before class was scheduled to start, but I wanted to make a good impression. That alone already made me a better teacher than I had been a student at any grade level.

I walked into the classroom and lay my briefcase on the desk at the front. No one else had arrived yet, of course, and I took the time to get acquainted with my surroundings so I wouldn't look like a beginner. Behind me was a large, empty blackboard with a fresh packet of chalk and two clean erasers—it was a blank slate, ready for a new start.

This was the first class that I had ever taught; in fact, it would be the first time I had ever stood in front of a group and spoken about anything. But, as with most of my first experiences, I was more excited than nervous.

Interestingly, it had been a relatively short amount of time since I'd decided to forego my evening college courses in mechanical engineering. So, it was somewhat odd to find myself stepping into the role of a teacher. But Josh had also assured me that teaching was a way to enhance my ability at public speaking—and as the owner of many large companies since then, I can confidently say that he was correct in his belief.

I just hoped that the role of teacher came as naturally to me as that of salesman. After all, it's one thing to *know* your subject inside and out. It's quite another to *teach* it.

Before long, students gradually began to trickle into the classroom, and I introduced myself as they arrived. Having never taught a class before, I wasn't quite sure what approach would be the best to take. But, like with everything else I have ever done in my life, I went with my gut instinct.

"Okay, everyone," I stated after all the students had taken their seats. "If you're here to learn about hydraulics and mechanical devices, then you're in the right place."

No one got up and left, so I supposed that was a good start.

"Let's go around the room and have everyone introduce themselves. Tell us a little about yourself and your background, and what you already know about hydraulics," I continued. "Let's start over on this side."

"Hello, my name is Paul and I work for Ford Motor in the technical lab," the first student stated.

"Hi, my name is Ray. I also work in the automotive field in the design department," said another.

As we went around the room, I found out that the majority of students were employed by companies already working with hydraulics. As a result, they had a solid foundation of knowledge already and asked good, detailed questions about things they didn't know. Reciting a prepared lecture is quite different from having to think on your feet in response to thoughtful questions—and I knew this group was going to keep me on my toes.

For the first several classes, I taught material from an outline, drew hydraulic circuits on the blackboard and answered a few questions at the end of each period. But something about that structure just didn't feel like *me*. I was a salesperson and an engineer. I was used to quick thinking and dynamic action. There was more to me and my chosen fields than a rigid outline and a standard teaching plan. Teaching hydraulics and mechanical concepts shouldn't have been dry—we were on the cutting edge, after all.

So, one day, I decided to be more spontaneous and approach the class from a different perspective, combining theory with real-world application. That, I believe, is the definition of "invention."

"Alright," I began. "Tonight we're going to design a hydraulic system. What are we interested in designing?"

The room was silent. Not a word.

"C'mon gang. Anything's possible—the sky's the limit. Use your imagination."

"How about a robot that can lift a car?" one student said, grinning.

"Okay," I replied with a straight face. "Let's start with the weight of the car. How much does an average one weigh?"

From there, the entire class participated in the design of a robotic system complete with hydraulic motors, pumps, hoses and lines that could accomplish the task at hand. We discussed open- and closed-looped circuits, and we talked about why our designs might or might not have worked in the real world due to logistic limitations. It was all pretty intense.

After that, every week, we tackled another unusual design project. Through this interactive process, everyone had fun and learned mechanical systems in a practical, comprehensive way. That was more like it!

Not only did I enjoy being a professor, but the supplemental pay wasn't bad at all. I ended up teaching hydraulics and mechanical devices at the college for three years—and the students actually ended up *learning.*

Putting my own personality into the lessons made the experience more rewarding, and teaching gave me the confidence to know I could speak well in front of other people—a skill that became very important later in my life.

I also learned that there are many different ways to accomplish any task, but choosing the way that fits your style makes your chances of success that much greater. Plus, knowing how to build your own robot couldn't hurt, either.

———

A lot of what I've accomplished throughout my career has been generational. My son Scott is now working with me on updating nuclear missile silos. I've bought out other family-owned companies to keep them running the way the original owners intended. I've passed on my knowledge to my employees and children so that I know my companies will be around for generations to come. Teaching is the same thing. You do it with an eye toward improving the future.

If you take your responsibilities seriously and look past the short term, you'll realize that business can be about a lot more than making products. If done right, you can create a legacy.

CHAPTER 33

The Dangers
of Hitchhiking

Most salespeople have a couple of things in common: They're never at a loss for stories, and, most the time, these stories are so incredible that listeners have a hard time believing that they're true. Trust me, you couldn't make up half the stuff that happens in sales.

Natural-born salespeople can talk to anyone at any time about any subject, and the talented ones know how to leverage those conversations into the messages they want to give and the sales they want to get. That makes sales a very dynamic field wherein you think on your feet and there's hardly ever a dull moment.

Now, I'm not the only salesperson who knows that, of course. But some of us find out the hard way.

By 1967, Josh and I had continued to grow his business progressively to the point that we could no longer keep up with the volume, and our geographic areas of service were becoming ever larger. For better or worse, we decided that the sales-and-design volume was too much for just the two of us to handle. The time had come to hire additional sales staff so we could keep our heads above water.

I was in the office, talking to a customer about their hydraulic system, when a sales candidate arrived for his two o'clock job interview. His name was Harlan. He looked to be about five foot ten and was neatly dressed in a pressed, white shirt, traditional gray tie and navy blue suit. He looked to be about thirty years old and had an honest face—an advantage for anyone in sales. I could tell from his appearance that he had the ability to make people feel comfortable, which was also a big plus.

He waited patiently while I concluded my conversation, and I invited him to have a seat in my office when the customer left.

"So, Harlan," I began. "Have you worked in sales before?"

"Yes," he replied. "I've worked for a company out of Toledo, selling automotive parts, and I just left a job selling factory machinery to automotive plants."

"Why did you leave?" I asked.

"The company was bought out and I was let go. The new owners already had a sales staff."

I'd been through layoffs before. I understood. "I see. Well, our territory is pretty broad. Are you able to travel?"

"I am. What's the territory?"

"Pretty much all of Michigan and into Ohio. But you'd have a company car to drive."

"That would be fine with me. My last territory was bigger than that. Plus, I live in Lamberton, so Ohio is a quick trip from home."

Harlan seemed personable and it was clear from his prior positions that he was technically savvy. Because of his experience, teaching him the intricacies of hydraulic systems would be pretty simple. That was a huge benefit for both Josh and me.

After checking his references and previous employers, everything seemed to be in order. I arranged a second interview for him to meet Josh but was already convinced that Harlan would be a good fit for the company. With a subsequent nod of approval from Josh, Harlan became our first new salesperson.

A year later, he was doing well in his job. In fact, we hadn't had any problems with him at all. He was always punctual and dependable, and he was a quick study when it came to hydraulics.

But the one thing I have learned about salespeople is that all of them are characters—you just never know what to expect from one day to the next. The most reliable salesperson in the world can suddenly surprise you with the craziest story. This turned out to be true for Harlan, too.

It was a seemingly normal Friday morning and Josh was at the office, working on designs, while I drove around Detroit, making sales calls. I had just finished a meeting with one of our clients and decided to stop in for a cup of coffee at a diner outside the financial district. The little place was literally sandwiched between two large skyscrapers. Every stool was occupied at the counter, despite it being midmorning. For the place to be that crowded, I figured the coffee had to be good.

And it was. While drinking a much-needed mug of it, I decided to throw a dime in the pay phone and touch base with Josh. If nothing else, he might have wanted me to bring him a cup of coffee, too.

"Bill, I'm glad you called," he said when he answered the phone. "I got a call from the Flint police department a few minutes ago."

"Flint?" I said. "What on Earth did they want?"

"It seems Harlan got himself into a bit of a mess. He wrecked the company car and got rolled by two guys last night. The police arrested him for being drunk."

"Great," I said sarcastically. "So, what do they want you to do about it?"

"I'm gonna drive up there, bail him out and have the car towed back here, I guess."

"Okay. I'll go back and stay at the office while you're gone."

The day before, Harlan had driven to Flint, about thirty miles north of Detroit, to make his usual sales calls. After he was done for the day, he booked a room rather than head all the way back home to Lamberton, then decided to go out to a local bar to have a few beers. Apparently, he met a couple of guys at the bar who were hitchhiking and needed a ride. After a few rounds of drinks, Harlan happily agreed to give them one. Hell, we should have been happy that he hadn't just given them the car.

Unfortunately for Harlan, his two new friends weren't so friendly after all. They jumped him for his wallet while he was driving, and Harlan ended up wrecking the company car while trying to fight them off. The fight then continued outside, where Harlan ended up lying on the side of the road, beaten and bruised, with empty pockets—and with our car wrapped around a tree.

By the time the police came, the two men had vanished, leaving Harlan alone to answer their questions. I guess he didn't do such a good job of answering them.

～～～

While Josh went to Flint to pick up our salesman, I went back to the office and worked on charting sales. From my desk, I could see the front door. The office wasn't that large and whenever someone entered, I had a good view, as did the girls at our reception counter.

Around three o'clock, when the front door swung open, I immediately looked up and saw Josh walking briskly, straight to his office. He was alone and didn't stop to speak to anyone. About a minute later, Harlan came in behind him.

He looked like he had been dragged in the dirt behind a tractor—only worse. His face was bruised and scratched; his collared shirt, which at one time had been white and starched, was now dusty brown with a long rip down the right sleeve. One side was untucked and grass stains covered his pants, torn over both knees. The expression on his face showed that he knew he was in big trouble.

The receptionists couldn't help but stare as he rounded the corner into the conference room like a teenager who'd be grounded. I stood up and walked back to Josh's office, closing the door behind me.

"What should we do with him, Bill?" Josh asked, clearly irritated.

"Fire him," I replied.

"On what grounds?"

"On the grounds that he picked up hitchhikers in a company car."

"Is that in the business policies?" Josh asked.

"It will be as soon as I call our attorney and have him put it in there."

Josh stood up and went to get Harlan. Slowly, with his head hung low, he walked into Josh's office. I was already standing by the time he came in.

"Harlan, we're gonna have to fire you," I said.

"I figured that was coming," he responded.

"Alright," I said. "Get your things and I'll drive you to the bus station downtown. You can get a bus home from there."

That was about all that was said. Harlan packed his personal items, then met me outside where I was waiting for him.

I stepped into my car and Harlan glumly took the passenger's side seat. It was rush hour, and we hit a lot of congestion on the way to the bus station. As you might expect, the ride was pretty quiet. All that had to be said had already been said, and I suspected that Harlan, after spending the night in jail, was just looking forward to a shower and a more comfortable bed. Unfortunately, he still had a long bus ride ahead of him.

Inch by inch, we crawled along in silence, hitting every stoplight imaginable. Just as we were about to reach our destination, I pulled up to the final stoplight and, there, to the right of the intersection, stood a hitchhiker with his thumb stuck out.

Throughout the entire trip, from the office to downtown, hardly a word had been spoken. But when Harlan looked up now and saw the man trying to hitch a ride, he calmly reached over and rolled down the window. The next thing I heard was his yelling, "Walk, you son of a bitch! Walk!"

It was all I could do to contain myself until Harlan got out of the car at the bus station, but as soon as I pulled away, I busted out laughing. I laughed all the way back to the office, and then Josh and I laughed about it some more.

Harlan had felt about as low as anybody could; he had wrecked a company car, been beaten up and arrested, spent the night in jail and lost his job all within twenty-four hours. But despite it all, he'd still had the energy to muster up a bit of profanity for that poor hitch-hiker who represented all the misfortune that he had suffered in the last day.

It turned out not to be such bad advice, either, though it came a little too late.

Those are salespeople for you. They always know what to say.

PART IV

Out on My Own

CHAPTER 34

The Start of PSI

In a relationship, things change as people grow. Sometimes, you hope you can change in the same ways in order to hold it together. Other times, you realize that individual space is what you need to realize your own potential.

If you think I'm talking about a personal relationship here, you're close. Business *is* personal.

<hr />

By 1968, Josh Shay and I had been working together for almost six years. Our business relationship and friendship were solid, though it was becoming clearer to me that we differed in more and more ways.

Josh was twelve years older than I was, and I had greater ambition at that point in my career than he did. I had gradually become a more proficient engineering designer, and my abilities in sales had continued to improve. I wanted the company to improve along with me—to become more involved in the design business and to be more aggressive in our sales strategies. Josh, on the other hand, was content with the way things were.

I could put up with our differences in ambition, vision and drive for the time being, although I did eventually want something more for myself. It was another point entirely, however, that put me over the edge.

When Josh had called to recruit me at Bendix several years earlier, he had promised me many things if I went to work for him. One was an increase in salary and another was the opportunity to get back into sales. I was happy to have gotten both. Additionally, he had promised to award me stock in his company after two years if I had grown his business significantly. Since I had begun working with Josh, his sales had more than doubled in volume and revenues.

Mission accomplished and stocks awarded. Or so I thought.

One day, it was business as usual, but for no specific reason, I became curious about the value of my stock in the company. So, before I left for the evening, I asked Josh's bookkeeper about what I'd earned. That was when I found out that I had no stock whatsoever.

"What do you mean I have no stock?" I asked her.

"Josh never distributed any to you," she replied. "I asked him about it several times, but he didn't issue any."

"But we had an agreement."

She shrugged. "You'll have to talk to him about that."

Damn straight I will, I thought. It was time to take stock of my situation.

That night, I lay awake, stewing over what had taken place—upset with myself for depending on someone else to keep their word and equally angry at Josh for not keeping it.

On my drive to work the next morning, it seemed like I hit every traffic jam, every red light and every slow car imaginable. I simply couldn't get there fast enough.

I arrived at our office at eight-thirty—the first one there, so I took a moment to look around. Josh's office was stacked with papers, drawings and projects, as was mine. A new desk had replaced his old one. There was a new radio in the reception area for our clients to listen to while waiting. There were even *receptionists* now.

Compared to the office I had entered six years earlier, nothing looked the same. But I owned none of those changes, none of those improvements for which I had worked so hard. Josh had backed out on his promise and had taken advantage of me.

After taking a deep breath, I went to work in my office. I rolled up my sleeves and poured myself into one of the designs on which I had been working. Temporarily, it took my mind off my anger and frustration. But only temporarily. Then, I heard Josh come through the door.

As usual, he walked into his office and I gave him about a minute to get settled, but then I couldn't wait any longer. I stood up from my desk and marched into his office.

"You lied to me, Josh," I announced as I stood in front of his dark, oak desk.

He was startled not only by what I had said but also by the tone of my voice. I was clearly mad. Fighting mad.

"What are you talking about, Bill?" he said, looking bewildered.

"You know damn well what I'm talking about!"

Josh looked uncomfortable, to say the least, repeatedly shifting his eyes from me to the floor.

"Bill, honestly, I don't know what you mean," he pleaded.

"Did you or did you not issue me stock in this company?" I asked point blank.

Though he tried to appear calm, his expression became a little more strained as he sat back in his chair. "Now, Bill, you and I never agreed on issuing an exact amount of stock."

"The hell we didn't! That was part of the deal when I came here and you know it! You gave me your word."

"When it came time for me to issue you the stock, I just couldn't do it. Honestly, the company hasn't grown that much."

It was a piss-poor excuse. Hell, I'll never know how he could even say that with a straight face, considering the stacks of papers on his desk representing all the projects we were working on, all the business coming his way, to *his* company.

"Listen, Bill, we can work this out man to man," he continued.

"Josh, you can make all the excuses you want, but as far as I'm concerned, there's only one real man in this room right now."

He just sat there, not saying a word. There was nothing he could say.

"I want out," I stated, and left his office.

Other than our different abilities in design, Josh and I differed in two major ways when it came to running a business. One of my business philosophies was—and has always been—to collect what the traffic would bear. In other words, I believed in maximizing profits. I never thought prices should be based on what others charged or what covered your expenses, but on what people would pay. Josh was never comfortable with that mindset and was too timid to test the market in that way.

We also differed in the areas of strength and courage. I had no problem being forthright and telling someone how I felt or what I thought. Josh, on the other hand, often shied away from confrontation. He was terrible at firing employees or breaking bad news, and I'm sure he was too scared to tell me about the company stock. But, despite his fears, he knew that if I left, I would form my own company, which would compete against his. And that alone was enough incentive for him to try to work things out with me.

"Look, Bill," he said, following me into my office. "How about I increase your salary—give you a raise?"

I was angry, but I wasn't in any financial position to leave or start my own company—yet. Knowing that I wasn't going to get my stock, I figured that getting a raise might have been the only chance I had to recoup some of what I had lost and some of the value I had added to the company.

"How much?" I asked warily.

"Fifteen percent."

"Make it twenty," I said. No negotiation. "But just so you know, you aren't the man I thought you were."

A seed of distrust had been planted between us, and regaining a level of friendship with him was difficult. We continued to work together and tackle new projects, but things between us had changed. He had taught me many skills through the years, but my trust in him had been broken. And it wouldn't be rebuilt.

Like I said, business is personal. Keeping your word, even in business, is a mark of who you are as a person.

———

When I'd told Josh that I wanted out that day, I'd meant it. Even saying the words made me realize how much I wanted to be out on my own. I had already made the decision. It was just a matter of time before I had the means to do it. And about a year later, I finally made the move.

"Josh, I've decided to form my own company," I told him one day.

"I can't say I'm surprised," he responded. "But there's really no need for you to do that. We have plenty of business, and I'd be willing to increase your salary again."

"No, thanks," I replied. "I've made my decision. It's something I want to do."

I could see he didn't want me to leave for obvious reasons. It's like the old adage—it's good to keep your friends close and your enemies closer. I wasn't an enemy but I would be a competitor, and Josh knew that my design skills had become better than his.

"How about this?" he proposed. "I'm sure you're going to need cash for startup. I'll give you some money in exchange for stock in your new company."

As much as I would have liked to be autonomous from the beginning, I did need capital to start the business. But I wasn't going to get into a situation where Josh—or anyone else—had any decision-making power. The biggest reason for leaving was so I could direct the business the way I wanted. It was something I needed to do for myself.

It was going to be *my* business.

As it turned out, Josh, another investor and I split the new company's stock three ways. Josh and I both put in $3,000 and the third partner provided free rent and utilities for my new office space for a year. My new company's name was PSI with the "P" standing for "Phillips," the "S" for "Shay" and the "I" for "incorporated." I might have shared the name, but as far as I was concerned, the company was all mine.

PSI handled designs for all types of hydraulics systems and mechanical devices. And, believe it or not, we also performed design services for Josh's company. He was primarily focused on sales, but I had begun to temporarily specialize in design.

During this time, I also kept selling for his business, so, to some extent, I had the best of both worlds, keeping my feet firmly planted in both fields. I was still using my talents in sales and engineering but I was finally enjoying more independence.

For an entrepreneur, nothing is more satisfying than being able to direct your own company. I was now able to charge what I wanted for my services and could shoot for the moon. Whereas Josh wouldn't ask for top dollar, I could now get what I was worth.

Even though I still worked part-time for Josh, being able to run my own business was incredibly rewarding. I hired my own assistants, managed my own clients and created a company that matched my personality and philosophy. If you have an entrepreneurial spirit, nothing will ever feel quite right until you have that level of self-determination. That, I had always had. But now I had a business to go along with it.

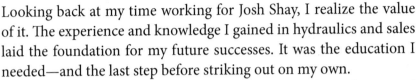

Looking back at my time working for Josh Shay, I realize the value of it. The experience and knowledge I gained in hydraulics and sales laid the foundation for my future successes. It was the education I needed—and the last step before striking out on my own.

By the time I formed PSI, I knew a lot about the industry and how to handle people. I had also learned that sometimes you can't trust even those who you thought had your best interests at heart. But all things happen for a reason—and the key is to be ready to act when the time comes.

If you don't take your future into your own hands, all you're left with are other people's words and promises, and your own wasted opportunities. And there's no one to blame for that but yourself.

CHAPTER 35

Fool Me Once,
Shame on You...

Like the rest of the world, Detroit was changing in the late '60s. Call it growing pains.

There were riots, the most notable in 1967, with looting and increased violence among inner-city neighborhoods. There were times when we came together, too, like when the Detroit Tigers pulled off an upset to win the 1968 World Series against the St. Louis Cardinals. Suburban growth had reached double-digit figures. The automotive industries were basking in the peak of their success, since foreign competitors such as Toyota had not yet entered the picture. Overall, the city's growth was tremendous and many industries were prospering. There were opportunities everywhere, as well as people ready to rip you off.

These changes were significant—both the positive and the negative—and PSI was born in the midst of it all, creating even more change for me.

Betty and I had increased the size of our family to six children in 1968—and that was *before* the minivan had been invented. Needless to say, our lives were on full throttle and with the advent of my new business, I found myself becoming busier than ever. Not only was I still making sales calls for Josh's company, but PSI was also handling all of his design jobs—on top of receiving business from other companies as well.

Fortunately, I had plenty of energy—and a wife who did an amazing job of caring for our children and managing the daily affairs of our home. Betty and I both had aspirations of making a better life for ourselves and our family. Isn't that the American dream? We wanted a better style of living and the chance to create even greater opportunities for our children. And we were willing to work at it.

Growing up in Detroit during tough financial times drove me to seek greater success for the benefit of my family—and, I'm not going to lie, for myself. Having an entrepreneurial spirit means having the drive to want to succeed. Without that, you would have gone to work for someone else and stayed content with the security. All entrepreneurs have that drive to succeed and I was thankful I had it—along with the energy and skills to make those dreams a reality.

One morning, I was sitting at my desk at PSI, working on a design, when Josh dropped in for a visit. He was neatly dressed in a shirt and tie, as usual, and was carrying his leather folder, which typically held his current projects and sales. After greeting me, he sat down and opened up his folder, revealing a project he was working on for a client.

"I need your help on the drawings for a project," he stated.

"Okay," I said. "What exactly does it need?"

"I've made some sketches for this hydraulic system and circuitry. I need it completed to finish the sale. I thought you might look it over and give me a quote for doing the full design drawings."

"Let me take a look at 'em and I'll give you a call this afternoon," I replied.

"Sounds good. I'll be in the office after two."

By that afternoon, my shop foreman and I had reviewed Josh's circuitry and estimations, and we quoted him a price for the entire set of formalized designs. Josh agreed to it and said he would send over the final specs and details so we could proceed. I had handled many similar projects in the same manner with Josh, and there was no reason to suspect that this one would be any different.

Fool me twice, shame on me.

Two weeks later, my shop foreman knocked on my office door and asked to see me. His name was Marvin and he was a large, burly man who completely filled the doorway as he entered my office. I had known him for years; he was a loyal worker and a good guy. I never had to question his word or whether he would finish a task.

I motioned for him to sit down while I finished a phone call.

"What's up, Marvin?" I asked as I hung up the phone.

"I wanted to talk to you about those new specs on Josh Shay's machine that were sent over to us recently," he stated plainly.

"Is there a problem?"

"Well, yeah, there is," he continued. "The specs of this machine are much larger than the one we first quoted."

"What do you mean?"

"I don't think we would have ever quoted such a low price for a design this size. The markings don't seem the same as before."

"Did you compare these to the original specs?"

"We don't have the original specs. We sent them back with the quote."

Since I'd dealt with Josh over the stock issue, my level of trust in him had not been as high as it once was. Given that he hadn't kept his word about that, he might very likely have been less than honest about other things as well.

I thought about picking up the phone and calling him, but that would have given him time to prepare an answer before we met. Instead, I took the drawings and specs from Marvin, put on my jacket and drove over to Josh's office immediately. If he was trying to pull a fast one, I was going to move even faster to stop it.

After working with someone for several years, you learn little things about how they conduct their daily lives. Josh always had a large, black, three-ring binder on his desk; inside it was every single notation he had ever made. He wrote down his appointments in the binder, he scribbled notes about various jobs there, and he even made cursory design drawings in it every day. Furthermore, it was organized chronologically so that on any given date, you could flip through it and see what Josh had been doing at that exact moment in time. What he lacked in forthrightness he made up for in organization.

Without any announcement of my visit, I got out of my car, drawings in hand, and went straight into Josh's office. There he sat, as I'd expected, writing in his three-ring binder.

"Afternoon, Josh," I said pleasantly.

"Bill, how are you? What can I do for you?" he asked, closing the folder in front of him.

"It seems there's a bit of a problem with this machine sketch you sent over."

"What's the matter with it?" he asked innocently.

"It appears to be a lot larger than the one we quoted for you a couple weeks ago."

"I don't think so, Bill."

"I'm almost certain," I persisted.

"Do you have the original drawings that show the discrepancy?"

Josh knew perfectly well that I didn't have the original set of drawings because we had sent them back over to him with the quote. He must have felt pretty confident at that point in our conversation.

Like he was the one holding all the cards. But I had an ace in the hole.

"I don't have the original specs right now, but I know where I can find them," I stated.

I walked around to Josh's side of the desk and slid the binder over to me so I could take a look inside it. Josh sat by helplessly, squirming as if he wanted to leave, but the look I gave him told him to stay put.

Page by page, I flipped backwards through the binder, moving closer toward the date when Josh had originally come over to PSI with his designs. And there they were, three weeks back: the drawings with all the dimensions and specifications detailing a machine half the size of the one he had later submitted to us.

It seemed that Josh had made a miscalculation in his original designs and had to increase the size of the machine later to cover up his mistake. But, he hadn't had the guts to call and let Marvin or me know—and, frankly, I don't think he wanted to let us have his cash, either. Instead, he'd simply kept the quote for the smaller machine, hoping that we would create designs for the larger specifications at the same price.

"Does this drawing look familiar?" I asked, thumping my finger on the page.

"Hmmm," he said, as if he were considering it. "Yes. I suppose it was a little smaller."

"You'll get another quote today for the larger machine. I'll expect a quick response if you want me to design it to the real specifications."

I stormed out of his office and slammed the door behind me. Josh didn't like confrontation and again had shown little courage in taking responsibility for his actions. It was no different from when he had denied me stock in his company—except that had been the first strike. This was the second. There wouldn't be a third.

After that incident, Josh knew he had burned a bridge between us permanently. It wasn't the first time he had failed to be forthcoming with me, and he had only himself to blame.

There are relationships that last forever and others that just seem to run their course over time. Our business relationship was coming to an end. But it was only *my* beginning.

Some change is hard. Some is easy. Breaking out on my own was the exact change I'd wanted. And I wouldn't have changed it for the world.

CHAPTER 36

When the Tough Get Going

The office at PSI was *my* space—so would it surprise you to hear that I kept it basic? That was how I conducted business, after all: according to the basics—hard work, integrity and simplicity. If it worked as a business philosophy, it was sure as hell good enough in terms of décor.

On my desk was an array of pencils and erasers, a few drawings and sketches, a small stack of invoices and a black, rotary-dial phone. There was a picture of Betty and our children because they were the driving force behind everything I did. But, mostly, my desk was a workspace. The only other thing I had in my office was a small transistor radio that I used occasionally to catch the news or a Tigers game, both of which were equally important.

I was alone in my office and that was the way I liked it. I'd come to the conclusion that partners were great—for dancing. But in business, I followed my own gut and my own instincts. Of course, I learned a lot from other people, but I always stuck to my own core beliefs and values, and that made me an entrepreneur in spirit, no matter who else's initial was in the company name.

Most mornings at PSI, I sat at my desk, working on drawings and design calculations. On one particular day, I was startled from my focus by the ringing phone. It had a loud bell, nothing musical about it. The bare walls almost shook as the noise bounced off them.

The phone and the mail were the lifelines of my business, so when I got a call or the mailman showed up, everything else came to a temporary halt.

"Hello, PSI," I answered.

"Bill," the familiar voice said, "are you free to talk?"

"Yes, I'm free," I replied.

It was Josh. Three days had passed since I had confronted him about the changes he'd made to his drawings. We hadn't spoken since.

"I've done some thinking, and I'd like to give up my partnership in PSI," he stated.

"I'd like that, too," I said.

"As it stands now, we're both on the bank note for about eighteen grand."

"Yeah, that's about right," I agreed.

"If you can get me off that loan, then I'll sell you my stock in PSI for one dollar."

"Alright," I said. "Let me see what I can do."

It doesn't get much better than that as far as a buyout goes. Getting complete control of my own company and the majority of the stock for a dollar was a dream. But figuring out how to come up with half of the bank note to get Josh off the loan was another thing altogether.

Somehow, I had to come up with $9,000. Where was I going to get that much money?

Nine thousand dollars in the late 1960s was a big sum—the equivalent of about $50,000 today. I had never tried to raise that much money before, let alone in a short period of time. I was still in the struggling phase of my life, with a large family, a mortgage payment and no real assets other than the business. So, I decided to start with some of my close friends. Even though they were in the same situation that I was, I didn't have too many choices.

I called most of my friends and was amazed by how many were willing to take a chance on me. Even if they didn't know too much about the technical part of my industry, they knew they could trust me, and that was enough for them.

I didn't come close to getting the entire amount I needed, but almost all of my friends bought some amount of stock. I was even more surprised by how many of them told me they were happy to hear that Josh would be out of the business. They saw him as a pure salesman who said anything he could in order to make a sale. Until recently, I had seen him as a mentor and partner, but now I had to agree with their assessment: He was a liability.

After collecting the money from my friends, I was still well short of my goal. The only other option I could think of was leveraging my home against a loan. I needed a second mortgage in order to raise the rest of the capital. Unlike today, second mortgages weren't common then. In fact, none of the banks in Detroit even offered them. Those were the days when banking made sense, and banks only loaned you what they thought you could pay back. Mortgages rarely exceeded eighty percent of the house's value; high-percentage loans and second mortgages were simply considered too risky. It's unfortunate that we didn't maintain that mindset over the last decade or so.

Still, at the time, it was an obstacle. So, I talked with several loan officers and was eventually referred to a bank in Atlanta that did offer second mortgages. After all the due diligence, I was able to get the rest of the money I needed to free Josh from the business loan. It looked like I was going to be the majority shareholder in PSI and would finally have the complete autonomy I needed to take the business in whatever direction I wanted.

Taking the second mortgage on our home never really worried me. Despite the inherent risk, I knew I could make it work. I had confidence in my ability to earn a living and pay my debts. I was committed to doing whatever it took to be successful, no matter how many hours a day I needed to put in or what projects I had to figure out. What I wouldn't do, however, was take shortcuts or go back on my word. And that made me a safe bet for success.

I had everything else in place. All I needed now was a buyout contract and a one-dollar bill for Josh.

When the deal was ready, I called Josh to let him know. Sounding almost as eager as I felt, he said he would come over to my office that afternoon. He arrived around four o'clock for what would be our final appointment together.

We had been working side by side for nearly nine years, and it was hard not to feel nostalgic as we sat across from each other. But, at the same time, a tension had developed between us—a gulf in how we practiced business—and that was impossible to ignore.

Josh put on his reading glasses and methodically looked over the contract and the loan papers. After a few minutes, satisfied with everything, he signed the documents and laid them on my desk. Then, he looked at me as I leaned back in my chair.

"Okay. Everything's set. Do you have my dollar?" he said with a slight grin.

I stood and reached into my wallet, then handed him the money.

"Here you go, Josh," I said.

He looked at what I had given him. "This is *two* dollars."

I shrugged and smiled. "How 'bout that? You just doubled your money! Now get the hell out of here!"

Our business relationship was officially over, but there was no need for it to end more bitterly than it had already been. After all, we had helped each other out a lot over the years, so the best way to finish it off was with some humor, a handshake and a smile.

That's one of the things about being successful in business: You have to know when to be tough and when to take it easy. Knowing how to react in a given situation can make all the difference in the world. Certain circumstances call for different strengths, and calling upon the right strength at the right time is crucial.

Sometimes, not being too tough can be a strength, just like losing a partner can be your biggest gain.

CHAPTER 37

Collecting From Kalamazoo

Of course, in business, there are times when you have to get tough. And I don't just mean talking a tough game. I mean taking a stand and then actually backing it up with action. Fighting for your chocolate milk, in other words, especially when someone's messing with your money.

I'm not afraid to throw a punch in any situation. But throwing a punch—the *first* punch, anyway—is generally out of the question in business unless you want to get hit right back with a nasty lawsuit. So, you just have to find another way of making your point loud and clear—even if you have to pull out all the stops.

———

In addition to my office at PSI, there was a main shop where we designed, repaired and built various machines. For the most part, a hydraulics lab wasn't like a typical industrial plant. Hydraulic components required a significant degree of precision, so hydraulic fluids were purified to eliminate contaminants, making the shop look more like a chemist's lab than a factory.

Many machines in the shop had hydraulic components, but some of the projects I accepted didn't. In order to survive in my new business venture, I accepted a variety of jobs—anything that came my way. So, on any given day, we would work on numerous projects in the shop, which was also home to one of my earliest albatrosses.

Having been in the business of hydraulics and mechanical engineering for more than a decade, I took pride in being able to accurately bid a project. I not only knew the cost of parts and labor; I also knew the potential pitfalls a project might encounter. Most of the time, I managed to avoid those as best I could. However, every now and then, something happened to keep my ego in check. That one machine that could be found sitting in the corner of the shop— that damned albatross around my neck—had taught me a lesson in humility, if not much else.

For better or worse, I'm not a quitter. Once I commit to completing a project, I will see it through to the end. On the bad side, this meant that if I bid a project poorly, I would ultimately be the one to suffer the consequences. This machine was one of those rare jobs. I had already spent over $50,000 on labor, parts and materials to repair it, yet the owner kept returning it to my shop because of further malfunctions.

The catch was that the machine never worked well and was poorly designed from the start. I suspect it had always operated badly, even when it was newly purchased. Regardless, my job was to get it back in working order each time it came to me. And, boy, that thing came back more times than a boomerang.

But, the repeated repairs weren't the worst of it. The owner of the machine, who was based in Kalamazoo, Michigan, owed me a large sum of money for past invoices. Not only had I underbid the project, but I also wasn't getting paid for the work I *had* done on it. I called him repeatedly and sent countless letters requesting payment, but the money never came. Even after my last repair, when the machine was out of my shop, out of my sight and back in working order, I kept seeing the unpaid invoices on my desk day after day, and my blood pressure kept creeping upwards. Finally, I decided it was time to do something about it.

Marvin was still my shop foreman, and he knew all about the Kalamazoo machine, so one afternoon I asked him to come into my office to talk about it. Now, as I said, Marvin was a big man—six foot two and built like a refrigerator. No one in their right mind would ever think to cross him unless they had nerves of steel or a death wish. I suspected the business owner from Kalamazoo had neither.

"Marvin, I have something I want you to do," I said as he took a seat in a chair that suddenly looked too small and un-sturdy. "I want you to take this set of drawings. They belong to that machine from Kalamazoo. I want you to head up there tonight and take a look at it."

"Is it broken again?" he asked.

"Not yet."

He gave me a confused look but sat silently.

"You're gonna open up the electrical panel and disconnect the main wires. Then, you're gonna take those wires and these drawings and leave," I told him.

"That's it? Just take out the wires?"

"Yep. Once you've done that, give me a call. Oh, and go ahead and book a room in a motel up there for the night. I'll call you when you can put the wires back in."

That evening, after he finished at the shop, Marvin headed to Kalamazoo to carry out his orders. The company there ran twenty-four hours a day, so he had no difficulty getting there late, getting to the machine and disconnecting the wires. Before I went to bed that evening, he had completed his task and checked in at a motel.

The next morning, I hadn't been sitting in my office for more than fifteen minutes when the phone rang. It was the owner of the company in Kalamazoo.

"Bill," he said, "that machine's not working again."

"I know," I replied.

"You know? Did someone else already call about it?"

"No."

"Then how did you know?" he asked.

"I had it disabled."

"What do you mean you had it disabled?"

"I figure since you haven't paid for the repairs to make the machine work, then it shouldn't work," I told him.

"You've gotta be kiddin' me! I need it back up and running."

"As soon as you pay, I'll get it running again."

The owner was absolutely dumbfounded. He couldn't believe that I'd had the nerve to send someone to his company to intentionally disable his equipment. Imagine—someone was holding up his production, which meant holding up *his* cash flow. How dare I do such a thing?

"Fine. I'll mail the payment out today," he said, but he didn't sound very convincing.

"If you want it running anytime soon, I'll need you here in my office with a cashier's check in your hand for thirty-seven thousand dollars," I told him. "When that happens, I'll get your machine running again."

"I'll send someone today," he conceded.

"No, I want you to bring it to me personally."

He sighed. "Are you serious?"

"Do I sound like I'm kidding?"

That was around nine-thirty in the morning and at four o'clock in the afternoon, the owner stepped into my office with a cashier's check for the balance of his bill. Looking worn out from the ride and like a dog holding its tail between its legs, he looked more humbled than I had ever seen him.

"Here's the payment," he said. "Now, can we get the machine running?"

"Sure thing," I replied as I examined the check. "It all looks to be in order. Have a seat."

He sat down and I called Marvin, who had been waiting in the motel room to hear from me.

"Marvin, we've received payment for the machine. You can go over there and put the wires back in place," I instructed him.

"When will it be working again?" the owner asked after I had hung up the phone.

"Oh, probably within fifteen minutes or so," I replied.

"You mean your man is in Kalamazoo?"

"Yeah. Just down the road from your place."

"Unbelievable," he said, shaking his head. "And I had to travel all the way to Detroit? I've been in business a long time and no one has ever dealt with me like this before!" He appeared to be amazed, irritated and half amused all at the same time.

"I don't like it when people don't keep their end of the bargain," I stated plainly.

"I can certainly see that," he said.

"Good, then you'll know where I'm coming from next time."

Luckily, there wasn't a next time.

The owner went back to Kalamazoo, where Marvin had replaced the machine's wires, and I never had the misfortune of seeing that clunker again. My hope was that they just got rid of it after a while and no one else got saddled with trying to repair it again—or had to deal with that owner's delinquent payments. Because I sure wasn't going to put up with it.

Once again, someone had tried to get in the way of what I'd earned and, once again, I'd fought for it. That kind of thing just doesn't fly with me. The business owner and I had an agreement and he failed to keep it—which, as far as I'm concerned, is no different from lying right to my face. He found out the hard way that I hold people to their words and accountable for what they say.

I lost plenty of money on that project, but it reminded me that you have to constantly stand up for yourself and fight for what's right. Getting ahead doesn't mean trying to take advantage of any-one—especially someone who's willing to pull out all the stops (not to mention all the plugs and wires) to get his point across.

CHAPTER 38

Flying the Coop

Around that time, in 1969, I was under a lot of pressure from the business. My partnership had dissolved, I had taken out a mortgage, clients weren't paying up on time, and it all began to take a toll on the one thing I wanted most to preserve: my marriage.

Betty was as understanding as ever, but she could also feel my frustration. That was when I decided to take some drastic action. I called my Uncle Hutch.

Hutch was a really good guy and, like quite a few of my family members, an entrepreneur. The problem was that none of his entrepreneurial endeavors ever seemed to succeed for long.

Like all entrepreneurs, Hutch was a bit of a risk taker. But, he liked to risk his money on gambling as well. You never knew what to expect with him—he was liable to drive up in a Cadillac one day then lose it the next and have to walk home.

At that time, Hutch and his wife had a shack on a little farm outside of Branson, Missouri. When I called him for some advice, he told me to come down and stay for a while.

And that was exactly what Betty and I did.

I arrived first to get things ready and spend some time with the family. Hutch took me out to fish in the middle of a lake to help me relax and get my mind off my business problems. Out there, in a small boat, he proceeded to tell me some of the wisest words I'd ever heard:

"You know, Bill, there are a lot of people in this world who'd think you're the greatest person that ever lived...if you'd just go out of business!"

That was country wisdom at its best—and he was right. I couldn't let the competition get to me.

———

Betty arrived in Branson a few days later. She was pregnant with our eighth child at the time and had come alone by Greyhound bus—that was what a tough lady she was. When she arrived, she could already see the change that had come over me.

Hutch and his wife decided to give us some time to ourselves and go stay at their trailer home. Before leaving, Hutch pointed to the chicken coop on the farm. "Help yourself to all the eggs you want," he said.

That trip to Branson turned out to be one of the most memorable vacations of our lives—not to mention the best marriage therapy ever!

Each morning, Betty and I would go into the coop, collect the eggs and have fresh omelets for breakfast. Then, we'd leave the shack, hop into Uncle Hutch's old Chevy truck from the '40s and head into town. The time alone together, without any outside pressure or work-related stress, was exactly what we needed.

It took a week of the simple life to bring me back to basics—which, after all, was how I always ran my business.

CHAPTER 39

Fishing With a New Lure

West of Detroit, in the town of Dearborn, there used to be a great little place where all the local salesmen would stop for lunch. Located on West Warren Avenue, the Gas Buggy Lounge was a landmark for years. Today, a strip mall sits where this once-popular watering hole used to be. But that doesn't mean it has been forgotten.

The Gas Buggy was legendary for having the best burgers in town. You walked into the diner and sat on a bar stool at the crowded counter, elbow to elbow with a variety of people, from business professionals to local contractors. It was a place where a salesman could always keep his fingers on the pulse of what was happening around town.

My office wasn't too far from the Gas Buggy, and several times a week I would eat lunch there. That was especially important during the early years of PSI, when networking and talking with local businesspeople was necessary for attaining new customers and projects. I was putting in so many hours at the office, working on designs and machines, that I needed to take every opportunity I could to meet new clients. And the Gas Buggy was my lifeline to the outside world.

Of course, no one would have gone to the Gas Buggy if the food hadn't been something else. Your mouth would start watering from the smell of the burgers before you even got out of your car. But a lot of the men ate lunch there for another reason as well: Her name was Kay Lech, and she was the tavern's barmaid.

Kay was an absolute knockout. Men sat in a line at the long, wooden bar that took up half the room, eating their sandwiches slowly so they could admire Kay a bit longer as she came around to serve everyone. She had long, brown hair and stunning, green eyes, and her figure was as fantastic as her face. She was also skilled at handling a crowd. If someone made a suggestive comment to her, Kay put him in his place before he even had time to retract it. But, Kay made those who came for a good meal and good conversation feel right at home. She had a natural way with people.

The Gas Buggy was my regular lunch stop, so I had known Kay for a long time. She came from a bar-and-restaurant background; her family had owned a pub for most of her life and she was well accustomed to the service industry. Still, one day, as I sat eating lunch, I wondered if she'd ever thought about getting out of the bar business and doing some other type of work. I asked her that very question as she was cleaning off the counter.

"What's wrong with working in a bar?" she joked.

"Nothing, if that's what you enjoy," I said. "I just wonder if you ever have thoughts about doing something else."

"Well, I tried to go to night school a few years back, but it just didn't work out."

"Oh, yeah? What were you studying?"

"Nothing in particular. I was just thinking about getting into a different line of work. You know, something with nights off, a regular schedule."

Now, I had a specific motivation for asking Kay about her future plans: I was toying with the notion that she might be an ideal assistant for me in the office. I was running PSI all by myself at the time, and I had several good contracts who gave me fairly steady business. But in the hydraulics field, receiving a contract for a system design or a machine repair was just the beginning. It was a long time before you saw any actual cash once a project was accepted.

After my bid on a project was accepted, there was still the work to be completed and an invoice to be sent; payment would usually come thirty days later in the form of a corporate check. But even after that, I still wouldn't have immediate access to it. I would take the check to the bank, and the bank would place a hold on it for five business days to ensure that the funds were available to cover the check. To put it short, I was having a problem with cash flow. While work was steady, available cash wasn't.

On a typical day, I sat in my office, trying to work on designs or make some sales calls while Marvin and the other technicians handled repairs in the shop. But every time I started to work on a project, a creditor called me about a past-due bill I owed. I felt like I was spending more time on the phone than doing any actual work. However, after receiving the large payment from the owner of the machine in Kalamazoo, I was considering hiring someone to manage the phones and the creditors' calls, so I would have more time to devote to conducting business. From what I had seen, Kay looked to be the right person for the job.

"Kay, would you like to come work for me?" I asked.

"For you? What would I be doing?"

"Type a little, answer calls and mostly help me stay off the phone so I can get some work done."

"Maybe. Let me think about it. I'll let you know."

Kay thought about it for only a few hours; before the afternoon was over she called me, wanting to know about the pay and the hours. My answers must have been good enough for her because she agreed to give it a try. The following Monday morning, she was at the office promptly at nine o'clock, ready to get started. I imagine I disappointed some of the regulars at the Gas Buggy when they realized she was no longer working there. But, their loss was my gain.

When Kay saw the office, she probably wondered if she had made the wrong decision. The walls were a dingy shade of beige, begging for a new paint job, and the absence of any personal décor was painfully obvious. It might have looked like we were ready to pack up and leave at a moment's notice. In my office, there was only a wooden desk that I had purchased for five dollars at the Salvation Army and a chair that cost about the same. I had little to invest in office furniture. If something couldn't generate revenue, it wasn't a priority. Times were tough then and for me, a chair didn't have to be comfortable. It was just a place to park yourself while you got some work done.

I had recently relocated from the east side of Detroit to Dearborn, on the west side of the metropolitan area. I had finally cut my ties with Josh Shay altogether and had also broken away from my other partner, Walter Shank, who had provided me with office space for a year. I was now truly solo in running PSI. And it showed.

In the common area of the small office, I had arranged an oak worktable and a pine chair with a tie-on cushion where Kay could sit. I had even gone to the store and gotten office supplies for her and equipped her with a typewriter and a phone. Kay didn't seem to mind the less-than-cozy feel of the place; I supposed that after working in a bar for most of her life, she was ready for a change. And she certainly brightened up the office.

The following day, I told Kay about the problems I was having with the creditors and cash flow, and she understood immediately. Before she was even settled at her desk, the phone began ringing.

"Good morning, PSI. This is Kay speaking. How may I help you?"

"This is John Rutherford of Vickers. Is Bill Phillips available?" the man on the phone asked.

"I'm sorry sir, but he is busy at the moment. May I help you?"

"I don't think so. When will he be available to speak?"

"I'm not sure. Could you tell me what this is regarding?" she asked.

"Well, it's about a bill he owes us."

"I'd be happy to help you then."

Before I knew what was happening, Kay was in the middle of explaining to this man the process of our billing, our delay in invoice receipts, and the hold-ups with the bank. She went through it all so nicely that it would have been difficult for anyone to be hard-nosed with her. The creditor was probably caught so off guard that he didn't even know how to respond.

A couple of minutes later, Kay hung up the phone.

"What did he say?" I asked.

"He said he would call again next week and see how we were doing," she casually replied.

"Okay, I'm impressed," I told her, knowing I had made the right choice.

Later that week, I accidentally ran into the caller, John Rutherford, while I was out making sales calls.

"Bill, how are things going?" he asked.

"Steady," I replied. "Business is good, but I wish I could just get my invoices paid faster."

He nodded in agreement. "By the way, who do you have working for you now?"

"You mean Kay?"

"Yeah, that was her name. She did a really nice job for you the other day on the phone. Am I going to be talking to her from now on?"

"Did she keep you from talking to me?"

"She did."

"Then I suspect you'll be talking to her quite a lot," I said with a laugh.

Kay not only had good looks, but she had a great telephone voice and was really good with people. That's a combination that can be hard to find.

She worked out exceptionally well in her new position and I

began getting a lot more done each day. The creditors also began calling less often, and mostly they were happy just to talk to her.

I also noticed that our mailman seemed to be spending a lot of time in the office, chatting with her when he dropped off the mail. Within another week or so, she had convinced him to bring us our mail first on his route so the checks we received would get to the bank the same day. Even a few hours made a huge difference when it came to freeing up cash. The business was surviving check to check back then, and I was keeping it alive in any way possible.

Sometimes you have to use different tactics in order to get things accomplished. I had asked Kay to come to work for me because she was great with customers at the Gas Buggy and I knew she would be a good fit for my business. She was bright, thought fast on her feet and knew how to react to a challenging situation. Those were her most valuable skills, though her good looks and sweet voice didn't hurt any, either.

I always kept an eye out for anything that would be an asset to my business, and it took a different perspective and a forward vision to see things where others didn't. Dozens of other salesmen and business owners were at the Gas Buggy for the express purpose of eating burgers and shooting the breeze. Yes, I did that, too, but at the same time I was looking for ways to improve my company. And, in this case, I found her.

Even today, I try to surround myself with the best people for the job. I have amassed a core circle of employees and friends, some of whom have been working with me for over thirty-five years. In that sense, PSI is a family business—and in the literal sense as well. My oldest son, Scott, is leading the charge on our project to install electromechanical opening systems in missile silos, the ones that showed up as his "old man" was leaving the military. I want the top people for the job, those I can trust, because then I'm sure that the projects we take on will be done right. And, in that way, we're not just building a business; we're building a legacy.

I firmly believe in giving people the types of opportunities that match their talents and skills. That's the most beneficial arrangement for the both of us, our clients, and our company. Sure, Kay was one heck of a waitress. But I always knew she had something more to bring to the table than just burgers.

CHAPTER 40

The Cadillac
and the Banker

It was a perfect day for a bank job—summer of 1972 and not a cloud in the morning sky. A little nervous about what was coming up soon, I stepped into the mile-long, cherry-red Cadillac Eldorado, with its matching red-leather upholstery, and opened up the white-canvas top to let in the sunlight. With a 500-cubic-inch V8 engine, polished finish and yacht-sized dimensions, this was more than just a car—it was a showpiece. And I couldn't wait to get it out on the road, even if it was only going to be for a few short hours. What I needed it for wouldn't take too long.

The problem was that the car didn't belong to me but to my brother-in-law, the successful owner of a Midas muffler shop in Detroit, not too far from where I lived. My old jalopy, which I could usually count on, had broken down the night before and I needed wheels to get Kay and me over to the bank.

My brother-in-law understood the situation—once I swore on my life that I wouldn't put a scratch on his brand-spanking-new car, which he had only bought a few weeks before. This wasn't just a joy ride, after all. It had taken me months to set this up, but I had finally arranged it—and today was the day! Just a short time later, I'd have a meeting with my banker in the hope of easing my cash flow problems.

So far, all of the pieces had fallen into place. I'd gotten the appointment and the car; all I needed now was the girl.

Kay had been working for me for several weeks by then—and, without a doubt, I was getting more accomplished with her there to run interference for me. But, cash flow was still tight. The more work I did, the more I needed to invest in supplies and materials, and that quickly drained what little capital and cash I had on hand. I was still at the mercy of an incredibly slow process, waiting for invoices to get paid and for the bank to clear my deposited checks. Additionally, Kay was now on the payroll, so my expenditures were slightly higher. These were the struggling years for PSI, and I was always looking for ways to keep the company afloat and moving forward.

For months I had been trying to convince Sullivan, the banker I dealt with, that I wasn't some sort of fly-by-night crook. Still, every time I called, he treated me as if I were the worst kind of delinquent. New business owners always have a real challenge getting credibility. It's a dilemma that every entrepreneur has to face.

But it was worse in the 1970s. Back then, banking was nothing like today's world of instant, electronic fund transfers. When I deposited a check, my bank mailed it to the originating bank to verify that the account it was written from had sufficient funds to cover the amount. Once that was established, my bank would finally do me the favor of releasing *my* money into my account. Because the process was handled through regular mail, it took an average of five days for a check to be released. I might as well have been dealing with the Pony Express.

In business, five days is a lifetime, and since PSI was a new company, that delay was even more significant for us. I figured that if I could convince the bank to release the checks sooner, it would make almost a week's worth of cash instantly available to me, which was something I desperately needed.

But how would I convince Sullivan to do this? Well, my first thought was to bring Kay along with me. Given her recent successes with the mailman and my creditors, I figured her presence at the bank meeting might win us some points. In addition to being smart and savvy, it didn't hurt that Kay also happened to be so good looking. So, the night before, I laid out the plan to her and she readily agreed to go along with it. I was thrilled, but not surprised: She was that kind of team player.

"Oh, and Kay," I'd said just before leaving the office, "wear something you think he might like. I could use all the help I can get."

"I gotcha," she'd replied with a grin.

It was that night, as luck would have it, that my own car had decided to up and die on the ride home. Murphy's Law, right? But at least it landed me in the driver's seat of a sweet, sexy Cadillac.

So, there I was, on the morning of the meeting, hopping into that Caddy and heading to the office to pick up Kay. Man, when I say she went all out to help me, I really mean it. She wore a black miniskirt with a white blouse, sky-high heels and a bright, lipstick-red scarf wrapped around her hair to protect it from the open air. She was a showstopper for sure, and maybe proof that God was a man. But what I saw when I looked at her was a really good sport.

To do my part for the occasion, I was wearing my best, navy blue suit with a red tie, and the two of us matched the red-leather interior of that Cadillac like it had been custom made for us. As we cruised down Warren Avenue during rush hour and pulled up to an intersection, people couldn't help but stare. We literally stopped traffic. Even though I hardly had a penny to my name, we sure looked like we were rolling in dough.

I was really enjoying the ride—that was, until we got to the bank. When Kay and I pulled into the parking lot, the only empty space was right in front of the building's enormous picture window. And that was when it suddenly dawned on me: There I was, cruising up in this flaming-red Cadillac a half a block long, wearing a razor-sharp suit and with a gorgeous, young woman by my side. What was I thinking?

Worse, what was Sullivan going to think? All the pieces of the plan finally had come together—and they formed the perfect storm. The license plate on the Caddy might as well have read "HUSTLER."

But, there was no going back. So, we stepped out of the car—Kay adjusting her miniskirt for modesty's sake and me straightening my tie—and walked into the building. *Well,* I figured, *at least we'll give Sullivan a good show before he calls the vice squad.*

He was already there in the lobby to greet us. Heck, with an entrance like that, there was no way he could've missed us. I introduced Sullivan to Kay, and he gave her the kind of look a starving man gives a T-bone steak. At me, he threw a sideways glance that hardly concealed his suspicions. I hadn't heard any police sirens yet, which was always a good sign, but my one chance with the bank might have already been blown.

We all went into Sullivan's office and sat down, but the guy was so distracted by Kay that he almost missed his high-backed chair by inches.

"What can I do for you?" he finally asked, after attempting to compose himself.

"Well, I'm hoping to free up some cash for my company," I began in earnest. "I run an honest business, Mr. Sullivan, but I have to front a good bit of capital on all my projects before I ever get paid. If I could improve my cash flow, it would help my business significantly."

"What's your business again?" Sullivan asked, glancing skeptically out the window at the Cadillac. Even though we had had this conversation many times before, he never could seem to remember what I did for a living. But, I could see that he was forming some ideas of his own now.

"I design hydraulic systems," I stated. "The company is PSI. Most of my clients own large companies."

"I have no way to free up any cash for you, Mr. Phillips. You've been with our bank less than a year. A loan is out of the question."

"I understand. But I was hoping you could release the hold on my checks when they come in—"

"That's against bank policy," Sullivan stated bluntly while none-too-subtly watching Kay cross her legs.

"But the delay in getting the checks to clear is a big problem," I told him. "It puts everything on hold for another five days even after I get paid for work I've already completed."

He was stubbornly holding his ground. "I'm sorry, but that would be too risky for the bank." I assumed the comment was addressed to me, though he was still staring directly at Kay.

I paused for a moment to assess the situation. The fate of my business was hanging in the balance and we were going down in flames. I needed to turn it around—and quickly. It was clear that Sullivan had no intention of trying to make things easy for me, so I had to find a way to make this beneficial for *him* somehow. That was when it struck me like a bolt of lightning: The guy couldn't keep his eyes off of Kay.

"What if Kay were able to bring our checks down each day for you to review personally?" I blurted out, inspired. "Could you release them then?"

There was a silence while Sullivan chewed over the idea like a snake devouring a rat. "Well, that *is* one option," he finally said, rubbing his chin and glancing in Kay's direction. "No guarantees, of course. But if the checks were from reputable local companies, I might be able to release the holds."

I looked to my left. "Kay, would that be alright with you?"

"Of course," she replied gamely, smiling directly at Sullivan. That girl deserved a big bonus for going the extra mile, if not an Academy Award.

By the time we left the bank, Sullivan was more than happy about the prospect of seeing Kay every day—it seemed the buttoned-down banker didn't mind bending the rules as long as it benefited him in some way. Of course, I really couldn't blame him. That would have been like faulting a fish for eating the worm you used as bait.

It wasn't enough to give him my word that I ran an upstanding business, or even for him to review my accounts to see that I had never bounced a check in my life. What it took was a little personal incentive—and isn't that the way the world always works?

As Kay and I walked to the parking lot and got into the Cadillac, I couldn't tell if Sullivan saw me as any more honest or trustworthy a businessman. But I did know one thing for certain: He sure as heck saw me as one lucky S.O.B.

From that point on, Sullivan began releasing my checks the same day, as long as they were from companies in Michigan. It was clear that he had gotten something he wanted from our deal. I, in turn, got an increased cash flow, which was a huge help to my business. In addition, Kay got my undying gratitude and respect, and my brother-in-law got his beloved car back in one big, beautiful piece.

In the business world, there are always ways of going around obstacles to accomplish your goals and negotiating to get exactly what you want. And that's something you can take to the bank.

CHAPTER 41

As a Matter of Factor

For an entrepreneur just starting out, the problems can seem endless. You've constantly got to think on your feet and come up with quick solutions. Although you're the one out in the ring alone, it helps to have a good team in your corner—from creditors and managers to the person you marry.

<hr/>

Even though Kay had helped me convince the banker to cash most of our checks the same day, I still struggled with cash flow. The delay between when we completed work and when we received payments created inherent problems that often got in the way of my running the business the way I would have liked to. So, as usual, I considered a different solution—and that was how I met Cliff.

Cliff wasn't another banker or a loan shark; he was a factor. A lot of people have never heard of factors, which have been around since the 1400s in England and have been a part of the American financial system since the nineteenth century, when the textile industry first came of age.

Factoring is the process by which a person purchases an invoice from a company for a percentage of what is owed. For example, if PSI had invoiced a client for $1,000, a factor might buy the invoice for $800 cash. The client would pay the factor the $1,000 and the factor would make a $200 profit—and PSI would have $800 to work with. It was a way of making more cash available, even if there was some cost involved.

Factoring seemed a logical solution to my cash-flow problems, so I sought out Cliff, who was an interesting guy. My first meeting with him was in 1973, after a friend referred me to his services. I drove into downtown Detroit to meet him in a large, brick office building not far from the financial district. Though not elaborate, his office was certainly nicer than mine; he had even gone to the trouble of hanging inexpensive art prints on the walls of the lobby. A nice touch, but nothing too fancy, which made me feel like I could trust him.

I introduced myself to the receptionist and then took a seat while she let Cliff know I had arrived, and it wasn't long before he came out to greet me.

"Mr. Phillips," he announced in a booming voice as he rounded the corner. "I'm Cliff Jones. Nice to meet you."

"Call me Bill," I said, shaking his hand.

Cliff was a fairly young man; for some reason, I had assumed he would have been much older. His hair was jet black and slicked back, giving him a Dick Tracy kind of look, and he was dressed the part as well, in a pin-striped, blue suit and polished, black oxfords.

I followed him into his office and we immediately got down to business.

"So, you're interested in factoring some invoices," Cliff stated, cutting right to the chase.

"Yes," I replied. "I own a business that designs and builds hydraulic systems."

"And these projects are eating up your capital before your invoices get paid." I guessed mine wasn't the first story he'd heard along those lines. "That's right. I need more cash so I can take on new projects and *make* more cash."

"Well, let's see what you've got for me."

I handed Cliff a folder of invoices and financials for PSI, and he took a few minutes to look them over. As I waited, I began to take notice of his personal office. Outside his window was a nice view of Detroit's downtown skyline; on the wall to the right of his desk was a picture of the 1964 St. Louis Cardinals with the trophy from the World Series they'd won against the New York Yankees. Next to it was a picture of Cliff yachting with teammates on what appeared to be Lake Michigan. Several other pieces of memorabilia were scattered on the bookshelves and on his desk. He seemed the sporting type, willing to take risks to get ahead. I liked him immediately and could see why he'd gone into this line of business.

"It looks like we can do something here," he finally stated. "Your account receivables look pretty good."

Since PSI didn't yet have enough of a history to qualify for a bank line of credit, Cliff was my best option. Although his rate was on the high side at twelve percent, I had few other choices, plus he had come well recommended. For the time being, he would have to do, and so I made the decision to do what I felt was best for my business.

"How quickly can we get started?" I asked.

"We can start today," he said. "Which invoices do you want to factor?"

Just like that, I got my cash flow flowing!

Unlike many of his customers, including me, Cliff wasn't a self-made businessman. He hadn't struggled his way through the trenches to get to where he was. Instead, he had come from a very wealthy family, and his mother had bankrolled his entire business, hoping he would make something of himself.

He was originally from St. Louis, as the Cardinals picture implied, and had come to Detroit specifically to establish his factoring business. He seemed to have found his niche there and was doing fairly well. Not only that, but the service he ran was quite valuable to his customers and he charged what the market would bear. It showed he had good business sense, if not the battle scars to prove it.

Having Cliff as my factor for a few years really helped the financial end of my business, and during that time I got to know him not only as a businessman but also as a friend. Betty and I often went to dinner with him and whomever he was dating at the time—he wasn't much for sticking with the same girl for too long. But even though the girls changed, Cliff didn't. He was always quick with his wit and entertaining to be around. Let's just say our conversations were never dull.

One Saturday evening, Betty and I met Cliff downtown for dinner and drinks. We walked into the restaurant and he was standing in the lobby with a girl whom my wife and I had never met before. Nothing surprising about that. After introductions, a good steak dinner and even better conversation, we all moved to the lounge area—and after the third round of drinks, everyone was feeling a little loose…especially Cliff.

"Betty, you know Bill is the straightest client I have," he stated in his usual loud voice. "All these other jokers are always trying to finagle money from me or handing me phony invoices."

"Is that so?" Betty asked, arching her eyebrow.

"Absolutely," Cliff continued with a slight slur. "But I never have any trouble with Bill."

"Sounds like you should reward him for being such a good client," Betty said.

"I do. I give your husband my absolute best service," he stated proudly.

"Well, your rates *are* a little high," Betty replied casually. "Maybe you could lower them for PSI a little, considering the good business it brings you."

"Oh, yeah?" Cliff said, pausing momentarily. "You know, Betty, I think you're right!"

Cliff was quite accommodating at that point of the night, and Betty, brilliant woman that she is, knew exactly what she was doing. Before he could reconsider his comments, she grabbed a bar napkin and wrote, "I, Cliff Jones, on July 20, 1973, will effectively reduce the interest rate on all future factored invoices to ten percent for PSI." Then, she placed it in Cliff's hands along with a pen. Without batting an eye, Cliff happily signed the napkin, and we continued to enjoy the rest of our night.

That Monday morning, Betty brought the bar napkin to my office and made a few Xerox copies of it for PSI's files. She placed the original "contract" in a safe place and mailed one of the copies to Cliff.

A couple of days later, my office phone rang.

"Hello, PSI," I answered. "Bill, this is Cliff. What's this I have here in my hand?"

"I don't know," I answered honestly. "What do you have in your hand?"

"It's a bar napkin with something about lowering PSI's rate to ten percent."

"Yeah, that's right," I said smugly.

"Are you kiddin' me? You're gonna hold me to that?" he asked.

"A deal's a deal," I replied. "Besides, you signed it."

This was the moment of truth. It could have gone either way. Cliff could have been ticked off by the whole thing and told me to go find a good place to shove the napkin along with my invoices, and I would've been out in the cold. Or he could have acted like a man and stuck to his word. Either way, I wasn't backing down.

So, what did he do? Well, he surprised me completely: He cracked up.

"That Betty... I gotta watch that woman!" he said, practically choking with laughter.

"She's a tough one," I agreed. "That's why I married her."

"Well, I guess I better uphold my end of the bargain, then. Wouldn't want any trouble with her," he said.

Rest assured, he would've gotten plenty of trouble if he didn't— from both Betty and me.

For a long time afterward, Cliff and I laughed about Betty's shrewd maneuver that evening, and the three of us had many more great nights out together.

As my business history grew, Cliff eventually referred me to a bank that gave me a solid line of credit. Even though it meant I would no longer need his factoring services, he knew it was the right choice for me, and that being successful in business didn't mean you had to be cutthroat.

In return, I referred plenty of people to Cliff and we remained friends long after I needed any factoring services. He kept true to his word and earned my trust—and that was the best recommendation I could give anybody.

In business, it helps to get to know the people you work with— not just the degrees they have hanging on their office walls or the titles on their business cards but their *characters*. It also helps always to search for another way around obstacles—an edge, an advantage, a simple solution that can easily be overlooked if you're willing to simply settle or give in.

If it seems like you've run out of answers and exhausted your options, don't throw in the towel when all you might actually need is a napkin.

CHAPTER 42

Sales and Servo Valves

A ny opportunity might turn into a life-changing one. That's why I've always taken chances and tried to make the most of them. Who knew where they would lead? But I knew one thing for sure: If I didn't take them, I might not have gotten anywhere.

A lot of people say they're happy where they are. I say they're lazy. Most of them lack vision and imagination. They simply settle for what *is* over what *could be*. And that's one risk I just won't take.

———

During our early years, most of the work done at PSI was designing hydraulic systems and building machines. A couple of jobs involved converting one type of system into another that utilized hydraulics. We also did some repair work on hydraulic systems, but that was just a small part of our daily operations. I was an engineer and a salesperson, after all, not a repairman—but I also wasn't in the business of turning jobs away.

I had a pretty good handle on the direction I wanted my company to go and the services we'd provide. But, I also kept an open mind when it came to other opportunities. They say that opportunity knocks; I say that sometimes it calls. Sometimes, it hides in plain sight. And, sometimes, you have to go hunt it down for yourself.

One morning, I even found an opportunity just sitting on my desk in the form of a telephone message.

I had just returned to the office from my morning sales calls and saw a note that a servo valve repair company had called. I knew all about servo valves from my experience with hydraulic systems and from teaching at the community college. But these devices were typically manufactured in large plants that were exclusively dedicated to their production. I had never had a request to repair one or even design one. Still, that didn't stop me from returning the call.

The number was a local one, in Detroit, and I dialed it, not having any idea that this call would be a life changer.

The phone rang and a man answered without identifying his business. I introduced myself and he immediately knew who I was.

"We're in the business of repairing servo valves," he said. "And we've heard some good things about your company."

"What exactly can I do for you?" I asked.

"We're looking for someone who can help us find customers," he stated. "Would you be interested in doing some sales work for us?"

Business was steady at PSI, but you never know what might lie around the corner. And, I didn't believe in just waiting around to see what would happen.

Keeping an open mind about any opportunity could mean the difference between the survival and failure of a business. Sometimes it's as simple as not having acted on something when you should have. I wasn't sure that this particular opportunity had any legs, but I was definitely going to listen. Particularly since he was talking my language: sales.

"I'd like to hear what you have to say," I responded.

"How about coming down to our laboratory tomorrow morning, around ten o'clock?"

"Sounds good. I'll be there."

The following morning, I couldn't get into my car fast enough. It was pouring outside and I was trying to keep my suit and tie from getting soaked. As I started the car, I struggled to see through the dense fog and heavy rain. Did I entertain the thought of maybe blowing off this meeting and just doing some work in my nice, dry office?

Not for one second.

I knew there was no such thing as "business as usual." There was either progress or potential bankruptcy.

The industrial lab I was going to was just outside of Detroit, to the west of town. Visibility was miserable, and all the buildings along the street where I was driving were poorly labeled. Eventually, I found the one I was looking for, and I parked my car right outside it before quickly running in.

I swung open the solid, gray-metal door that stood at the top of three short steps, and the fluorescent lighting inside brightened a small entry room. At the other end of the room, a receptionist sat in front of a glass window. I told her I had an appointment at ten o'clock, then sat and waited.

Behind her desk, I could see a large portion of the laboratory: Technicians dressed in white smocks stood over tables, measuring and examining various pieces of equipment. Fluorescent bulbs lit the entire area and a low-level hum came from some of their calibration machinery. It all looked a little sci-fi, especially for servo valves.

In order to understand the concept of a servo valve, it's best to think of it as a control system that regulates some type of output. In engineering terms, this is called a "closed-loop system," which provides feedback to a control. The control then regulates the system's performance to attain results within a narrow range.

For example, cruise-control systems on automobiles are a common type of servo control system. You set the speed for sixty miles per hour, then a servo control system regulates the acceleration of the car accordingly. If the speed goes above a certain velocity, the servo system eases back on the acceleration. Likewise, the reverse occurs if the speed starts to become too slow.

While many servo valves use electrical power for their performance, it's also common to find ones that use hydraulic systems. In this instance, the servo valve controls the direction and flow of the hydraulic fluid to alter the performance of the entire system. It isn't rocket science (although it looked like that in the laboratory), but it is pretty technical, despite the fact that most people take its benefits for granted.

"Good morning," a man said, stepping into the reception area from the lab. "My name is Thomas." This was the one I had spoken to on the phone.

He was very tall and wore a white smock. I introduced myself, we shook hands, and then I followed him into the lab area, where I met two other technicians. As it turned out, these three men ran the whole operation together, even though Thomas did most of the talking during our meeting.

"What type of hydraulic work do you do?" he asked me.

"I do different types of things, but mostly I design and construct hydraulic systems for a variety of companies and contractors," I replied.

The other two men glanced at each other briefly.

"Ever do any work on servo valves?" Thomas continued.

"Not any repair work," I said. "But I have designed them into applications and machinery many times."

"How's your client base?"

Now I had some questions myself. "What's this all about?" I asked. "Why are you so interested in what I do?"

This meeting was beginning to feel more like an interrogation than a business discussion. Thomas glanced at his two partners, who stood by silently. Then, he finally showed his hand.

"We're looking for somebody with good contacts who can help us distribute the servo valves we repair and drum up business."

"And you'd like me to find these customers for you?" I asked.

"Yes," he replied. "We want to increase our volume."

"How much would I be compensated?"

"We want a hundred and seventy-five dollars for every servo valve we repair. Anything you collect over that price, you can keep."

It turned out that the three technicians had once worked for a company that manufactured new servo valves. As a result, they knew the industry pretty well. For instance, they knew that a new valve cost about $600, and when a valve broke, most companies typically had no choice but to buy a new one.

The manufacturers of servo valves made them with automated machinery, so it was cheaper for them to produce new valves than to repair broken ones. They would have to take away resources from their production of new servo valves in order to develop a repair division, and they didn't want to do that. Besides, new valves were more profitable, so manufacturers had little interest in offering repair services for their old ones.

These three technicians, however, had found a niche. They could repair the old valves and sell them for much less than the cost of new ones—but they didn't have the contacts or client base to which to distribute them. I did.

They needed my sales ability to market their services to the right clients and wanted me to act as a sort of middleman.

"When you find us clients, we'll pay you after we collect the money for repairing the valves," Thomas explained.

"How 'bout I find you clients and pay you the one hundred seventy-five for each valve repair I sell?" I offered instead. "That way all your payments are coming from me and not a bunch of different companies that you might have to chase down."

I could tell that proposition wasn't what Thomas had in mind and, by the way he reacted, I didn't think he trusted me completely. With all of their shifty eyes, I didn't totally trust these characters, either. But I knew I could get the payments from the clients.

"I guess that would be okay," Thomas answered after a few moments' thought. "Do we have a deal?"

"It sounds fair to me," I replied. After all, what did I have to lose?

A few days later, I started marketing servo valve repairs to various companies in the Michigan area, making calls to all of my current clients and soliciting many new ones to see if they had any interest in this sort of repair service. Turned out, there was a huge market that needed to be filled.

I was able to increase the price of the repaired servo valves to as much as $400—not a bad profit for an easy sales job. Because of my negotiation with Thomas on how I would collect the fees, I had a natural incentive to get as much as the market would bear. If I had let the technicians handle the finances, I would have been at their mercy not only with the collection procedures but also for the prices they determined. They weren't looking for much more than $175 to turn a nice little profit. I didn't bother with "nice little profits" when there were bigger ones to be made.

Even at $400 for a perfectly repaired servo valve, I knew I was saving the customer at least $200 compared to the price of a new valve. So, why not ask for the higher price—especially since they were willing to pay?

The one thing I always knew I could do well was make sales. It didn't matter if it was servo valves or vacuum-cleaning services. If I had a hot product in an underserved market, I knew how to make the most of the opportunity.

Within a couple of weeks, the technicians were already reaping the benefits of my sales abilities. They had nearly doubled their client base, and I was making some good money for my services.

That was one phone call I was certainly glad I'd returned—and one more way I found to make a return on the investment of my time and talents.

CHAPTER 43

Sometimes Opportunity Rattles

I was stuck in traffic. Worse, I felt a little stuck in my servo valve deal.

Sure, I was turning a profit on my sales. But being the middleman wasn't exactly sitting right with me. To me, the middle was a security zone. It wasn't the fast lane, where you could get ahead, and it wasn't the slow lane, where you could get off and try something new. You just sort of cruised along at whatever pace the traffic was setting. And I was getting fed up with the limitations.

On this particular day, I was trying to get to my next sales appointment, where I'd be meeting with one of my clients about a design project for PSI. I was already a little behind schedule because of the highway traffic, so I decided to take some back roads, hoping I'd be on time.

Back then, Betty and I were living on a shoestring budget and I was trying to keep as much money in the business as I could. Things were always pretty tight, but we tried our hardest to make ends meet. And that meant making it to my business meetings on time since being late could have been the deciding factor in whether the client chose to use my services or someone else's.

Back roads in Detroit didn't offer the smoothest of rides. Pot holes, railroad tracks, road construction and speed bumps all hindered my attempt to arrive promptly as I meandered slowly through the industrial areas of downtown. The traffic was lighter, but I wasn't making much additional time by taking the roads less traveled.

What made it worse as I bounced along was that I was also being tortured by the incessant rattling of six servo valves that I had shown to potential buyers and were now sitting on my backseat. The harder I tried to get to my PSI appointment, the louder the pieces of equipment rattled and the more irritated I became. I was almost ready to chuck them out the window.

Then, I had a revelation.

I had been selling servo valves for the technicians for a few months and had been doing quite well. I had convinced several of my existing clients to buy repaired valves instead of shelling out for new ones, and I had successfully solicited many new customers for the technicians. The number of repairs had skyrocketed in the last month, and the technicians had been enjoying the extra business, as had I. I'd been consistently selling the repaired valves for $400 and was making a profit of over $200 per sale.

But, as I rushed to my appointment, I realized that I wasn't using my time most efficiently. The meeting had been set up to discuss a design project that might have yielded the same amount of money as my profit on a single servo valve sale. And, the time to render a full set of hydraulic design drawings was significantly more than the time it took to sell one servo valve. So, I thought, what if I performed the repairs myself?

I had all the ability to learn how to perform the same service that the technicians were doing—plus I could take full advantage of my sales skills. Suddenly, my urgency to be on time for the appointment wasn't quite as strong.

As the valves continued to rattle at me in my backseat, I

realized that the technicians had set their scope too narrow. Servo valves were used for many other industries besides automated factories and automotives. From hydraulic to electrical systems, servo valves controlled many operations in the aerospace and automotive fields and more. Selling repaired valves to bigger corporations in other industries could generate enormous profits—and adding hydraulic repair to my services would help me gain even more clients and projects.

Once again, opportunity was rattling.

I arrived at the appointment ten minutes late, but by then my thoughts had shifted to the future. I was less concerned about selling my design services and more focused on my new venture in repairs.

But, I still had to deal with Thomas and the other technicians, who were becoming progressively restless. For the last couple of weeks, they had been pushing for a contractual partnership situation with me. They'd seen the increase in volume since I had begun selling their services to clients, and the bottom line was that they wanted to muscle in more on the sales. I knew that in a partnership, my percentage of the profits would undoubtedly decline while their level of control would increase. Where was the upside in that?

After my appointment that morning was completed, I drove straight over to the technicians' lab to drop off the valves that were in my backseat.

"Bill, come inside," one of the technicians said as I got out of my car. "Let's talk."

I left the valves where they were and walked inside to where the other two technicians were seated in the conference room, eating lunch.

"Have a seat," Thomas said with his mouth half full.

"I'm fine standing," I replied.

"Suit yourself." He shrugged. "Let's talk about this partnership deal."

"I'm not really looking for a partnership," I stated. "I've been down that road before, and I've got no interest in going back."

"I understand. But we brought you into our line of business. It's only right that you share the risk with us in this venture."

Thomas was once again doing most of the talking for the three of them. He'd said "share the risk," but what he'd meant was "share your profits." They knew how to repair servo valves, but they had no idea how to sell their services—and without me, they had no opportunity to gain clients.

On the other hand, I could learn as much about repairing servo valves as they did. They didn't have any unique expertise in which I didn't already have a foundation.

"I'll think it over," I replied, wanting to get out of there. "But don't get your hopes up. I'm pretty set on flying solo."

"Either we have some type of partnership arrangement or you won't be selling any more repair work for us after this week," Thomas stated bluntly.

Ultimatums are doled out by those who are scared of something. They are afraid that if things don't change the way they want them to, something bad will happen or they'll lose the upper hand. Therefore, they try to force the situation by threatening the other party. It's no different from a bully who threatens a smart kid into helping him cheat on a test. Only one really has something to gain.

It was obvious to me now that the technicians were scared of my taking over their business. They had tipped their cards.

"I'll tell you what," I said. "Here's a deal for you. How about I quit selling for you today? I've doubled your business since I came onboard. You can go screw yourselves and your servo valves."

I walked straight to my car, started the engine and drove away. I didn't turn around to see their expressions, although I heard one shout "Bill!" a couple of times behind me. I wasn't in the habit of looking back—and I sure as hell wasn't going to start now. So I just kept on driving.

The rattle of those servo valves in the backseat was now music to my ears—the sound of a new opportunity knocking.

I hadn't invested much time in repairing servo valves before, but I was about to take a crash course in it and get up to speed. When I arrived at my office, I got out of my car, grabbed the box of valves and walked straight back into the shop area, where Marvin was hard at work. I plopped the box down on the closest worktable and the noise immediately caught Marvin's attention.

"We're getting into the servo valve repair business," I announced.

"The what?" he asked.

"Servo valves," I repeated. "I'm not dealing with those small-time technicians any longer. We're gonna start repairing them ourselves."

"Well, somebody'd better get smart in a hurry," Marvin replied. "'Cause I don't know a darn thing about them."

That was an understatement.

Repairing servo valves took special skills and special equipment. But, like I always said, physics is physics, so we'd figure it out somehow.

Besides, I told him that between the two of us and my contacts in the industry, we could learn how to do it in no time.

And "no time" was all we really had to get this business up and running.

Through the years, I had met many colleagues who, like me, had done a little of this and a little of that. Some had worked with companies that built servo valves. Others had equipment and parts they were willing to donate.

One thing I have learned in life is that the people you expect to help often don't, and people you hardly know often help you the most. From electrical control boxes to laboratory tables, many close friends and colleagues helped me prepare PSI to compete in the servo valve repair industry. I gave them my thanks and then got right to work.

Within a week or so, I was set. The lab looked professional, and I now had the skills to match. I was not only selling but also repairing servo valves myself.

It was a little bit of "old school" business savvy mixed with "home school" self-teaching. And with a combo like that, there was nothing that could stop me.

1937

Bill and cousin, Anna, 1939

1935

With grandfather, William Phillips, 1934

Bill with his parents,
Asa and Dorothy Phillips, 1935

Bill with grandmother, Elizabeth Phillips, and
cousins, Anna and Jean, 1938

Bill and cousin, Anna, 1936

Bill and Gail with mother,
Dorothy, 1942

Bill and younger sister, Gail, 1942

Having fun with a cousin,
1945

Parents with Gail, 1945

The gang, 1948

Grandparents Tom and Nancy Keeter, 1945

Bill's first wool suit, 1943

The Irving School, 1944

Observe Golden Wedding Day

Grandparents' fiftieth wedding anniversary

Above is a picture of Mr. and Mrs. W. S. Phillips, taken a few days before they observed their 50th wedding anniversary at their home here Saturday. They were married at the Blake farm on Swann Pond, three miles east of Tuckerman on August 16, 1891, by the late W. G. Hogan, justice of the peace. Mr. Phillips was born at Vandale, Ill, and Mrs. Phillips, daughter of the late, Rev. and Mrs. I. W. West, was born in Mississippi, both in 1870, there being only two months difference in their ages.

From a youth, Mr. Phillips has been mechanically inclined and has played a large part in promoting the use of modern and labor-saving devises on the farms, gins and mills in this section. He was operating a sawmill at the time of his marriage and paid the J. P. for his services with gum fencing lumber, he said. "They didn't use much money at that time," he continued, "but swapped their products and labor with neighbors for their needs." Mr. Phillips has been ginning cotton the past 22 years. He has also operated threshing machines, combines, flour mills, in addition to sawmills.

On their farm at the east edge of town Mr. and Mrs. Phillips en-joy many modern conveniences due to the mechanical inclination of Mr. Phillips. In their barnlot he has installed an electric pump which furnishes water for their stock, and from a large pressure tank water is forced through pipes to the vegetable garden, the kitchen and bathroom. In a nearby field he has a gasoline pump which furnishes water for irrigating truck crops and a portion of his field crops. When the drouth came this year he turned the water on a 14-acre patch of cotton which if stopped producing now would yield more than a bale to the acre. A two-and-a-half-acre plot of early corn has 125 bushels to the acre where only nubbins would have grown had it not been irrigated.

Mr. Phillips says no cotton worms have appeared in his field this year, but he is ready for them. On a two-wheeled cart he has mounted a rotary pump, geared to the axle, and a fifty-gallon tank from which two men can spray 8 rows of cotton at a time.

Mr. and Mrs. Phillips have six living children. They are: Oscar Phillips and Mrs. Harry Lawrence of Tuckerman; Lawrence Phillips, Sheridan; Neil Phillips, Avondale, Ariz.; and Asa and Hughie Phillips, Detroit, Michigan.

Gail and Bill, 1945

Grandmother Nancy Keeter, 1953

Bill with family car, 1950

Asa and Dorothy Phillips, 1956

Betty with her brother, Bill, 1954

Bill and Betty Phillips' wedding, St. John's, Newfoundland, January 1955

The wedding cake, 1955

Their first house, 1955

Bill, Betty and Lynn, 1956

Bill in uniform, 1952

Torbay, Newfoundland, summer 1955

The Hed Shed, Torbay,
6622nd Air Transport Squadron Headquarters

Bill in Sonderstrom, Greenland,
December 1953

Greenland, 1952

Torbay maintenance hangar

Air Force passengers on a transport plane out of Greenland

Thule Air Base:
Transportation is where you find it

Mechanics at Thule Air Base

Relax wherever the opportunity presents itself

Torbay hangar

Goose Bay Labrador Air Base

Aircraft Hydraulic Technician School, Bill Phillips third from right

Photo taken from a transport plane

Pepperell AFB, 1953

Repairing the braking system on a C-54D at -30°F

Landing on the ice cap

F-89s from Goose Bay Air Base

Barrel drop at a station

Colonel Bill Bower, former Doolittle Raider

General Meyers' aircraft

BW-8 Air Base, Greenland

DEW line
radar station

Alert radar station

Landing on the ice cap

Ye Olde Coffee Shoppe: Everyone had their own mug that hung on the wall.
Bill's mug is circled in blue.

Thule and "B" Site Air Base

First PSI building in Dearborn, Michigan, 1969

Kay Lech

National Fluid Power Society, 1960s

National Fluid Power Society, 1970s

Scott, Betty and Bob fishing, 1970

Asa Phillips at Westland house, 1965

Terry and Lisa, 1961

Lynn and Donna, 1960

Bill and parents, 1969

Lisa, Scott, Donna and Bob, 1965

Amy, 1974

Sean, 1978

Livonia house, 1970

Bill with first plane, Aero Commander

Bill and Jim Allen, pilot, Durango, Colorado, 1978

Sabreliner

First grandchild, Sarah, 1980

Bill and Blake Northrop,
Ascot, England, 1980

Amy, Lisa, Betty and Bill in Barbados, 1986

The gang on the Golden Horn, Alaska, 1984

Bill and Betty, July 1986

Betty, Dorothy and Gail, Mother's Day 1986

Jaguar, 1986

Back: Amy, Scott, Lisa, Sean, Terry, Bob
Front: Lynn, Donna
1986

Bill with grandchildren, Andy, Ben, Amy and Lauren, 1991

Bill with daughter, Amy, in Barbados, 1987

Bill and Betty holding Andy, 1989

Buck

Bill and Betty with Sr. Mary Francilene, Madonna University president (center)

Betty, 1994

Fishing in Alaska, 1992

Bill and Betty meet the Pope, 1997

MADONNA UNIVERSITY

Bill and Betty with daughter, Amy, at the National Cherry Blossom Festival, Washington, DC, April 1991

BRIDGET DR.

Bill receiving doctorate, becoming Dr. William T. Phillips, May 1995

Bill, Amy, Matthew, Terry, Andy and Steve, 1995

Camp

Bill with Jack and Owen, 1999

Bill and his mother, Dorothy, 1994

Sarah, Meghan, Donna and Erin, 1999

Terry, 2001

Gail Johnston and Dorothy Phillips

Lisa

Terry, Donna, Bob, Scott, Sean, Lynn, Lisa and Amy, 2003

Back row: Amy holding Will, Laine, Ben, Lauren
Middle row: Jarred, Matthew, Andy, Alia
Front row: Molly, Zane, Haley, Jack, Caleb, Max

Amy, Betty, Sabine, Lisa, Terry, Lynn, 2004

Hal Keeter and Bill Phillips, Camp 2008

Bill and Hal, 2002

St. Mary's, 2007: Steve, Ben, Terry, Bill, Lynn, Betty, Amy, Matthew, Max

Bill and Betty awaiting the president—just another day at the office, July 2003

President Bush with Bill Phillips, Mike Fitzpatrick, Scott Phillips, Betty Phillips and Bob Phillips

Bob Phillips introducing President Bush

President Bush with Scott, Betty and Bill

Scott Phillips escorting President Bush through the facility

Bill and Betty with
President Bush

Back row: Bill, Betty, Terry, Jane, Sean, Alia, Sabine, Scott, Sarah, Erin, Steve, Donna, Steve
Front row: Amy, Laine, Meghan, Matthew, Andy
Beaver Creek, Colorado

Annual family football game, Thanksgiving 2007

Terry, Bill and Betty
Beaver Creek, Colorado

Bill fishing on the Sturgeon River in Northern Michigan

Home, 2009

Phillips Service Industries, Inc.
World Headquarters, Livonia, Michigan

Bill and Betty at the PSI
20th anniversary party, 1987

John McCain's visit to PSI, August 2008
Left to right: John McCain, Scott Phillips, Bill Phillips and Bob Phillips

PSI corporate jet

Beaver Aerospace & Defense, Inc.
Livonia, Michigan

Mountain Secure Systems
Longmont, Colorado

Sciaky, Inc.
Chicago, Illinois

PSI Repair Services, Inc.
Livonia, Michigan

Evana Automation Specialists
Evansville, Indiana

St. Mary's Gala, October 2009
Top left: Bill Phillips, Ben Phillips, Mike Fitzpatrick,
Andy Cauzillo, Steve Cauzillo, Bob Phillips
Seated: Amy Fitzpatrick, Terry Cauzillo, Betty Phillips,
Amy Cauzillo

St. Mary 17th Annual Gala

Event raises $200k for graduate medical ed program

Betty and Bill at the St. Mary's
Annual Gala, October 2009

St. Mary Mercy's 17th Annual Gala celebrated the hospital's Golden Anniversary on Oct. 9 at the Laurel Manor Banquet and Conference Center, and was well attended with over 600 guests who enjoyed the fabulous music of the Simone Vitale Band. This black-tie affair raised over ___ ___ in support of clinical

difference to this hospital and the communities we serve," said Sara Stauffer, director of Development, St. Mary Mercy Hospital. "The proceeds from this year's event will assist in building a vital component of St. Mary Mercy's residency program—clinical research."

"With the proceeds from the

of Saint Joseph Mercy Health System) and University of Toledo College of Medicine (UTCOM) have collaborated on approximately 10 new residency and fellowship programs and will host nearly 150 new residents. Internal Medicine and Family Medicine programs have been established and interviews for residency positions have already

The Phillips family, 2009

CHAPTER 44

My Introduction to the Legal System

≋

How to repair servo valves wasn't the only thing I learned. I also got a firsthand education in the legal system.

The lab I had set up for servo valve repairs at PSI was connected to the main office, and everything was enclosed within the confines of cement-block walls. One metal exit door was located on the west side of the lab, and a set of double doors separated the laboratory from the office area. The few windows throughout the lab were covered with shades to prevent anyone from seeing the contents of the building.

Although we weren't working on anything top secret, it wasn't exactly something I wanted to advertise to the competition.

So, when we started our repair service, I specifically instructed Marvin to keep the doors to the shop locked at all times. There was a lot of expensive equipment in there and I didn't trust those three shifty-eyed technicians too much. I suspected that I hadn't seen the last of them, and my intuition was right.

Late one evening, while I was out on sales calls, there was a loud banging on the office door. Marvin was there but he was alone, so he reached for a hammer and approached the door.

"Who is it?" he asked before opening it.

"Thomas McAlister," a voice replied. "I'm here to talk with Phillips."

"He's not here," Marvin said. "I suggest you call him tomorrow and make an appointment." By the way he said it, you could tell it was meant as more than a friendly suggestion.

"Tell you what," Thomas continued. "How about you let me leave him a note with my number on it?"

"I'm sure he has your number."

"Well, I'd like to leave it anyway to be sure."

Marvin cracked opened the door just enough to see who was on the other side. Thomas wasn't alone. He stood there with one of his partners.

"Give me the note and I'll be glad to give it to him," Marvin stated.

"Sure. Hey, how about a tour of the place first? I've never seen Bill's office before," Thomas asked.

"Do you have a note or not?"

"I'd like to see the inside of the shop," Thomas said in a more serious tone.

"Then you'll have to get past me," Marvin said, thumping the hammer against the palm of his hand.

Thomas didn't leave a note, nor did he get past Marvin. In fact, he knew enough not to try.

Those technicians didn't return the next day to meet with me, either. They finally figured out that there was nothing to talk about at that point, and they also had a pretty good idea that something was going on inside PSI.

The fact was that I was skilled in mechanical engineering and sales—and the technicians' skills were less unique than they'd originally thought. But, by having become a sales engineer, I had positioned myself to have singular talents, which reduces the number of real competitors in any business.

I had called Thomas and the company's bluff, and they had no choice but to sit by and watch as their market share declined. But, they didn't simply sit by for long.

≈

"Bill, our insurance company just called us," Betty said as I answered the phone in my office one day.

"About what?" I asked.

"They said the check we sent them bounced."

"Bounced? That's impossible."

"Well, they said it did, and they're canceling our policy."

Every couple handles their finances differently, I suppose—however it happens to work for them. In our marriage, I paid the bills and managed our bank accounts while Betty managed the rest of the household. She had enough to do with our eight children while I was in the office. Besides, my business account was at the same bank as our personal account, so it just made sense that I handled both.

Even though money was tight, Betty and I always paid our bills on time: our mortgage, our utilities, our medical bills and, of course, our insurance premiums. Something was strange. There had to have been a mistake. I had never bounced a check as long as Betty and I had been married.

So, I drove down to the bank to see what had happened to our account. Sullivan was out for the afternoon, so I tried one of the bank tellers to get an update. But it was the lunch hour and the bank was very busy; there were nearly a dozen people waiting in line and all of the loan officers were already helping clients. Wrapped in a maze of stanchions, we all waited our turns, moving closer to our goals inch by inch.

In the 1970s, tellers didn't have computers. If you wanted to know your account balance, they had to go into the back of the bank and check a master ledger, which was updated daily from a batch of

microfilm sent by a main branch or from information sent by telegraph. It wasn't exactly the most efficient process. Keep in mind how far bank services have come in the last thirty-odd years the next time you're waiting for the guy in front of you to finish using the ATM.

Anyway, I finally made my way to the front of the line.

"May I help you?" the young lady asked.

"Yes, I would like to check on my personal checking account," I replied. "Here's my account number."

"Just a minute, please," she stated.

She took my information and went to the back. After a few minutes, I saw her walk around to the side where the loan officers were weeding through a line of people to whom they could and couldn't loan money. After getting the attention of one of the officers, the teller promptly returned to her window.

"Please have a seat and a bank officer will be right with you," she told me.

Those are never words you want to hear. If a teller couldn't tell me the current status of my account, that meant either it was overdrawn or a mistake had been made.

The lack of information was beginning to make me a little frustrated when, finally, a bank officer approached me.

"Are you Bill Phillips?" he asked.

"Yes."

"I'm Ted Reynolds. Please have a seat in my office."

I followed him and sat down, awaiting an explanation.

"Mr. Phillips, I'm afraid your account has been frozen," he stated bluntly.

"Frozen? What on Earth for?"

"We received a judicial order placing your accounts on hold."

He reached into a file and handed me a copy of a judicial order from the nineteenth district court out of Dearborn, requiring that all my personal and PSI's commercial accounts be placed on hold.

A judge had signed the order two days earlier and a case number

had been assigned. There was even an official stamp on the front of the document.

I wrote down the case number, thanked the banker and left.

At that point, a couple of weeks had passed since the servo valve technicians had tried to force their way into my lab, and I had nearly forgotten about them. But, when I saw the judicial order, I knew those clowns were up to no good.

I drove back to the office and called the civil courts division where the order had originated. After a few redirects, I finally got the information I needed.

A John Davidson, Esq., had solicited the judge to freeze my accounts, citing "delinquency of payment to Mechanical Repair Specialists, Inc." as the reason. It was the name of the technicians' company. My hunch had been right.

I picked up my phone and called them immediately. "I want to speak with Thomas," I demanded.

"Who's calling?" the receptionist asked.

"Never mind who's calling. Get Thomas on the phone now!"

It seemed like five minutes passed before he came on, though it probably was less than a minute. I was raring to get a hold of him.

"Hello?" he finally answered.

"I want the hold on my accounts released immediately."

"Then all you need to do is pay us the ten thousand dollars you owe us," he replied snidely, referring to their cut of the servo valve sales I'd made.

"What are you talking about? I don't owe you any money for another twenty days!"

"Bring us a check or your accounts stay frozen," he threatened.

"Forget the check. I've got a better idea."

I slammed the phone down so loudly that Kay, Marvin and everyone else in the office heard it reverberate off the bare walls.

For the several months I had worked with the servo valve technicians, I had always paid their invoices within thirty days of

submission. I had never once been delinquent. And, despite their accusations, I was still up to date on my present payment. They were simply trying to limit my financial resources and strong-arm me so I'd have trouble competing with them. If they'd known me better, they'd have realized that was just the kind of dirty trick that only made me fight back harder.

I was already involved in litigation with some other joker who had approached me about designing hydrostatic transmissions for conveyor-belt machinery. He had supplied the basic design drawings for me to elaborate on, but he had stolen those drawings from a company where he used to work.

His old company found out about it, and they were suing both him and me for stealing trade secrets. Once I found out that the guy had stolen the drawings, I stopped working with him immediately—but that didn't stop the lawsuit against me.

As a result, I had already been forced to find an attorney. His name was Elliot Pearlman and he was my kind of guy: simple, straightforward and unlikely to back down from a fight. I hired him because he told it like it was and because he was tenacious. I didn't need a wimpy pencil pusher trying to negotiate a resolution. I wanted someone with a backbone and the sense to stand up for what was right.

So, right after talking to Thomas, I called Elliot. I was in his office the next day, going over the details.

"Here's the last invoices the technicians sent me and here's the case number I got from the bank," I said, handing him some papers. "And here's what they owe me for my sales commissions."

"They've gone way over the line on this one," he replied, shaking his head. "And that judge had no grounds to freeze your accounts."

"I want to take these guys to the cleaners."

"We will. Let me set up a meeting—me, you and their attorney. When are you available?"

"Any time. I want this done quickly. I can't run my business with my accounts on hold."

I got back to my office at about five o'clock, when the sun was beginning to drop. I had spent the whole day handling this mess and hadn't gotten one thing accomplished at work. That made me even madder. They were screwing up my business now, and I couldn't wait to confront those greedy bastards. Let them know they were messing with the wrong guy.

I could have predicted that being new to the servo valve repair business was going to mean I'd be tested by some guys who thought I was entering their turf. That's the way it always is, from being the new kid at school to the new name in business.

But proving myself was never a problem. No matter how many times I had to do it.

CHAPTER 45

Showdown With the Servo Techs

Most showdowns take place at high noon outside the saloon of a small, Western town, between two guys in cowboy hats and holsters. Mine was scheduled to take place at nine on a Saturday morning in an attorney's office in Detroit—me against three guys in white lab coats.

Elliot had made the appointment and there was no way, come hell or high water, that I was going to miss it.

There was just one small problem.

Weeks earlier, Betty and I had made plans to spend the upcoming weekend alone together. We had an array of children ranging from high school students to kindergarteners, and even though our home was well managed and rather peaceful, a getaway every now and then was a good way to preserve our sanity.

We had booked a hotel a few hours outside the city and would go to some nice restaurants, maybe catch a movie, do some shopping and, best of all, sleep in late. Meanwhile, my mother would be watching the kids. The plan was that for forty-eight hours, both Betty and I would catch up on some much-needed relaxation. Of course, you know what they say about the best made plans...

The day before my legal showdown, I had learned that six checks from our bank had bounced as a result of the action taken by the servo valve technicians, and my anger had only deepened since I'd first figured out what they'd done. Despite that, I hadn't told Betty

anything except that I was handling it. She wasn't aware of the meeting I had scheduled with my attorney on Saturday morning, since I didn't want to disrupt the trip we had looked forward to for so long.

As planned, my mother came over that Friday and Betty and I drove off to the hotel. During the first hour of the drive, we caught up with what was happening in our daily lives. In the second hour, we simply enjoyed the peacefulness of the highway and the colors of the changing leaves. The tranquility was soothing after the hectic week we had both had. It was just what I needed to keep my mind off things.

The next morning, however, I somehow had to make it to the meeting in Detroit without letting my wife know what I was up against. Secretly, I set my alarm for six o'clock and when it rang, I stealthily got up, got dressed and tiptoed out of the hotel room without disturbing Betty. Since my days in the Air Force, I'd always woken up early anyway, and even if she awoke without me there, she would assume I was out getting coffee and a newspaper. The goal was not to disturb her in any way so that she could enjoy a peaceful weekend.

There was almost no traffic heading into downtown Detroit at that time. It would have been a very serene morning if it weren't for the burning anger in my gut brought about by the week's occurrences. The closer I got to the attorney's office, the more the anger won out over the serenity. I was ready for a fight by the time I arrived there at nine o'clock. If I had worn a gun to this showdown, I would have walked in with it blazing.

"Bill, let me do most of the talking," Elliot counseled me the second he saw me enter the building. I guess he could tell from my expression that I was already worked up. I didn't respond because I knew I wouldn't refrain from saying exactly what was on my mind.

We walked to the conference room and opened the door. Seated at a large table were all three of the technicians and their attorney, a short man with wire-rimmed glasses. He stood as Elliot and I entered

the room, and he came up to about our shoulders. Brief introductions were made and their attorney began talking.

"Given the facts of this matter," he said, "my clients are owed a total of fifteen thousand dollars."

"For what?" I exclaimed, unable to refrain. Elliot shot me a look but said nothing.

"Ten thousand for invoiced services and an additional five thousand for legal fees and penalties related to delinquency," the man declared, reading notes off a piece of paper.

"We can take this outside and settle this right now," I threatened, standing up.

"What?" the attorney asked. "Are you serious?"

"You bet I'm serious," I replied. I didn't like being referred to as "delinquent."

"I'm sure your client doesn't mean that," the short man stated, directing his gaze at Elliot.

"Watch me!" I said as I started to walk to his side of the table.

"Now, wait just a minute, here," the attorney exclaimed with a look of fear on his face—the same look each of the three technicians was wearing. They realized I wasn't kidding, either.

"C'mon, Bill," Elliot said as he stood up. "Let's leave. This meeting was a waste of our time."

Elliot made his way to the door, turned to the other attorney and said, "Expect a suit to be filed Monday against you and your clients."

"Hold on. What do you mean?" the attorney asked, clearly rattled.

"Bill is not delinquent on anything," Elliot retorted. "He's paid all the submitted invoices on time, and the current invoice for ten thousand dollars is not due for another week. We'll be filing a countersuit for wrongful tampering with his business and personal accounts and for all the pain, suffering and costs associated with that. In fact, the suit will name you personally, as well as your clients."

"Now—now, look," the attorney stammered. "Things have gotten off to a bad start. Let's calm down a bit and start over."

Elliot and I looked at each other, knowing we had made some headway. We both sat back down.

About thirty minutes into our meeting, I stepped out to call Betty. She was awake by then and, without going into too many details, I gave her the lowdown on where I was. I suggested she go shopping until I could catch up with her. It couldn't have been soon enough.

I went back into the conference room and for the next two and a half hours, Elliot made their heads spin. The other attorney had been misinformed by the lab technicians. He had failed to perform his due diligence and didn't realize that the invoices weren't actually delinquent. As a result, he spent the entire rest of the time trying to weasel out of the predicament into which he had gotten himself. Not only did he have to backtrack on his own actions as a licensed attorney, but he also had to convince the technicians that they had no real legal grounds for freezing my accounts.

By the end of our meeting, the technicians agreed to release the hold on my bank accounts and, as compensation for my troubles, to forgive the $10,000 I owed them. Never mind that I'd *made* them that money in the first place. They went from demanding $15,000 to awarding me $10,000. It was a pretty productive morning.

After everything was settled, Elliot and I stood up to leave. But, just before I walked out the door, I turned to the three technicians and stared them down.

"If you bother me again, I promise I will find you and make you pay dearly."

"Is that a threat?" their attorney asked in astonishment.

"Call it what you want, but they'd better steer clear."

I doubt that attorney had ever been in a fist fight. He couldn't fathom taking someone outside to settle things man to man. But by the time I left, I had no doubt that he was convinced I would

do whatever it took to protect my business. And I was sure that the technicians knew the same thing.

———

By the time I made it back to the hotel, Betty had just returned from a morning of shopping and was ready to spend some time with me, relaxing together—and so was I. Without any kids, and without any technicians, we were both finally free to enjoy ourselves.

When I got back to work the next week, I purchased a second machine to repair servo valves and hired a second salesman with the extra $10,000 I'd been awarded. I personally handled sales from Detroit to the Atlantic Ocean, and the other salesman's territory was from Chicago to the Pacific Ocean.

The technician's little stunt had turned into just the thing I'd needed to successfully launch my own servo valve repair business from coast to coast.

I'd say that justice had been served.

PART V

Achieving the American Dream

CHAPTER 46

Milestone

By the time I turned forty-one, I had come a long way. I had overcome the adversity of post-Depression-era Detroit. I had survived the challenges of the Air Force and the brutal climate of Newfoundland, Labrador and Greenland. I had married the girl of my dreams and had eight children. I had worked my way up through various companies to own my own corporation. And I had fought legal battles and more to attain a strong position in my field of expertise. Getting to where I was with PSI had been a long, tough road, but nothing worthwhile in life ever comes easily.

———

Midway through 1974, I owned the majority share of PSI; the only other serious shareholder was Ray Rosberg, a friend of mine for many years. When I'd had the opportunity to buy my way out of the business loan, Ray had stepped up to help me. He'd contributed $3,000 in exchange for a small percentage in the corporation.

Additionally, Ray became PSI's sales representative for the western half of the country. He had been born in Detroit but now lived in Chicago. Therefore, all the territory from Chicago to the West Coast was under his domain. I handled the other half of the country, from Detroit to the East Coast.

At this point, I was pouring all of my energy and assets into the

servo valve repair business. I finally realized that within the field of hydraulics, design and machinery development was much less lucrative than repairs. So, I learned what I had to learn, made the necessary adjustments to my business and rolled with the punches.

At that time, no one was performing repairs for servo valves on a large scale and, more importantly, nobody was performing hydraulic repairs in general. To fill the niche, PSI began tailoring to the servo valve repair needs of different industries as well as the repair needs of all types of hydraulic equipment. In addition to servo valves, I began repairing pumps, cylinders and much more. Repair services were where it was at—and, as always, I went where the money was.

I also thought big. If markets within the Detroit area needed these services, it made perfect sense to me that other areas throughout the country would need them as well. I knew that the aerospace and automotive industries had strong market potentials, but I assumed there were others. For instance, the petroleum industry routinely used various hydraulic and servo valve control equipment in its operations, so I figured it could use our repair services, too.

With a little market research, PSI opened a duplicate facility in the Houston area to provide regional services there. Shortly thereafter, I opened another facility in Los Angeles for the same reason. Like many businesses, once you have an algorithm that works, there's no need to reinvent the wheel—and no reason to think small. I simply packaged the Detroit model and took it on the road.

The facility in Houston was a 20,000-square-foot building. The plant there employed four servo valve technicians, six hydraulics repair experts and another ten or so administrative and shipping personnel. Each facility was designed as a laboratory with workstations and precision equipment. Employees wore white smocks and performed their tasks in a professional manner.

Even though the lab environment wasn't sterilized, you would have thought you were in a science lab if you visited. Hydraulic and high-tech equipment repairs had to be done in a setting that was

clean and conducive to high-level performance. Therefore, all of PSI's labs and offices maintained stringent standards—and they all excelled.

Due in part to the oil boom of the 1970s, the Houston office was a success, just as Detroit was. Expansion was a gamble that paid off.

As a sales engineer, I had recognized a niche in the market and worked hard and fast to take advantage of it. Because of that, I attained my first real taste of success. After eighteen years of struggling, the fruits of my labors were finally paying off.

It was July of 1974 when I was presented with my first tangible evidence of having achieved a milestone on the road to success. Ray and I were closing out the financial figures for PSI's fiscal year. We were in Detroit, in my family room, analyzing our sales and our accounts receivable for the past twelve months.

"Bill, how old are you?" Ray asked out of the blue.

"Forty-one," I replied. "Why?"

"How much were sales for PSI last year?"

"Just over two million," I answered.

"You know what that means, right?"

"No, what?"

"At the age of forty-one, with your stock in PSI and the current receivables, you're a millionaire."

I knew PSI was doing well, but I had never taken the time to label myself a member of the millionaires' club. Ray was right, though—I had made over a million and had earned it the hard way. Still, I was a little shocked by his statement.

I looked around my home and thought of all the years of struggle that Betty and I had gone through to get to that point in our lives. The dream of wanting more not only for ourselves but for our children and, eventually, *their* children was the constant incentive that pushed us both forward toward our goals. Deep inside, I'd always believed I would be a success. A thought to the contrary had never even entered my mind—I wouldn't let it, not for one moment. Through

my dedication to hard work, persistence and optimism, I made sure I stacked the odds in my favor.

It also had helped that I had been doing something about which I was passionate. I had found an area in which I was talented and had managed to create a lucrative enterprise out of it. I had made myself invaluable by becoming good not only at sales but also mechanical engineering. I had a niche in an area where few others were looking—let alone providing service—and, like any good entrepreneur, I'd exploited it to the very best of my abilities.

After all that, I must admit that in the middle of my family room, without any fuss or ceremony, I experienced one of my proudest moments.

I looked at Ray and said, "I guess you're right. I *am* a millionaire."

CHAPTER 47

Play Ball

Achieving a certain level of success doesn't mean you can let up. It means you have to work that much harder to maintain it and improve upon it.

But, you can also enjoy yourself along the way.

—————

George Benz was the first person, and the only one I can recall, who I had to fire more than once. This speaks of his abilities as a sales manager on one hand, since I decided to hire him on two separate occasions. But the fact that I fired him a second time also tells you a little about his character.

George was a former Marine who had been in the Korean War and had spent some time in the stockades. I think he might have been a little off all along, but that didn't necessarily mean much in sales.

Originally, I'd hired him as a salesperson while I was still working with Josh Shay. He performed well for a while, but he always got in trouble or had something go awry in his personal life. His wife, of all people, had gotten him arrested and thrown in jail, and I had gone to bail him out and subsequently fire him. Despite George's sales talents, he was one of those guys you might say was just full of shit.

Betty knew George well and would begin laughing as soon as she saw him coming. He was a true character through and through.

With the opening of the other office in Houston and the expansion of my business into Los Angeles, I had to increase my technical staff as well as my sales staff. Whenever a new location opened, we had to hit the ground running. That was the way my business worked. The expense of the location, lab equipment, personnel and capital wouldn't allow for a trickle of projects here and there. Each location needed high volume to keep up with the scale of the business. Houston had started off well, and it was time for me to invest in some sales talent in the Los Angeles market. I had kept George in mind and brought him back onboard to help fuel sales in that area.

It was a Monday afternoon and I had arranged to travel from Detroit to Los Angeles with George that evening. American Airlines had one direct flight to LA every day at five, so the plan was for us to be on it. We were both at the airport and ready to board the plane a little after four.

We were traveling to Los Angeles on a McDonald Douglas DC-10. This wide-bodied airliner was first released in 1970 as the premier comfort plane for passengers. Its spacious aisles and leg room made the interior of today's commercial planes look like a closet. George and I were able to secure the last two first-class seats, and we comfortably settled into our leather chairs. Three two-seat sections spanned the massive first-class area, which totaled forty seats altogether. With such high-quality accommodations and a full flight attendant staff there to serve us, I didn't think our flight could have been much better.

But, there was something on which I hadn't counted.

"George, you notice anything funny?" I asked after we took our seats.

"No. What?" he replied.

"Isn't that Joe Coleman from the Tigers?" I asked, nodding in a fellow passenger's direction.

"Yeah, it is. Hey, there's Ralph Houk, the manager!"

In fact, exactly thirty-eight people were on the Detroit Tigers' traveling roster that year, and all of them were there with us in first class. With a game against the Angels the following day, they were making the trip to the West Coast. I couldn't believe our good luck.

The DC-10 took off and soon we were flying at over 500 miles an hour. In the 1970s, especially in first class, drinks were served pretty efficiently and flowed freely. Scotch and waters, vodka tonics, martinis—you name it. Shortly into the flight, everyone was feeling pretty relaxed—including George and me.

"Hey, George," I said, "we've both got a couple of sons who'd love some autographs. We should make the rounds and see if we can collect a few for them."

"Great idea," he agreed. "Let's go."

I grabbed a notepad and we went up and down the aisles, asking the players for their autographs. Everyone we asked—Gates Brown, Mickey Stanley and several others—graciously obliged. Happy with the memorabilia we were able to amass, George and I made our way back to our seats, passing two flight attendants who were chatting nearby.

"These ballplayers are drinking like fish," one complained.

"Yeah, and these guys here are going around taking their names. They must be with management," the other woman said, pointing to George and me.

"I wouldn't be making any wagers on the Tigers tomorrow," the first woman scoffed.

"Thank goodness they're not playing tonight."

The flight attendants walked toward the front of the section, and I leaned over to George. "Hey, did you hear that?" I whispered quietly.

"Yeah, they think we're with management," he answered.

We got a good laugh out of that but didn't think too much more about it. The flight was smooth and the drinks kept coming. By the

time we were past Chicago, several of the players were really getting pretty soused—and George and I weren't too far behind.

A few moments later, the two flight attendants came back to where we were seated.

"Excuse me," one of them said. "Don't you think they've had enough to drink?"

"They certainly have!" George exclaimed with a newfound sense of authority.

"They're going to be in poor shape to play baseball," the other flight attendant commented.

"Yeah, that guy there drinks way too much," I said, pointing to one of the players. "We've been trying to get him to lose some weight, too. He's making over one hundred thousand a year and we can't keep him in shape."

"Hmm." She glanced over, nodding in agreement. "When are you going to cut them off?"

I looked at George with an expression that said, *Are you thinking what I'm thinking?*

"You can cut 'em off anytime now," I stated in a managerial voice.

When any baseball team travels by bus, the seating arrangements are always the same: The coaching staff sits in the front on the right side. Within the first-class section of the plane, the seating for the Tigers' management was arranged in the same way. George and I, on the other hand, were farthest from that area, all the way at the back and to the left. But I guess the flight attendants weren't aware of any of that.

Ralph Houk, the current manager of the Tigers, sat in the management area in the front. Houk had come to the Tigers after his previous experience with the dominating Yankees of the 1960s. Nicknamed "The Major," he was known as a player's manager, but he had a terrible temper. So, when he spoke, the players listened.

Almost immediately after I had instructed the flight attendant to

stop serving the players drinks, Houk stood up and made eye contact with the other attendant. He then took his right forefinger and ran it across his throat, indicating that it was time to stop serving drinks to the team. But he was a bit too late—I had already beaten him to the punch.

The rest of the flight was a load of laughs. George and I became friendly with several of the Detroit Tigers by the trip's end, and as we disembarked to collect our bags, we wished all of them good luck against the Angels and shook hands. Then, George and I took the autographs we'd collected and went about our own business. Those guys never knew that it was us who had cut them off from their drinks.

Even though it's not on my official business résumé, I would like it known now that, for a very brief time, I had been a co-manager of the Detroit Tigers. Being at the right place at the right time really does have its advantages.

CHAPTER 48

The Music Industry

Most people know Houston as a center of the petroleum industry and for its aeronautical endeavors. I knew it as one of the newest sites for PSI. But Houston, more than anything, is all about Texas.

It's home to the largest rodeo in the country and gave birth to many famous blues and country singers, such as Lyle Lovett and Johnny "Guitar" Watson. So, it's hard to be in Houston for any length of time without some of its culture rubbing off on you. I suppose it's the same anywhere with a strong heritage—you can't avoid adopting some of its traditions.

PSI became well established in Houston's oil and aerospace industries. But, even though operations were seemingly on autopilot, it took a lot of hard work to make it look that easy, and I liked to visit the offices and the plant periodically to make sure everything was running as smoothly as possible. I did this at all of PSI's locations; regardless of their degrees of success, I always looked for improvements and liked to get a feel for the local markets and their people.

During my many business trips to Houston, I had progressively become a fan of country-and-western music. The songs have simple and honest meanings, which suits me well. Country songs tell it like it is, and so do I.

On a hot, sunny morning sometime in 1981, I made one of my usual trips to Houston. I toured its different labs and offices, met several executives and employees and checked to be sure that operations were carrying on without a hitch. As the morning was coming to an end, one of my managers and I were walking along the loading docks, discussing different aspects of the business. As we walked, I began to hear the twang of a guitar and a man's voice coming from one of the loading bays.

A few of the employees were scattered around the area, taking their lunch breaks and enjoying the nice weather. Up ahead, I spotted the source of the music and started walking in that direction.

"It's you that I love," the man sang in a Texas twang to his small audience, the lyrics becoming more audible as I got closer. He was dangling his feet off a platform while strumming an acoustic guitar. His voice was more of a tenor than a bass, and the song had a nice melody.

"There is no other that I adore," he continued singing.

The man was in his early thirties and wore his sandy-brown hair short and tight, as did many Texans. He was dressed in jeans and a blue, collared work shirt, identifying him as a worker in the company's shipping-and-loading area.

I stood and listened for several minutes with my manager before the guitar player finally noticed I was standing there. Recognizing me, he jumped to his feet and slung his guitar over his shoulder as if coming to full attention in front of a drill sergeant.

"Mr. Phillips," he said. "I hope my guitar playing wasn't bothering you."

"Not at all," I replied, "and call me Bill. I was enjoying listening to it. If you don't mind, I'd like to hear some more."

"I'd be glad to," he stated.

"What's your name?" I asked.

"Jimmy Middleton."

I sat and listened to Jimmy play a little Hank Williams and a few songs he had written himself. He was a very good guitar player and his vocals weren't bad, either. The more I listened, the more his music grew on me. By the time he had finished the third song, I was beginning to have some ideas for Jimmy that went beyond the loading bays.

"Have you ever cut your own songs?" I asked him.

"No," he replied. "I just play for the fun of it."

"How about I arrange a recording studio for you to record some songs in?"

"That'd be great," he said with enthusiasm. "What would I play?"

"Play your own songs," I said. "Then we'll make a few thousand forty-fives and distribute them."

Jimmy was all for it and while I had absolutely no experience in the music business, I was willing to help him get a start if it was meant to be. Nothing ventured, nothing gained.

I called a few people in the Houston area and had soon arranged for Jimmy to record his songs in a recording studio. He played the one I'd heard in the loading area and another original entitled "I Won't Cry Anymore." You gotta love the names of country songs!

Once Jimmy completed the recording session, we had 2,000 forty-fives made of his songs. I then had PSI's salespeople distribute them as they went to different places around the country. It was a nice gesture for our sales team to give these records to our customers; it was good for PSI's public relations, plus Jimmy's music got a little attention at the same time.

I honestly thought he had great potential and I enjoyed what he was doing. It's easy to invest in something you like and believe will be successful; even if it's not a hit, it's never a mistake.

"Jimmy, I've got a proposition for you," I told him one day.

"What's that?" he replied.

"I'll take you off the docks, put you in a rehearsal room and keep

your pay the same," I said. "But there's a catch—you have to practice eight hours a day, just like putting in a full day's work."

"You mean play guitar and sing eight hours every day instead of working the docks?"

"That's right."

"Let me give it some thought," he said.

Jimmy didn't need much time before agreeing to give it a try. He and three other band members began practicing every day. My thought was to treat it like any other profession: Commit the hours to your craft, get good at it, and then you can excel.

In addition, I located a manager for Jimmy and his band so they could get some gigs. He was the same manager who had arranged Freddy Fender's venues, and pretty soon Jimmy was playing at hotel ballrooms and Steak and Ale restaurants in the Houston area. It wasn't the Grand Ole Opry, but at least it was progress.

Despite these small steps and my organized approach to improving Jimmy's talent and exposure, things weren't moving along very fast—at least, not fast enough for my liking. His paying gigs were pretty infrequent and the practice sessions didn't seem to be working out as scheduled. A couple of the band members weren't used to working eight-hour shifts and maybe it was too structured for their free-spirited, creative sides. Either way, the business-development approach to Jimmy's musical success didn't seem to be the right one. So, I decided to take a sales-and-marketing approach.

"Jimmy, I expect you've heard of Loretta Lynn," I said.

"Of course," he answered.

"I think you'd be better off getting out there like she did. Hit the road and go to all the little towns. Talk with the DJs and get 'em to play your songs."

"Alright. I'll give that a try."

Jimmy went to all the small cities in west Texas, Oklahoma and Louisiana, plugging his songs and talking to DJs. A few played his records, but not very many. By the 1980s, the music industry was

becoming very political and corporate. Compared to the '60s, when Loretta Lynn had been promoting her music on the road, DJs no longer had much control over what they played. It was hard to discover the next big thing without going through the usual channels.

Jimmy wasn't making much headway, and I was beginning to get a little frustrated by the situation. Not only had I invested a fair amount of money in him but none of the traditional approaches to business that I was accustomed to had been very productive. It was time to take it to the next level.

"Jimmy, I'd like you on a flight to Nashville on Monday morning," I said to him over the phone. "We have an audition with RCA at one o'clock."

"Really?" he exclaimed. "What do I bring?"

"Bring anything you think they might want to hear or see," I said. "I'll meet you at the airport there."

If Jimmy was going to make it in country-and-western music, the road would likely have to go through Nashville. Houston was a good start, but it was time to see if he had what it took to be a success.

A friend of mine had helped arrange the audition, and Jimmy was excited about the opportunity, but he wasn't the only one. Betty was pretty excited, too, as she and I got on the plane to meet Jimmy in Music City. This was a chance for both of us to see the inner workings of the country music industry.

That Monday, Betty, Jimmy and I walked into the RCA offices for his audition. We were in the heart of Nashville, right next to Vanderbilt University. The brick office building wasn't anything like I'd expected; I'd envisioned something a little flashier, considering the industry. But, once inside, the studio-and-audition area was almost identical to the one Jimmy had used in Houston.

While Betty and I watched, three gentlemen gave some introductions, then eventually asked Jimmy to play some of his own songs as they listened intently. The songs sounded pretty good to me, but then again, what did I know about the music industry?

"Jimmy," one of the RCA executives began, "leave us your cassette and we'll think it over."

"How do you think he sounds?" I asked.

"You never can tell what the public might like," he stated very matter-of-factly. "We'll consider it."

With that, the men said their goodbyes and we left. I had never been involved in the entertainment industry before, but I could tell we were getting a polite brush-off.

I was already frustrated by the lack of progress, but now I was even more aggravated by the lack of any real answers. Did Jimmy have promotable talent or not? That was what we had come to Nashville to find out. If he didn't, then those guys at RCA should have said so. I just wanted the same simplicity and honesty from them that was heard in Jimmy's songs.

"C'mon, Jimmy," I said as we all walked outside the RCA offices. "We're taking a ride around Nashville."

We drove around downtown and along Music Row. I was on a mission to find a studio that would give me straight answers. Any studio that was hungry for a good country-and-western singer would have done. I didn't want an agency that had so many singers it leveraged one against another.

After a little while, I spotted one place that looked like it had potential. It was an old, converted house with white siding, a tiled roof and faded, green shutters. On the outside, a sign in bright red letters read "Rascal Recordings." I went inside to feel them out.

"I've got the best country-and-western singer with me since Willie Nelson," I announced in a booming voice as I walked toward the receptionist. "Get your boss, 'cause he's gonna want to hear him."

The young girl almost jumped out of her skin at the sound of my voice. Then, she smiled cautiously at me and climbed up a creaky set of stairs framed by an old, wooden handrail.

While I waited, I noticed that the walls were covered with all sorts of framed albums from many singers, most of whom I had never

heard of before, and haven't since. A few seconds later, she returned with a man whom I presumed to be her boss following behind her.

"I'm Jeff Ringer," the man said in a voice as loud as mine. "Who do we have here?"

"Bill Phillips," I said, shaking his hand. "And in my limousine, I have the next new country-and-western star. His name is Jimmy Middleton."

Ringer was what I'd imagined Nashville to look like. He wore red knit pants as bright as the lettering on the sign outside and had on a white shirt that matched his white vinyl loafers. His hair was wavy and black, slicked back behind his ears in a bad imitation of Elvis, and he wore lightly tinted sunglasses. He couldn't stop moving from the time he walked in until the time I left.

"Let's give him a listen," he exclaimed, taking the cassette from my hand.

The next thing I knew, Jimmy's music was blaring from a stereo conveniently located in the reception lobby. Betty and Jimmy made their way inside the building as the music began to play, and Ringer didn't just listen to Jimmy's music but also began dancing to it at the same time.

By the end of the first song, Ringer was swinging Betty around by the arm and the rest of us were all tapping our toes. It was quite a contrast from the corporate atmosphere at RCA.

Ringer was certainly a character, but he also knew the industry inside and out. After the cassette was over, he explained to us that the style of music Jimmy had created was called "country swing." And while songs of that type were popular in the 1950s, times had changed. No longer was there a big demand for that classic kind of sound. He was very complimentary of Jimmy's talents but told him flat out that his style of music was no longer in vogue and therefore wouldn't sell. A straight answer from a straight shooter—red pants and all.

Jimmy continued to play and occasionally did some small performances, but our days in the country-and-western music industry came to a close after the trip to Nashville.

He continued to work in the shipping area at PSI in Houston for many years, and I always made a point to see him when I went there on my routine visits. He and his wife had a daughter who was later accidentally struck by a car and killed. Knowing his financial situation, I made sure she had proper funeral services, and every year after that, at our company picnic, Jimmy's wife came to find me and thank me. They were honest and sincere people, as was reflected in Jimmy's songs—and those are qualities that are always important in both the music and business worlds.

Not every investment works out in the way you expect. But, I still believe that Jimmy was exceptionally talented, and I personally loved hearing him play. It was worth it to me to have given him a chance at the big time. Even though the record contract didn't work out, I was a much richer man for having known Jimmy and his family, and for having had that experience and foray into the music industry.

Success sometimes comes in ways that aren't financial. If I had it to do all over again, I undoubtedly would take the same chance on Jimmy. In business, you have to go with what you believe in.

CHAPTER 49

An "Overnight" Success

There are some things that you absolutely, positively have to have overnight. Other things take a little more time, like experience and expertise in the business world. Sometimes, however, the two intersect.

Part of keeping up with your trade is reading about your industry as well as staying current on what others in the business world are doing.

I remember sitting in my office in Detroit in the late 1970s and reading an entrepreneurial journal about a businessman named Fred Smith. The Computer Age was just beginning to make an impact in terms of business planning, and this man's approach to and perspective on business were very similar to my own.

Like I had, Fred Smith had enrolled in the military earlier in his life. From 1966 until 1969, he had served in the Marines as a grounds officer. However, his passion was airplanes. He had become an amateur pilot as a teenager and, in the Marines, had ridden as a forward air controller in more than 200 combat missions. That alone earned him two purple hearts during the Vietnam War.

While I parlayed my knowledge of and experience in hydraulic

systems into my own career, Smith transferred his expertise of airplanes and logistics systems into his own company as well. He gained several skills in the military and was able to utilize them when opportunities in civilian life presented themselves.

After I left the Air Force, I began working in the fields of mechanical engineering and hydraulics, which ultimately led to the formation of PSI and my sole ownership of the corporation. Smith, likewise, purchased the majority of shares in an aircraft maintenance company in 1970, after leaving the Marines. He then began trading used jets before moving on to bigger and better things. His experience in dealing with jets, added to his prior experience in the military, eventually led him to realize his true entrepreneurial potential.

In 1971, Smith took a $4-million inheritance and invested it in his idea for a new company. Prior to that, he had attended Yale and written an economics paper detailing a concept for delivery services in the Computer Age. So, combining that idea with his military knowledge and civilian experience, he created an integrative system through which air and ground delivery services could guarantee overnight shipping. He named his company Federal Express and, in 1973, it began providing services to twenty-five cities. The rest is history.

I sat back in my chair after reading the article and couldn't help but feel as if I knew Fred Smith personally. He had traveled a path very similar to my own to achieve success, and I knew we shared a strong entrepreneurial spirit. Smith had located his company in Memphis, Tennessee; he had grown up in Mississippi and had Southern roots, just as I did. The more I thought about his story, the more I wanted to meet him. Not only that but I thought of a way it could benefit my business.

I picked up the phone and decided to give him a call.

"May I speak with Fred Smith?" I asked.

"One moment, please," the receptionist replied.

After a few seconds, she returned to the phone and transferred

me to his office line. A man who could be easily reached? I liked him already.

"Hello, this is Fred Smith," he said.

"Hi, I'm Bill Phillips of PSI," I stated. "I was just reading about your company in a business journal and I have some problems of my own that I think you can help me solve."

At this point, PSI's labs and offices were doing large volumes of business in Detroit and Houston. The company was receiving servo valves and other hydraulic system parts for repair from major corporations around the country. While most of those companies had backup spare parts, on occasion both the regular and backup pieces of equipment would break down. When this happened, speed was a critical issue because, essentially, these companies would be shut down completely until the parts were back in service. For a large corporation, that could have meant tens of thousands of dollars a day, if not more.

For local services around the area, we would use our own vans or trucks to pick up equipment to repair as needed. For regional deliveries, UPS or other ground-delivery services were effective in getting repaired equipment back to the companies the next day. However, getting equipment to companies that were out of state required air transport. Before the days of ground-air integrated delivery services, it would often take three days or more before a delivery would be received. For PSI, that meant a company might have chosen to purchase a new piece of equipment rather than having it repaired and losing money while waiting for it to come back.

In addition to our similar roots, Fred Smith and I had some common interests: We were both interested in getting items delivered quickly and guaranteeing their arrivals. Speed and dependability were key elements in order for both of our businesses to be successful. I knew I was speaking to the right guy.

"I need a way to get equipment to my customers the next day, no matter where it's going," I stated after explaining my situation.

"I understand, Bill," he said. "We can handle that for you, and we can handle your ground shipping, too. Pretty soon, we're going to be international as well."

Just as I had found an area that was not being serviced in the equipment repair industry, Smith had found a similar situation in package deliveries. The opportunity let him offer a service that was drastically needed but that no one had thought to provide before (and as the Internet age sped up the efficiency of information processing, his deliveries were able to keep that pace). Smith's experience and knowledge—as well as making the most of a nice inheritance—had made him uniquely able to pull it off, just as my experience and knowledge had led me to my own entrepreneurial path.

For many entrepreneurs I have met throughout my life, the combination of experience, knowledge and opportunity created doorways through which success could be attained. The key to opening those doors is being ready and willing to jump at the opportunity when it comes—or when you create it.

FedEx Corporation now has a quarter of a million employees and handles annual revenues of almost $38 billion—not bad for an amateur pilot and former Marine who just happened to know a little about logistics systems. It makes you wonder how many opportunities might have come along in life that you never recognized or that you let pass by without taking action.

I believe that opportunities are out there for everyone, and all it takes to turn these chances into success is paying attention to what the market is missing and being ready to act. Entrepreneurs are like artists: They see things that others don't, then create from there. That ability, along with knowledge, experience and persistence, is the total package.

CHAPTER 50

The Right Staff

If you're in business for yourself, you always keep an eye out for anything that can benefit your company and raise your bottom line: a niche in the marketplace, a good product, new customers, the right staff. Entrepreneurs look everywhere for such assets—and sometimes find them where they least expect.

On a gloomy Monday morning in Detroit, I was on my way to the office as usual. But, on this particular day, I had planned to stop at a local mechanic's shop to have a routine tune-up done on my car. I had woken up early, as always, and arrived at the auto shop when it opened at seven-thirty. I didn't think it would take very long, giving me just enough time to read the newspaper and have a cup of coffee before heading to work. As crazy as my schedule was, it would have been nice to have an hour to myself, even if it was in a mechanic's shop.

I grabbed the *Detroit News* and poured a cup of black coffee from the shop's coffee maker. Then, I tried to make myself comfortable in the orange-plastic seats that decorated the otherwise nondescript waiting area while my car was being worked on.

One by one the mechanics showed up, most trying to make the adjustment from the weekend to the workweek. But, one of them

stood out from the pack. His name was Bob, and he hit the ground running. The moment he entered the shop, the place automatically came to life. The level of energy and enthusiasm he brought made the other mechanics look literally half asleep.

"Let's go, Tony!" he said enthusiastically. "Time to rock 'n' roll. I've got the tune-up, you take the tire rotation."

I noticed him immediately. For one, he was taking care of my car. But, more importantly, he kept everyone else in the garage in line and motivated. Bob made sure all the mechanics were keeping on top of their work, and if they weren't, he didn't mind telling them.

I was reading the sports page when the bell on the shop's door rang. The door swung open suddenly and in walked a woman who looked quite upset. It had started raining hard, and she was soaking wet. She had her hair up in curlers and was clearly in a hurry to get somewhere—and I was guessing an auto shop wasn't it. The woman was almost frantic as she began calling out for someone in the shop to wait on her.

"Is there anyone here?" she shouted toward the back of the shop. "Hello! Is there anyone here at all?"

"Yes," Bob said cheerfully as he rounded the corner. "What can I help you with?"

"You can begin by getting my car to start!" the woman exclaimed.

"Okay," he said calmly. "Where is it?"

"Here it comes," she said pointing to a tow truck pulling a gold, 1973 Buick Skylark. "I'm in a rush."

"Okay, okay. Take a deep breath," Bob suggested. "What do you think is wrong with it?"

"How should I know? *You're* the mechanic." She wasn't the world's easiest customer to deal with, but that didn't faze Bob.

"Did it make a funny noise before it wouldn't start?" he asked patiently.

"It just wouldn't start at all this morning. No noise, no nothing. How long is this going to take? I'm in a hurry."

"Let me take a look at it. I'll get right on it. Have a cup of coffee and try to relax. I'll be back shortly."

Telling her to relax was like trying to tell someone to forget that their hair was on fire. It wasn't going to happen. Even so, Bob kept his cool and took care of business.

He got one of the other mechanics, who was working on another car at the time, to focus on the Skylark. Bob knew that the other car's owner wasn't coming back until the end of the day, so it made sense to take care of this lady's most pressing concerns first and place the other car's problem on hold for the time being. It showed good managerial skills—and common sense.

In about ten minutes, Bob came back into the waiting area to speak with the woman.

"Good news," he said. "You just need a new battery. We'll get you fixed up and you'll be out of here in about fifteen minutes."

"Alright," she replied, looking at her watch. "But if you could make it ten minutes, that would be better."

Bob just smiled in response. I'm not sure, but I think he had anticipated her request, because the car was ready in ten minutes flat.

What could have escalated into a fighting match between an angry customer on a Monday morning and a mechanic trying to ease into the workweek instead turned into a transaction with a satisfied—and, most likely, repeat—client. The woman couldn't have been more pleased and grateful as she left. I was impressed.

"Your car's ready," Bob said to me about thirty minutes later. "All tuned up."

As he handed me my keys, I handed him my card.

"If you ever need another job," I said, "look me up."

Bob studied the business card for a moment then thanked me.

Any man who could appease a disgruntled woman who was soaking wet and in a rush had to be pretty tough. That was the kind of guy I wanted working for me.

Sometimes, you can just tell someone's abilities by watching their everyday actions. Based on what I'd seen, I was willing to take a chance on Bob.

Not too long after that, he gave me a call. He was still working for the automotive shop but was interested in what I might have had to offer. I brought him in to PSI for an interview, and he began working with me on sales and various other projects shortly afterward. Not only was Bob equipped with an abundance of energy but he was very smart and a complete clown. He kept us laughing half the time we were working with him.

For one thing, Bob had dentures, and he would take them out and leave them in the strangest places for one of us to find. On our many trips to and from the Los Angeles facilities, Bob would entertain the entire crew with his jokes and pranks. You never knew what he was going to do next, but it would undoubtedly not be what you expected.

With all of his hijinks, I'm not sure Bob would have lasted very long with PSI if he hadn't been so bright and good at what he did. But, he managed to balance both fun and work exceptionally well.

A classic routine of his occurred every time we took off from John Wayne Airport, south of Los Angeles, en route to Detroit. The flight patterns from the airport required planes to fly out over the Pacific Ocean, then reduce the throttle to keep the noise level low for the surrounding areas. Our plane would always fly right over Richard Nixon's estate, which we could see well after takeoff. Everyone onboard knew the route well.

"Everyone," Bob would announce, "a moment of silence, please, while we pass over the estate of President Richard Nixon, our

glorious commander in chief and one of the best American leaders of all time!"

Bob would then get out of his seat and kneel on the floor in the aisle, raising his right hand to his forehead in a salute. He would hold that position until the plane had traveled well past Nixon's estate. In the meantime, everyone else just stared at him as if he were a lunatic.

"Thank you," Bob would say, getting up after the plane was past the area. "You may now resume your normal activities."

I think he admired President Nixon because he knew no one cared for him much after the Watergate scandal and Bob liked to be that one in the crowd. Besides, the whole scenario allowed him to get some attention from the group on the plane for his clowning around. He loved to make people laugh and liked the attention even more. When he was on the plane, I always knew our trip would not be dull.

Like many people I've chosen to work with over the years, Bob epitomized some of the key elements that I always looked for in an employee. First of all, he was smart and tough. I didn't want someone who was going to back down when things became difficult, and I wanted someone who could understand the details of a situation. Secondly, he was great with people. The sales profession is a customer-oriented industry. If you have limited social skills, you aren't going to get very far in sales. And, lastly, I liked people who could balance hard work with play. When it was time to get down to business, that was what needed to happen. But when it was time to relax, it was always good to have someone with a sense of humor around. They also tended to be the ones to keep perspective in tense situations.

These characteristics might not work for every business or employer, but they worked well for me. Once you define the type of people you need to make you and your business better, then it's just a

matter of getting them onboard. Bob hadn't come looking for me; I'd found him while I'd just happened to be taking care of my car.

Being observant and paying attention to what's going on around you is one of the best ways to get the most out of life. You never know what lies around the corner—or what you'll find if you check under the hood.

CHAPTER 51

The Royal Ascot

At that point in my life, I was definitely living the American dream: great family, nice house, successful business. The only thing was, I hadn't seen that much of America—let alone anywhere outside it. Except for business trips and my stint in the Air Force, I either didn't have the money to travel or the time. But, I always had the inclination. And you know what happens when I set my mind to something…

⸻

Though PSI now had facilities in Detroit, Houston and Los Angeles, neither Betty nor I did much traveling during its early years. Who could afford to? With success came more responsibility. And, who had the time to travel? She was taking care of the kids and the entire household and I was running my business.

But, in the summer of 1979, while sitting in my office in Detroit, a little bit of Europe came to me.

I was going through sales invoices and revenues for the quarter when my phone suddenly rang. "Bill," my receptionist said, "there's a John Head on the phone who would like to speak with you."

"John Head?" I answered. "I don't think I know him."

"He said he's a businessman from London," she responded. "And by his accent, I don't doubt him."

"Okay, ring him through."

That was a first. I had received many phone calls from company owners and businessmen who had wanted my services over the years, but I didn't remember ever receiving a call from London. I was impressed that my company's reputation was expanding internationally.

I answered the phone, and a man with a thick, British accent identified himself and proceeded to tell me his interest in speaking with me.

"I am chairman of a company that operates in London and Scotland, and we've been following your company's success for a while. I would very much like to visit you and discuss a potential purchase offer."

"Well, that's great...but PSI isn't for sale," I replied.

"I see. Would you mind if I came for a visit all the same? I would like to speak with you in person."

As it turned out, John chaired a large corporation that sought up-and-coming companies to purchase as investments. He had done his homework and knew a lot about PSI. The more we talked on the phone, the more I enjoyed the conversation. We spoke the same language in business and we seemed to share a similar perspective on life. Before I hung up, we set a time for John to visit Detroit and see the company.

He came a couple of weeks later and we spent the day discussing the operations and facilities that PSI managed, as well as many other things. John had been in the Royal Navy, of which he was extremely proud, and of course I was equally proud of my experience with the U.S. Air Force. It didn't take much time for us to develop a friendly rivalry between our two branches of the military. By the end of the day, it was clear we had more in common than we'd initially thought, so I invited John to stay longer and get to know my family as well as the Michigan area.

"John, come have dinner at my house this evening," I suggested. "I want you to meet my wife, Betty, and my children."

"I'd love to," John replied in his polite-sounding English accent.

"And, I'll tell you what," I continued. "We should head up north and do some fishing before you go. I think you'd enjoy that."

He did. In fact, John stayed with Betty and me for four days before going back to England. We fished, shared business stories and had a good time all around. The two of us really hit it off. He tried to make a few more pitches to buy PSI, but by the end of the trip he was certain of the fact that I wasn't going to change my mind (I was certain of that fact all along). He might not have gotten my company, but he gained a friend.

A year later, Betty and I decided to take our first international trip together. We were planning to go to the UK with some friends, and I immediately recalled John saying that if we were ever in London, we should be sure to let him know. I definitely wanted to look him up while we were there, so before we finalized our plans, I gave him a quick call.

"Bill!" he responded. "Great to hear from you. What are you doing these days?"

"Betty and I are coming to England with some friends in a few weeks," I explained. "I was hoping we could make some plans to see you if you're available."

"Absolutely. What dates are you going to be here?" he asked.

It turned out that John didn't just make plans to see Betty and me. He did much more than that: He invited all of us to the Royal Ascot in Berkshire, which was being held during our visit to London and for which he had his own suite.

The Royal Ascot is one of the premier thoroughbred horseracing

events in the United Kingdom. Though many races are held in Ascot all year long, this one is the most prestigious. More than 300,000 people attend this four-day social gathering, and the royal family is always in attendance. In fact, the racetrack is only six miles from Windsor Castle and is part of the Crown Estate.

Not just anyone can attend the Royal Ascot. You have to be either a member of the racetrack or a guest invited by a longstanding member, so Betty and I were pretty fortunate to have befriended someone who actually had a suite for the event. Who would have thought that a boy who grew up on the west side of Detroit would ever attend an event with the queen of England—and one where men had to wear top hats and tuxedos with tails ("full morning dress") to boot?

When we arrived in Berkshire, it was a perfect day to bet on the ponies. We rode up in a Rolls-Royce limousine with John and made our way through the fashionable crowd to his suite. The British tradition of formality, decorum, pomp and grace was showcased to its fullest, and the experience was one I will never forget.

Just as we made our entrance into John's section of the racetrack, the crowd all stood and began applauding loudly. Betty and I turned around and saw four beautiful, white horses pulling the royal carriage. Inside sat Queen Elizabeth, Prince Phillip and other members of the royal family. One by one, the carriages brought them to the royal suite, which was separated from the rest of the field. Even though they were well protected by the Royal Guard, the attention they received from everyone in attendance was tremendous. As I saw all the people surrounding them and watching their every move, something occurred to me that I wanted to share with John.

"John, you know, Prince Phillip has a really great wife," I commented.

"Indeed," he replied.

"But with all these loyal subjects and staff constantly crowding around, he has to have a pretty poor sex life," I continued.

"Oh, to the contrary," John said emphatically.

"Why do you think that?"

"Because, ol' chap," he stated with a smile, "he's Navy, just like me."

Score one for Navy!

The entire day was spectacular. We watched the races, as well as all the elegant people at Ascot, Betty picked the winning horse and I got to enjoy the company of a friend.

Friendships and experiences like those are what make life richer. I've always said that with success, it's not about how much money you can hoard. It's about how many great moments you can have.

CHAPTER 52

Not Such Sweet Dreams of Success

People always talk about their dreams of success. I say it's much better to have a *plan for* success. But that didn't mean I didn't have dreams. I had them almost every night.

I recently learned that approximately thirty percent of the population has difficulty sleeping. From insomnia to teeth grinding, sleep disorders are increasingly common, but I didn't have them for most of my life. In the early 1980s, however, I began having changes in my sleep pattern that bothered me. Strange, recurring dreams disrupted my sleep at night and left me wondering about them during the day. After months of having these dreams regularly, I wanted to know what they meant. As with everything else, I needed to get to the bottom of things.

At that time, the country was in a significant recession. Following the 1973 oil crisis and the 1979 energy crisis, the inflation rate rose progressively higher, hitting 13.5 percent in 1980. Of the industries affected, housing, steel and automotive were the hardest hit.

Federal Reserve Chairman Paul Volcker invoked contractionary policies in 1981 to control inflation and as a result, the prime lending rate hit 21.5 percent. All of these factors triggered a severe recession, with unemployment rates eventually reaching almost eight percent.

With PSI in a growth phase, I was worried about the potential reduction in business. A large drop in revenues and an inherently high overhead could have triggered the worst: a company failure.

Everything I had worked so hard for could have gone up in smoke. And the hardest part to take was that it would have been completely out of my control.

That was when I began having the recurring dreams. At first, they were occasional, but eventually, they came almost every night. The same scenario played out each time, over and over again. In the first dream, I drove down the road where I currently live. At the time I had this dream, Betty and I had just moved there, into a large home on several acres west of Detroit. The setting was beautiful, with manicured lawns and custom-built houses.

In the dream, as in reality, nothing was out of place. I slowly drove up to our house, but when I tried to go inside, something held me back. I couldn't see anything physically preventing me from going in, but even so, some barrier was present. Feelings of anxiety accompanied the frustration of not being able to enter my own home.

As soon as that dream ended, a second one would occur. It was always in sequence with the first. In this dream, instead of driving up to my new home, I would be standing inside the first house that Betty and I had ever bought. After moving out of my parents' home in the late 1950s, we'd purchased a small house on the GI Bill and lived there for about ten years. In the dream, I was looking out the window of this house at our neighbors as they mowed their lawns or sat and relaxed on their porches. All the while, I was commenting to Betty, "It's okay, we'll get this house back into shape." I could see that the walls needed to be painted and the floors had to be repaired, but I was resigned to the fact that we had to live there even though I didn't like it. We were stuck.

After the second dream finished, I woke up rattled. This went on for four months. Every time, I would dream first about our new house then our old one and feel anxious for different reasons: either not being able to get in or not being able to get out.

I never dreamed about the other house Betty and I bought, where we stayed for nine years in between the starter home and our current

one. It was a nice, large Colonial of excellent quality, but it never entered into my subconscious.

I assumed that my financial worries had something to do with these dreams, but for the life of me I couldn't quite figure out their meaning. I decided to have my head shrunk to figure it out. I made an appointment with a psychiatrist, to see if a professional could make sense of my psyche.

I'm a self-reliant guy, but when I have a problem, I do not hesitate to seek the right help. I don't see that as a sign of weakness, like some men do. I see it as a strategy. For me, it's no different from taking your car to a mechanic if it's not running properly. My dreams were messing with my sleep, so it made perfect sense to go to someone who understood how the mind worked and could help me with the issue.

During the first two appointments with the psychiatrist, she asked me a lot of questions and listened to the details of my dreams. There wasn't any sort of couch to lie down on and it was nothing like I'd imagined from having watched such scenes in movies. Instead, she sat at her desk while I sat across from her in a regular office chair. I did most of the talking, and she would ask an occasional, directed question. In other words, she got to know me a little during the first couple of visits. On the third visit, I finally received the answer I sought.

"You're easy to figure out," she stated that morning.

It was pretty much the first time I had heard that in any context. I'm not an easy guy to pigeonhole. Sure, I like to keep things simple, but I also keep people guessing. Anyway, I figured that in this case, that was a good sign.

"Okay. So what do the dreams mean, then?" I asked.

"You're very black and white—all or none," she stated.

"How so?"

"The new house represents success. The old house represents failure. It's either one or the other with you."

"Why don't I dream about my second home?" I asked.

"Because it doesn't represent success or failure. So, it means nothing to you."

"Why am I having these dreams now?"

"Because you're worried about losing your success," she said.

And she was right.

I learned a great deal about myself from those three visits to the psychiatrist and from my dreams. I had never really thought much about it, but the struggles of my childhood had created a very strong drive for success within me.

Growing up in Detroit hadn't been a walk in the park. It had been rough. I'd constantly had to prove myself, to either stand up or get beaten up. If a kid wasn't thick-skinned and quick on his feet, he was likely to get nowhere fast.

Running my own business and making money were the means by which I escaped all of that. Success meant I could shield my family from that environment, and money, as always, meant power and freedom. And, more than anything else, I always wanted my freedom.

On top of that, I'd seen my parents struggle all their lives. My dad had worked incredibly hard at General Motors for thirty-five years. My mom had made the most with what we'd had while raising my sister and me. Growing up in such an environment can either inspire you to overcome it or cause you to accept it as your fate. I definitely chose to fight that fate. Having money meant not having to struggle like my parents had and giving my own kids more than I'd had, just like my parents had wanted to do for me. That's a big part of the American dream.

Even though I mostly attended inner-city Detroit schools, I saw plenty of kids who hadn't struggled with the challenges I had. I knew there was another way, and I resolved early in life not to become one of those kids who had to fight every day of their lives just to survive.

For all of these reasons, success became more than just a business goal; it was a very personal issue for me.

When the recession hit hard in the early 1980s, the threat of losing everything I had worked so hard for affected me to my core. Until then, I'd never realized how much I valued my success. Because I had such an all-or-nothing philosophy, losing any ground meant a loss of success to me, and the dreams were simply a manifestation of those deeply rooted concerns and that conditioning.

Not long afterwards, the recession passed, the dreams went away and I was getting a good night's sleep again. But, I now had a better idea of what drove and has always driven me: on the one hand was success and on the other, the threat of that success being taken away. I didn't care if it was one individual trying to screw me out of what I'd earned or an economic downturn; I wanted to keep what I'd built and continue providing for my family the best I could.

And, rest assured, that was exactly what I did.

CHAPTER 53

Mining Your Own Business

To find ways to expand your business and adapt to a changing world, you sometimes need to dig a little deeper.

Beginning in the early 1980s, declines in the oil industry were being felt nationwide. Undoubtedly, this affected the number of equipment repairs for PSI, since many servo valves and other hydraulic equipment parts on oil rigs, platforms and refineries were being used less or had decreased in number.

In 1981, I was approached by a group that wanted to purchase my Los Angeles facility. Because the timing was right, letting go of that plant made a lot of sense. But, selling that facility highlighted the writing on the wall: If the oil industry continued to decline in the country, that portion of PSI's services would go down with it. One thing you can always count on in business and in life is that nothing stays the same. It was time to roll with the changes.

The most obvious solution to me was to consider other industries that utilized hydraulic and servo valve equipment and include them in our service market. While the dynamics of the industry were much different from petroleum and aerospace, making equipment repairs to mining operations was one area that had yet to be tapped. And, believe me, whatever was being overlooked was exactly where I was looking.

Coal, copper and uranium mining were prevalent in the West

during the 1980s, so exploring this area of potential business seemed like a wise move. Not only that, but the idea of going out West always appealed to me, so I also partly did it for the fun of it. You've got to enjoy yourself in business, too. Otherwise, what's the point?

Within a week, I planned a trip out West to investigate new business opportunities for PSI and do a little exploring myself.

It's funny how people tend to enter and re-enter your life at just the right times. Just after I made my plans to go to Colorado to explore the local mining operations, I received a call at the office. It was a Friday afternoon, and I was wrapping up the affairs of the week. If it had been just a little later, I would have been already home for the weekend. Instead, I picked up the phone and heard a familiar voice.

"Bill, this is Weldon Franks."

"Weldon," I exclaimed. "How are you?"

"I just thought I'd call and say hello."

Weldon had worked for me in Houston for about a year, handling sales and operations. But, eventually, the traveling had become too much for him. He'd resigned from PSI, fallen back on his part-time career as a Baptist preacher and worked in some other sales positions closer to home. The timing of his phone call was impeccable, considering why he had called.

"What have you been up to, Bill?" Weldon asked.

"I've been thinking about looking into the mining business," I stated. "I believe there might be an opportunity there for equipment repairs."

"I was wondering if you have any work opening up," he said. "I'm looking for something new."

"Tell you what... If you'd like, you can come out to Colorado with me next week and investigate."

Weldon and I finalized our travel plans and the following Tuesday, we landed in Vail, Colorado, to do some exploring. Colorado has an

incredibly rich mining history. It was one of the earliest places to have its own gold rush and in the 1800s, several mines in the state yielded significant amounts of silver.

But, the mines I was interested in didn't involve either of those elements. Other minerals and precious materials were more common at the time. Colorado supplied large amounts of coal to many states in the country, and it also had mines that drilled for uranium, copper, molybdenum and more. If I could get these facilities onboard for the repair of their equipment, PSI would be well established in the mining business in no time. Which would, in effect, be a gold mine!

Vail is, of course, known for its skiing and recreation, and not far from there were several coal mines where I thought we could make some sales calls. Ever since I'd first started out in sales, I'd realized that the best way to convince someone that your product or service was the best was to tell them exactly that, face to face. And, even more importantly, I needed to see what these mining operations looked like before I pulled the trigger on a new niche market for PSI. I appreciate research and fact finding, but nothing replaces the instinctual feeling you get from being hands on.

Weldon and I leased a car and headed south through Leadville, then further west through the Gunnison National Forest. Fortunately, it was summer. Otherwise, many of the mountain passes on which we traveled would have been closed, and having to travel other highways would have significantly lengthened our driving time.

The scenery was incredible along the way, with aspens and evergreens decorating the majestic mountains and hillsides. I think we saw every tree there by the time we finally came to the coal mines along West Elk Bank. It was time to see if this idea of mine had any merit.

We stepped out of the car and onto the dusty ground, making our way toward the entrance of a large, sheet metal building. Workers were everywhere, with hardhats and fluorescent vests, and

the noise of heavy machinery could be heard well before we reached the offices.

Once inside the building, we sought someone who could help us.

"Where can we find one of your foremen?" I asked a large, burly man as he walked past.

"I'm a foreman," he replied. "What can I do for you?"

"My name's Bill Phillips. I run a hydraulic equipment repair company. I'd like to speak with someone who knows how you handle your equipment."

"That would be Mike," the guy said. "Have a seat over there and I'll see if I can find him."

Weldon and I found some folding chairs on the other side of the room and took a seat. About ten minutes later, another man walked into the area and introduced himself as Mike. He was in charge of West Elk Mine's invoicing and equipment operations.

As it turned out, Mike used only the original equipment manufacturers, known in our industry as the OEMs, for all his equipment needs, from repairs to new purchases. But, they did have several pieces of equipment that utilized hydraulic pumps, cylinders and servo valves—which meant, without a doubt, that there was an opportunity for PSI.

"I'm sure we can handle your repairs much faster than the OEMs," I told him. "They typically take a while to repair their own parts. They think they've got no competition and no reason to hurry."

"That's true," Mike agreed. "What kind of turnaround are we talking about here?"

"Well, I'm looking to open operations here in the state. If you give me all of your repair business, we can pick up the equipment within twenty-four hours and return it as soon as the problem is fixed. Probably an average of a week or two for most repairs."

"I'll tell you what," Mike said, clearly impressed. "Let's take a walk

around the mine and I'll show you our equipment. If you still think it'll work for you, I'll definitely give you a try."

Mike, Weldon and I walked around for the next thirty minutes, surveying all the equipment in the mine. I was convinced that PSI could handle the work. Their equipment was nothing we hadn't seen before, and the repairs would be identical to those in other industries we serviced.

The volume of equipment there was pretty impressive, and Mike knew a couple of operations managers at other mines that we might be able to establish business with as well. If we could get him onboard first and do a good job, establishing ourselves within the mining network sounded simple. We would only be competing with the original equipment manufacturers, and PSI was faster and hungrier.

After that brief tour, I made the decision to begin repair operations in Colorado. And, before long, I decided to provide services to the mining industries in New Mexico and Wyoming as well.

When one door closes, look for another opening. The oil industry was winding down, but the mining industry provided a market to take its place—and PSI was the first to move. You have to be ready to change when the climate changes or you'll definitely be left out in the cold.

With the expansion of operations, I needed a manager to help coordinate everything—and that was where Weldon came in. Like me, he was in the right place at the right time, and all the pieces seemed to fall perfectly into place.

The time was right to explore new options, and PSI was ready to give the mining industry a try. It was a new frontier for both me and my business. So, what better place than the wild West?

CHAPTER 54

Doing Business in Durango

I was convinced that the mining business had great potential for PSI's repair services, so I then needed to determine where to set up shop. While searching for a location, it didn't take long for me to realize that most destinations weren't in close proximity to one another in Colorado. To go from one mine to another within the state usually took hours.

Other than knowing that the West was a wide-open space full of opportunities, I didn't know much about the area. But, Weldon had been to Colorado a few times and suggested taking a look at Durango. Originally, it been established as a mining town, but those days were long past. With a population of about 10,000 people, most of its trade now revolved around tourism and recreation. It was a beautiful town surrounded by tall mountains on all sides.

After what seemed like a full day of driving, Weldon and I arrived in Durango in the afternoon, a little after three o'clock. I didn't want to waste any more time. Once I make a decision, I act, so the first thing I did in Durango was find the local bank to get things started.

"Good afternoon," I said, walking into the small lobby of the First National Bank.

"Good afternoon," a man replied, getting up from his desk. "Welcome to First National. May I help you?"

"I hope so," I told him. "I'm thinking about opening up a business here in town. What can you tell me about buildings for rent?"

In small towns like Durango, the opening of new businesses didn't occur very often, so the man fell all over himself trying to cater to any need I had. I could practically see the dollar signs in his eyes. He turned out to be the bank's branch manager and was more than knowledgeable about what I needed. Before closing time, I had made contact with a commercial realtor, established a bank account and found out where to purchase a vehicle. It was one-stop shopping as far as I was concerned.

As it is with any new equipment facility, time was of the essence. In order to be profitable, the new location had to be fully operational as quickly as possible. At the most, I usually only allowed a month or so to get a new facility off the ground—and this new venture into mining equipment repairs wouldn't be any different. My goal for the trip was to establish a foundation before Weldon and I left.

With one of those famous Western sunsets in the sky, Weldon and I left the bank and checked into a local hotel. We needed to get some rest because the next day was going to be busy—but with the new industry and territory PSI would be serving, I already felt refreshed and energized. Every now and then, even a successful entrepreneur needs a new adventure.

The next morning, the crisp, dry air felt good as Weldon and I went to work on setting up shop. Durango was a tourist haven and we fit right in with the other visitors in town. But, the regulars could tell the out-of-towners from the locals by their attire, if nothing else. Since I was going to be established in town, I was already eyeing a pair of cowboy boots for myself, and I was pretty sure I'd end up with a cowboy hat, too, before the trip was complete. But, there was a more pressing purchase I needed to make.

"Let's go buy a truck, Weldon," I said.

Based on the amount of driving we'd done the day before, it was clear that we would need some solid transportation.

"Sounds like a good first step," he replied.

Weldon and his family had visited Durango on vacation several times, and he liked the area. He was planning to relocate his wife and children there as soon as possible once he started working, so he would have to find a place to live; at least getting a truck now would provide him with some means of getting around.

We drove our rental car west of the city, eventually coming to a Ford dealership on the outskirts of town. Being from Detroit, I was used to seeing huge inventories of cars and trucks at auto dealerships. But, in Durango, that wasn't the case. I had seen more cars in a strip-mall parking lot than I saw at this sales lot. It seemed as though high-volume sales weren't the strategy for this dealership.

Weldon and I walked toward the small office in the showroom area. Surprisingly, no one rushed out to greet us. The sales vultures that you usually have to beat off with a stick were nowhere to be found. It was so desolate, I expected a tumbleweed to roll by at any moment.

Just before I was about to walk into the office, I saw a man in jeans sitting outside, tilted back on a chair with his feet propped up on a railing. He had lowered his newspaper just enough to notice that someone had come into the lot. Seeing that there was no one else around, I headed toward him, though he appeared to have little interest in making a sale.

"Do you work here?" I asked when I was about ten yards away.

"Yes, I do," he replied.

"I wanna buy a truck," I stated.

"What kind of truck?" he asked, finally lowering his newspaper further. "Used or new? Our finance guy is out today, so you might have to wait until tomorrow."

"A new one...and I'm paying cash."

The noise his chair made as it slammed down and struck the floor could have woken the entire town of Durango. He jumped to his feet and was shaking my hand before I could blink an eye.

"My name is Joe Hillman," he said, pumping my hand up and down. "What kind of truck are you looking for?"

"Something with some towing power," I said. "Nothing too fancy, but one with some muscle."

"Alright, good. What color?"

"Any color that matches four black tires."

He smiled, sensing that I wanted to get down to business. "We have this nice white one here that would suit you. She's decked out and has a Windsor V8 engine. That's three hundred fifty-one horses."

Now the guy was really moving, like we did back East. I guessed that actual sales and actual cash were rare in car dealerships around there. I called our accountant in the Detroit office and had money wired directly to the Ford dealership. The salesman couldn't have been more excited.

The next step was to find a building for operations. Weldon and I easily found the industrial park in town, where we secured a 2,000-square-foot space with a small office attached. I had another check wired to a realtor so PSI could lease the building, and the realtor's reaction was about the same as the car salesman's. It seemed that I was making a lot of new friends in Durango.

Wherever I expanded, I always tried to take the local economy into consideration. I tried to use local people for employment whenever possible, and I certainly used local businesses and services for our supplies when reasonable. It had a good impact on the region and made things easier for PSI. In any new market I entered, I used the same formula for expansion. If it wasn't broke, I didn't try to fix it (which is usually a good rule for repairs).

I knew other nationwide companies in larger cities that could have handled all of my needs regardless of where I decided to locate

my businesses. But, supporting the local communities was an investment worth making. Having scratched my way up from the bottom, I appreciated what it meant to have a chance to prove myself, and I liked giving people the opportunity to show what they could do. Usually, I was pleasantly surprised.

Weldon continued to make his plans to relocate to Durango, and I went back to Detroit to assemble a core team that would get the mining operations division off the ground. One of my more tenured engineers began looking for the machinery we needed and ended up getting some great bargains at an auction in North Carolina. I hired some employees from the Durango area and some from Michigan and, before long, PSI was officially in the mining repairs business, which remained lucrative for many years to come.

My intuition and hands-on planning style proved to be effective, allowing the vision of the company to become a reality before it could get bogged down in a never-ending research-and-planning phase. Of course, there's nothing inherently wrong with research and planning, but all too often companies and people get so busy working out the details that they never take action. At least flying by the seat of your pants gets you places.

Making a final decision and executing your plans are the most important steps in any business—otherwise, you're just left with blueprints. Fortunately, I've never had a problem with either of those actions. The key is to put aside your fears and doubts, go with your gut instinct and never look back. That doesn't mean that you won't make any mistakes, but at least you'll be making some strides forward.

And, for that, you might want to invest in a nice pair of cowboy boots.

CHAPTER 55

Home on the Range

They call Colorado "Big Country" for a reason. Our salespeople soon found that out.

Distances were vast and the time required to go from PSI's centrally located facility in Durango to a remote mine where a piece of equipment was located could have been three hours or more. That meant a great deal of time on the road for the sales force. And, more time driving meant less time selling.

In addition, the salespeople had to be capable of loading heavy pieces of equipment into their vehicles so they could carry them back to the main facility for repair. Commercial transportation wasn't available to many of these remote areas, so our sales vehicles had to be heavy-hauling trucks instead of cars.

Before weigh stations and transfer stations were built along Colorado's state highways, allowing equipment to be weighed and stored closer to the mining facilities, the sales team had to handle all the transportation tasks as well. Once these stations were established, however, a salesperson could deliver a piece of equipment to a storage location and one of PSI's trucks could collect it the following day.

What all of this showed me was that PSI's original, successful formula would have to be tweaked a bit when we implemented it somewhere else—and this was particularly true of our operations

in the mining industry. But, the small adjustments were no big deal, especially since the business basics and our blueprint for expansion were working out well. I wasn't about to turn molehills into mountains or let the mountains themselves keep me from entering the mining industry.

Once we became comfortable with the Durango facility and its idiosyncrasies, I felt it was time to expand even further. New Mexico had numerous uranium mines that lay just south of Durango, and Arizona had a few copper mines that I knew could use our repair services. But, the best opportunity was actually in Wyoming. It had an even greater number of coal producers and mines than Colorado.

So, I decided to explore Wyoming for a site for a second facility.

This time, I decided to take Betty along and show her how a new operation was opened. More importantly, I really wanted her company. Most of our children were adults and with PSI being successful, we were finally able to enjoy some time together.

After Betty and I landed at Wyoming's Natrona County International Airport, only a few hours' flight from our home, we headed into Casper. The city's population was less than 50,000 and, typical of most Western towns, its pace was slow and relaxed. We could feel the change in the air as soon as we stepped off the plane. The silence that surrounded us, the spaciousness of the landscape and the mountains rising in the not-so-far distance told us we weren't in Detroit any longer.

We rented a car, then I took Betty to where I always start when moving into a new area: the local bank. As I mentioned, I like to invest in the local economy and support businesses within the community. In addition, I have found banks to be a wealth of information when developing a new market. They have all the resources necessary to facilitate a growing company.

"Good morning," I said to one of the bank tellers as I walked into the Bank of the West.

"Good morning," the woman replied pleasantly. "What can I do for you?"

"I would like to open up a new plant in Casper," I stated. "Could I speak to one of your managers?"

Betty's head practically spun as two managers overheard my request and rushed right over to attend to our needs. Another employee went to make fresh coffee for us while the two managers escorted Betty and me to an office with leather chairs and deep-maroon carpeting and made sure we were comfortable. A luxury hotel in New York would hardly have had this kind of service.

"I'm looking to open a facility here to handle hydraulic equip-ment repairs," I explained. "I was hoping to get the name of a good contractor and some overall information about your town."

"We can certainly help you," one of the bankers said, smiling. "There's an industrial park in Casper, and I know several contractors who can do a good job for you."

In general, small banks are always short on cash. When their managers see an opportunity to gain a customer who can place a decent amount of money in the bank, they'll do just about anything to impress him, since that extra money allows them to make loans and profits.

Without question, businesses like PSI didn't just waltz into Casper on a regular basis. So, my being ready to start a large business in town certainly provided some extra incentive for their already-friendly service.

By the time we left the bank that morning I had placed $200,000 in an account to purchase some land later that week and gotten the names of a reputable contractor and an attorney. I had also received a crash course on the geographical layout of Casper as well as its politics, regulations and day-to-day operations. Like I said, banks are great places to begin.

"I don't believe I've ever been doted on like that," Betty said as we were driving away from the bank.

"That's why I wanted you to come," I replied. "I wanted you to see how it happens."

"Well, don't expect to get that kind of treatment all the time," she said with a grin.

"But, that was another reason I wanted you to come," I teased her.

As usual, I didn't waste any time. Later that afternoon, I met a contractor at the industrial park near the edge of town and, after looking over the available land, I found just the right lot on which to construct our new facilities. I literally took a stick and drew out the floor plan and basic construction design of the new building in the dirt. The contractor and I played around with the details a bit, but when we were done, that drawing on the ground was what ultimately became PSI's new facility. Now, that's my idea of how things get done out West.

As I expanded PSI's operations, Betty and I enjoyed traveling to the western United States quite often. Because I was constantly flying out to check on business operations, I grew tired of the hotels that made going out west with my family difficult. I ended up buying a condominium in Durango from a local builder named David Jones, who had developed almost the entire area. That made going back and forth much easier and more settled. In fact, a few years later, Betty and I purchased Jones' own house, completely furnished.

Durango became our home away from home for a few years; all the kids learned how to ski and took part in all the other recreation the town had to offer. Two of my children, Sean and Donna, even live in Colorado today.

After so many years of struggling in Detroit, it was nice finally to be able to enjoy the fruits of our labor together as a family. Betty and I had come a long way since those early days of living with my parents. And, a few Western sunsets made me realize it was all worth it.

CHAPTER 56

A Saloon Story

I always kept my finger on the pulse of the company, and the sales operations for our mining services division were a little different from PSI's prior protocols. The sales vehicles were different, the sales territories were larger and the equipment transport was more cumbersome. Even the mining supervisors were a little different from the typical petroleum or aerospace managers. These guys were true cowboys, accustomed to dealing with the harsh conditions that came along with the Western location. They had a sense of adventure and ruggedness about them. But, I wanted to have a firsthand feel for how things were handled on a daily basis.

So, I made plans to spend a full day with one of my general sales managers. Starting in Casper, Wyoming, he and I would make a few sales calls within his territory. His name was Joe Allen, and I had known him for some time. Joe was a Kent State graduate who was no stranger to the Western mentality and culture, not to mention controversy. He was also a good salesman.

He picked me up in Casper and we drove in his truck to our first sales call, which wasn't too far outside of town. An hour or so later, we had arrived at the first coal-mining plant to speak with the supervisors there.

The day was a scorcher; it was the middle of summer and by the look of things, it hadn't rained in a month or more. In between

stops, I noticed how beautiful the terrain was, with mountains in the distance separated by long spreads of flat land. What appeared to be just a few miles away was often more than fifty miles in the distance. Everything was vast and spacious out there and a few sales calls sure added up on the odometer.

Our second call was sixty miles from our first appointment, and the third one was even farther away. Without a doubt, Joe spent more time on the road than he did conducting business face to face. That was just the nature of how things worked out there given the geography he had to cover.

By five o'clock that evening I had seen enough to have a good understanding of exactly how everything was operating—and I was thirsty. That was when our real adventure began.

"Joe, how about we stop somewhere for an ice-cold beer?" I suggested.

"That sounds like a really great idea," he replied. "There's a town not too far away, on the way to Grand Junction."

Grand Junction was where I was to catch my airplane so I could fly back to Detroit that evening. A pit stop on the way was surely in order.

As we drove onwards, I saw road signs saying that Rock City and Green River were not too far ahead. I had never been to either of those two towns, but Rock City sounded very familiar. I just couldn't quite place where I had heard of it before.

"Let's try Rock City," Joe suggested.

"Okay. Have you ever been there?" I asked him.

"No, but it's five miles closer than Green River."

We pulled off the highway and into town. The streets were paved but otherwise the area we were driving through looked like the set of a John Ford film. Rock City was a small town with an old-fashioned general store and a swinging-door saloon. I'd never

been in that kind of classic Western bar before, so, I figured, why not give it a try?

It was then that I remembered where I had heard about Rock City. In the late 1970s, *60 Minutes* on CBS had done a special TV show about this little Wyoming town—though it had been more like an exposé. The program detailed Rock City's corruption with drugs, prostitution and other criminal dealings. I thought I remembered hearing that, at some point, one of the sheriffs in either Rock City or Green River had been shot. This wasn't simply a film set for a Western. It was the real thing.

Joe and I took our seats at the bar, doing our best John Wayne swaggers. Several wooden tables were scattered around the room, and about a third of them were occupied by grizzly looking patrons, all drinking beer or whiskey. Everyone had looked up for a second when we walked into the saloon then redirected their gazes back to their drinks. Joe and I just minded our own business.

"Hey, Joe," I whispered after we sat down.

"Yeah, Bill?" he replied.

"Don't ask for a glass with your beer. It isn't manly," I joked.

"You think I'm crazy? I know better than that."

When the bartender finally came around, we gave him our order and were soon relaxing with two cold bottles of beer in our hands. We were about halfway finished when the doors swung open again. Nothing could have prepared us for what walked in.

Standing just inside the doorway was a man with disheveled hair and a patch over his left eye. In one hand, he carried a wooden stick that, if I wasn't mistaken, was a sawed-off axe handle; his other hand held a leash that was attached to a huge German shepherd. He also had a pistol tucked inside his belt, resting in front of his stomach.

When he walked inside, Joe and I tried to keep from staring in

his direction or making eye contact, but it was difficult to ignore him. Because of the man's appearance, no one in the bar, including the bartender, thought about saying a word to him, and the guy himself stayed silent.

He walked straight to a table immediately to his right, where two people were sitting. Then, he put the axe handle under one man's chin and said something that neither Joe nor I could hear. All we could make out was that the man at the table responded, "No."

The guy then methodically went over to the two other tables in the room where customers were sitting and appeared to ask the same question. Each time, he received the same answer.

So far, Joe and I had avoided his gaze, but it was inevitable that he would eventually make his way to the bar. And, he did. The two of us kept drinking our beer and waiting for our turn.

"You fellas been sittin' here long?" the man asked in a gruff voice.

"About ten minutes," I replied.

"Either of you seen my woman?" he asked, looking each of us in the eye.

"Uh, no," Joe answered.

"No one else has been in since we got here," I said.

Without another word, he turned and left the saloon with his dog, his axe handle and his pistol. Everyone in the place seemed to breathe a collective sigh of relief.

About a minute passed as Joe and I resumed drinking our beers. Then, after the long, silent pause, Joe asked me a very thoughtful question.

"Can you imagine how ugly that poor woman must be?"

"Yeah. Who would want to take her in the first place?" I replied.

We finished our drinks and left Rock City, happy to have gotten

out alive. As the distance between Joe's truck and the town grew, so did our laughter about the one-eyed man looking for his woman.

The West was a different kind of place and after that trip, I definitely had a much better appreciation of that.

I also couldn't wait to do more business out there.

CHAPTER 57

An Expression of Faith

On the surface, there doesn't seem to be much connection between business and religion. But, I realize that both require faith and the ability to believe in something that isn't necessarily apparent to others. In both cases, faith takes guts and can often lead to glory.

Within three months of opening the mining operations in Durango, my lead manager, Weldon, had moved his wife and children to the area. He was managing all the sales and operations for the entire Western region for mining equipment repairs, but I was unsure how long he would stick with the position given that he had left PSI once before in Houston because of the traveling demands.

All in all, Weldon lasted a total of four years before choosing to explore other options. This time, the incentive wasn't to establish a job closer to home; he was close enough already. Instead, he decided to fulfill his true calling.

Weldon had served as a part-time Baptist preacher when he was in Texas, and he told me one time when I was in Colorado, "Bill, I've decided to open a church of my own."

"What do you mean, Weldon?" I asked, somewhat surprised.

"I've been preaching some at one of the local churches. I think the Lord has called me to open my own church to serve Him."

"Does that mean you're resigning?"

"I'm afraid it does. I've been happy at PSI and am very thankful to you, Bill, for allowing me to work here. But this is just something I have to do."

"Well, I wish you luck," I told him. "Just quit slowly. You can still do some work here while you get your church started."

He appreciated the offer—and took it. He continued working at PSI part-time while both he and his wife jumped into their new roles as ministers.

Despite Weldon's Baptist background, his line of religion was more evangelical; he was what people in the South referred to as a "holy roller." When I was growing up in Arkansas, that was the name given to people who attended churches where everyone danced in the pews and sang out as loudly as possible. Faith healing, exorcism and speaking in tongues were common parts of the services every Sunday, and seeing Weldon in action was impressive, to say the least.

A few weeks after he told me about his decision, Weldon found an old supermarket in Durango that had closed down. The owner of the property was willing to let him open his new church there, although strip-mall churches were rare, especially in the 1980s and in the West.

The lease was a decent sum of money and being that his church was new, Weldon didn't have the financial means on hand. He came to me for some assistance.

"Bill, I hate to ask you this," he began. "But is there any way you could help me with the initial deposit for the lease on the church building?"

"How many people are going to be attending?" I asked.

"I know of at least a hundred," Weldon replied. "We've been getting that many at our community gatherings already."

"Let's go look at this place," I said, approaching it as I would any business decision.

The building was on the outskirts of Durango and its layout was typical of a supermarket. The shelving and registers had all been removed, and the freezers and refrigerators were gone. However, the interior certainly didn't look like any church I had ever seen.

"Weldon," I said, "how are you going to make this place look like a church?"

"Oh, we're gonna have folding chairs in here for a while, and my wife and I already have a wooden pulpit to use. One of our members has an organ as well."

"Are you sure this is gonna work?"

"I know it will," Weldon said.

His confidence convinced me. I provided him with some startup money to get him and his congregation into the building and before long, Weldon got the small church off the ground. Attendance steadily increased and it seemed as though he was going to make his new career a success. I had lost a manager, but Durango had gained a preacher.

———

Ever since being declared an infidel by Father Murphy before my marriage in St. John's, I had continued to attend the Catholic Church. Betty and I attended Mass with our children and, over the years, I became very involved with church activities. In fact, I served as chairman of the advisory board at Madonna University, a Catholic college in Detroit, for several years.

Regardless, my belief was that religion was practiced in many different ways, and Weldon had his own way of expressing his faith. Just as there are different ways to achieve success in business, I am sure that different forms of expression achieve the same spiritual satisfaction.

But, of course, not everyone necessarily agrees with my viewpoint.

One of my dearest friends and mentors was Father Gerard Hadaad, a Catholic priest in Detroit whom I had the pleasure of knowing over the years. Unfortunately, he died not too long ago. He'd served in the military as an officer before he'd become a priest, so he and I immediately hit it off well.

I invited Father Gerry to come along with me on several of my trips out West. On one occasion, we flew to Durango to have lunch with Weldon. I assumed that since both were men of the cloth, they would have plenty of things in common to talk about.

"So, Weldon, Bill tells me you've started your own church in Durango," Gerry stated.

"I have," Weldon said with a certain pride. "My wife and I are ministering to a small congregation together."

"How has it been going, getting things started?"

"It was a little rocky at first, but things are picking up. Miracles keep happening all the time."

"What kind of miracles?" Gerry asked.

"Well, Bill was a blessing when it came to getting the church on its feet. And just last week, with the Lord's help, I healed a man."

"Healed a man? How so?"

"A man who had been paralyzed from the waist down for years was able to walk," Weldon explained.

"How did that happen?" Gerry asked. I could hear the skepticism in his voice.

"The entire congregation prayed and sang for him to be healed, and we offered him up to the Lord."

"Then he was able to stand and walk?"

"Popped right up out of his wheelchair!" Weldon said, satisfied.

"I see," Gerry replied, studying the other man's face for sincerity.

There was a long pause in the conversation before Gerry turned to me and said, "Bill, this is where I get off."

I suppose that both Weldon and Gerry could have been considered conservative based on their religious beliefs, but when it came to evangelical expressions of faith, Weldon was as far left as anyone could imagine. On the other hand, as a Catholic priest, Gerry sat well to the right, and the two had no chance of meeting in the middle. To each their own, I figured.

Weldon went his own way after leaving PSI. He served as a preacher for a while and tried to grow his church before he and his wife split up. Weldon took the children, and his wife moved to California. I kept in touch with him for a while, and he did return to sales at some point with a company close to where he was living. However, as time passed, we gradually lost touch.

Still, I was happy that I had once helped an employee and friend to realize his own dream. Whether you're building a church, a business or any other enterprise, you're shaping your future, which requires a lot of courage.

And, more than a little faith.

PART VI

Fighting the Battles to Win the War

CHAPTER 58

Rolling With the Punches

I believe that diversification is a good strategy in almost any business. Whether it applies to the number of services you provide or the number of different clients you have, diversification prevents you from putting all your eggs in one basket—and it keeps you on the cutting edge of an ever-changing business world.

Unfortunately, I haven't always followed my own advice—and in at least one instance, it could have cost me my company.

By the time the mid-1980s came along, PSI found itself heavily servicing the energy industry. Our Houston facility was significantly involved in the oil and petroleum industries and, of course, the mining operations out West dealt with coal to a large extent.

But, when the energy crisis hit during the middle of the decade, PSI saw a tremendous decline in the number of repair services needed.

Energy crises weren't the only changes that affected PSI's operations, however. In New Mexico, many uranium mines began to close as a result of popular and political pressure. Campaigns led by Jane Fonda, among others, caused several businesses in the uranium and nuclear industries to shut their doors. As a result, repair services for mining equipment declined.

In addition, Arizona saw several strikes occur among union workers in the copper mines in the 1980s. This resulted in reductions in the demand for PSI's services as some of the copper mines went out of business.

The culmination of all of these things prompted the eventual closure of PSI's mining and oil-based equipment repair services in those locations.

Our Los Angeles facility had already been sold to a group of engineers in 1981, so by 1986, PSI had consolidated its operations in Detroit, Houston, Durango and Casper. Industry declines then led to the closure of the Houston location in 1986 and the sale of the Durango facility in 1988. Casper subsequently closed shortly afterward, in 1988.

Despite some attempt at diversification on my part, several factors occurred that caused a lesser need for hydraulic and servo valve repair services. So, like any business during times of contraction, PSI had to cut back its overhead and operations.

But, as those doors closed, I knew to look for other openings. It wasn't just good business; it was a matter of survival.

As the coal and oil industries were declining, another area was rapidly advancing: electronics. The field began to boom and many pieces of equipment in the aerospace and manufacturing industries needed to incorporate electronic systems into their operations. This, of course, meant that electronic components would need repair services periodically. I was already a step ahead, having incorporated electronic repair into our offerings in 1977.

Just as the industries we serviced had changed to adapt to new technology, so had PSI been adapting all along. We were a corporation adept at repairing anything from hydraulic systems and electronics to large mining equipment. We had already been servic-

ing numerical and computer-controlled machines for a decade, and since electronic controls were actually a necessity for dealing with hydraulics, we were already well ahead of the game and well versed in the field.

Hydraulics and servo valves were fundamental; in fact, servo valves were the foundation around which equipment design revolved and upon which even the highest-tech equipment was built. Electronics is electronics; it can be applied to almost any arena. So it wasn't too far a stretch for PSI to be an all-service industry.

Our facilities were ideally equipped for all of our services. The Detroit laboratory was meticulously clean and had to handle hydraulic fluids that were microscopically filtered. It was the perfect laboratory setting for electronics work, as well, where technicians would be dealing with intricate repairs.

New technicians were occasionally hired to keep up with specialization and our offices and laboratories were sometimes modified to accommodate new service lines when the emphasis shifted. But we didn't need to reinvent the wheel. We just had to turn the wheel's direction a little bit every now and then in order to accommodate everything from hydraulic system repairs to replacing component parts of electronic circuit boards for various pieces of high-tech equipment. That kind of diversity and flexibility is how I augmented the business—and ensured its survival through whatever the next wave would be.

PSI adapted to the changes in the market and more than met its needs. But everything else about the business remained the same: We continued to have a national sales force and handle deliveries, service and repairs in our usual fashion. These basics always seemed to work and didn't need to be messed with.

When the market's paradigm shifted, however, so did we.

One of the biggest threats to success is complacency. Without a doubt, almost all companies will face serious changes over their lifetimes—and failing to adapt will result in quick declines. The one thing that never changes is change itself. You've got to learn how to recognize the signs of change and stay at least one step ahead. There will always be a next wave. Ride it or drown.

Someone will always be ready to provide a service and meet a need that no one else is providing—I should know because I was that guy. I jumped into the servo valve repair business as soon as I realized an opportunity existed, and I did the same with electronics. I know that if I hadn't adapted my business so quickly, some other entrepreneur would've beaten me to the punch.

The opportunity to act doesn't last very long. Complacency will cause you to miss it, and shortsightedness will assure that you don't see it at all.

No matter how successful you become, adapting to change and evolving your business are necessary skills to stay ahead of your competitors and keep your company alive. Attaining success is an advantage, but it is by no means a guarantee of future successes.

Every day, the market redefines its needs. Staying on top of those needs means that your business will also stay on top. You either stay one step ahead or you fall hopelessly behind; the market waits for no one.

Each entrepreneur has a choice: Roll with the punches or take a beating. The former means your business stays alive another day. The latter will have you packing up and heading home.

With the survival of a species, it's adapt or die. In the survival of a business, it's go forward…or go bankrupt. It's your choice. I've already made mine.

CHAPTER 59

A Matter of Trust— and Antitrust

"**B**ill," the letter concluded, "I am in my mid-fifties and upon some recent reflection on life in general, I came to the conclusion that you have had as profound an impact on my life as just about any single person outside of my family. For if you had never had the chutzpah to open PSI, God only knows what would have become of my life."

The letter came to me in March 2009 from a salesman named Doug who had worked for me many years earlier, back in the late 1980s. He had been with the company for a total of eight years and was, without question, one of the best salespeople I'd ever had. He was a tough kid, and his energy and enthusiasm gave him great sales abilities. Doug wasn't the kind of person you would go and put your arm around, but when he spoke, he got your attention. In a lot of ways, he reminded me of me.

———

Unfortunately, our parting had not been on the best of terms and had actually led to one of my most significant and serious legal battles. Perhaps, in part, that was the reason for the letter.

It was 1992, and PSI had long since successfully incorporated electronic-equipment repairs into its wide range of services. That

evolution meant my business had dodged a bullet and continued to thrive.

Though the facilities in Houston and out west had closed or been sold off, our sales offices still existed around the country. Otherwise, all base repair operations for PSI were conducted out of the Detroit laboratory. Despite all the changes, it was business as usual: Equipment would be sent to the company for repair, then we would collect the necessary component parts and eventually deliver the repaired piece back to the client. Operations were running smoothly and profitably.

Still, one day, one of my operation managers called to tell me that we seemed to have a problem.

"What's that?" I asked.

"Allen-Bradley is refusing to sell us any more components."

"Why?"

"Our account has been permanently closed. When I spoke with the supervisor he said there were conflicts of interest, so they weren't going to sell to us any longer."

That was definitely a problem. Allen-Bradley was our largest supplier of electronic components and if we couldn't get parts, then we weren't going to be able to render repairs.

Unfortunately, Allen-Bradley was one of the few suppliers that had the electronic components we needed, and my guess was that they were interested in taking over repair services themselves. By preventing PSI from getting components, they had fewer competitors and a better chance at being successful in the market.

My hunch turned out to be right. But, restricting our access to components wasn't their only strategy in taking over our client market. According to one of my sales managers, they had also hired my employee, Doug—though I hadn't even known that he'd quit.

"When did that happen?" I asked the manager over the phone.

"He resigned a couple of weeks ago. Said he was gonna take some time off and look for something a little different from sales. I guess he found it."

"I'd say he found it! He knew exactly where he was going when he left here. Allen-Bradley lured him over there to get to our clients."

"No doubt about that," the manager agreed.

"That isn't right. If they think they can take our customers without a fight, they've got another thing coming."

Choosing not to sell electronic components to me was their prerogative, but stealing my sales force to get insider information about my company and clients was crossing the line. Not only was it underhanded but I knew there had to be something illegal about it. I was a far cry from an attorney, yet my instinct told me that the judicial system had to provide some type of protection for honest businesspeople. As soon as I got off the phone with my sales manager, I called my corporate attorney to find out.

"I want to know what we can do about this," I demanded after explaining the situation.

"We could file a suit against Allen-Bradley," he replied. "But it will be a federal one, given the domain of the products and services we're talking about."

"Then it'll have to be. What they're doing is wrong, and I'll be damned if I'm gonna just sit around and let it happen."

"Alright, then, PSI will file an antitrust lawsuit against Allen-Bradley," he stated. "Have all the details sent to me. I'll draft a copy and meet you on Monday of next week to finalize."

"You'll have everything this afternoon," I told him.

To me, the choice was clear: Roll up my sleeves and fight for what was mine, or lie down like a dog and take it. The answer was even more obvious. You don't get into business if you're not willing to do battle.

One of PSI's key advantages when we added electronic repairs to our arsenal of services was our established client base—which I had earned with my own two hands in the first place. The equipment we had been servicing belonged to some of the biggest names in the aerospace, petroleum and automotive industries. It had taken

me decades to develop this network of clients through hard work, dedication and dependability. Allen-Bradley wasn't going to walk in, take one of my experienced sales reps and tap into that database without a fight—and having to deal with me first.

≈≈

I wasn't exactly sure how Doug had been lured from PSI to Allen-Bradley in the first place. Surely, a big bonus or pay incentive was part of the package—and the relationships he'd developed with PSI's customers were undoubtedly a great bargaining chip for him in the deal.

The damnedest thing was that I was the one who had always told Doug—and the rest of my workers—that no matter how large a corporation becomes, it is always important to stay in touch with your clients and customers, so he had a great working relationship with all of them.

One of the reasons I frequent the various locations of my businesses is so that I can remain hands-on and involved in the daily operations; in that way, I can respond to my clients just as well as I can to my sales representatives. In other words, I maintain the relationships that got me where I am today. Otherwise, I would simply be turning my success over to the people who work for me—and who might take advantage of that opportunity and those business connections. If I had anything to do with it—and I did—Doug wasn't going to be one of those people.

I knew if it came down to it, I could always beat him on the streets, but I didn't pour my blood and sweat into a business to have somebody steal it away from me. They might be wrong to even try, but I would be worse if I stood by and watched them do it.

In business, you either stand up for yourself or you stand aside. It's not simply a question of how successful you can become; it's a matter of what kind of person you want to be.

CHAPTER 60

Good Judgment

They say that everyone has their day in court. For business owners, it's likely to be a lot more than just one day.

There is always somebody gunning for a share of your market
and, legally or not, they'll find a way to go after it. If it's justice you're
after, you won't get it in the corporate world. You've got to settle the
issue like the best basketball players do: Quit the trash talking and
take it to the courts.

It was raining hard the day of the federal hearing regarding Allen-Bradley, but I barely noticed. I had waited six weeks for these
proceedings to begin and I was only focused on the arguments of my
case, replaying them over and over in my head.

I finally arrived at the Theodore Levin Courthouse, also known
as the Detroit Federal Building, which was a ten-story, limestone
structure overlooking downtown. Except for the ornate carvings of
eagles that sat above the entrance, the massive building looked quite
sterile and severe from the outside. The rain pouring down gave the
courthouse an ominous feel.

Accompanied by my chief operating officer, Eugene Lawrie, I
walked inside, down the marble-floored corridor to the elevators,
then went up to the fourth floor to meet my attorney, Rodger Young.

Our case was the first to be heard that morning, which was good since I wasn't sure how much longer I could wait. For weeks, I had literally been counting down to the hearing.

During that time, since Allen-Bradley had pulled their under-handed stunt, PSI had found other sources of electronic components but we'd lost some of our customers to them in the process. They had hit me where it hurt—in my wallet. Now, I was ready to strike back.

"Good morning, Bill," Rodger said, greeting me as I got off the elevator. "We can speak in this conference room."

Rodger was bright and always on top of his game. That was why I had retained him.

He led me down the hall a short distance and we went into a small, carpeted room where he explained the upcoming proceedings.

"The judge will hear both sides' briefs," he stated. "I'll present PSI's case, then they'll present theirs. Afterwards, the judge will make a ruling as to whether the issue will proceed to trial or to summary judgment."

"Make sure the judge understands exactly what these shysters did," I said.

"Don't worry… I'm ready."

"And make sure he knows exactly where I stand."

"I'm sure he will," Rodger said.

Inside the courtroom, the judge's bench sat elevated a few feet off the floor, and behind it were shelves of legal references and dockets. The appearance and atmosphere were austere.

My attorney and I took our seats at a table across from the stenographer, who was the only other person in the room at the time. A few minutes later, the Allen-Bradley team appeared. Each member of the opposing counsel was dressed in what looked like a custom-tailored suit, no doubt financed by a handsome retainer from Allen-Bradley.

Lastly, the bailiff walked into the room from the side door and waited for his cue to announce the start of the morning's proceedings.

"All rise," he commanded in a loud, deep voice. "The United States District Court of the Eastern Division of Michigan with the honorable Robert Friedman presiding. This courtroom is called to order."

As the bailiff made his announcement and we all stood, the judge walked in from the side room and sat behind his bench. He was a distinguished-looking man with thinning hair, probably in his early fifties. Without making eye contact with either party, he nodded to acknowledge our existence, studied some papers before him then immediately proceeded with customary protocol.

"In the case of Phillips Service Industries versus Allen-Bradley, who represents the plaintiff?" the judge asked in an authoritative tone.

My attorney stood and stated his name. At the judge's request, he then made opening remarks detailing my complaints, and Judge Friedman listened patiently. Rodger described my company's loss of revenue from our inability to get electronic components in a timely manner, Allen-Bradley's solicitation of one of my top salesmen to take him away from the company and provide insider information, and the loss of clients as a direct result of both. He then detailed how these actions culminated in violations of antitrust laws.

When he was done, the judge didn't ask any questions. He simply turned to the other attorneys and asked them to present their defense.

All I remember about Allen-Bradley's defense statement was that it was a bunch of bull as far as I was concerned. They cited some legal cases and precedents, but the bottom line was that they were in the wrong. They didn't refute that they had stopped selling components to PSI, nor did they deny the fact that my previous salesman worked for them now. Their defense was that the company's behavior had been legal and fair. And that just wasn't the case.

After the briefings, Judge Friedman rubbed his chin with his right hand and looked at each party while contemplating how best to proceed. Everyone else in the courtroom just sat quietly for what seemed to be an eternity. Then, finally, the judge spoke.

"We have a couple of options," he began. "One is that we proceed to trial, and each of you can present your testimony, witnesses and the like."

He paused to let that option sink in.

"Or, we could arrange a mediation date."

He explained that with mediation, both parties would return to the courthouse and work with a go-between who would try to arrive at some type of resolution, thus avoiding a trial.

"In my opinion, both sides have some legitimate arguments. My schedule is open next Friday for the entire day. I would offer to serve as mediator for both parties if everyone's in agreement."

At that point in my life I had experienced a few legal battles, but never before had I been to a federal courthouse, nor had I gone through a real mediation experience—except when I'd sat down with the servo valve technicians and their attorney in Detroit. Despite my lack of experience, though, I was pretty certain that federal judges didn't routinely offer to serve as mediators. That alone was surprising, but I was more than happy to let Judge Friedman attempt to resolve this mess expediently. The group for Allen-Bradley must have felt the same way because they also agreed, and the date for mediation was set for the following week.

Unfortunately, the weather was no better when we returned to the courthouse that Friday for mediation. Welcome to spring in Detroit.

My attorney and I waited silently in the courtroom for the mediation to start, as did the attorneys for Allen-Bradley. A few minutes later, Judge Friedman walked in and promptly began the

proceedings. He instructed each party to go into a separate room for the mediation process, during which he would serve as the go-between.

Young and I got settled into our own room and not long after, the judge entered and sat down with us.

"Alright, I've heard PSI's complaints and the defendant's rebuttal. What do you propose as a solution?" he asked.

"I expect them to compensate me for my losses," I stated plainly.

"We would propose complete compensation for the list of damages detailed in our brief," my attorney added and mentioned a figure upon which he and I had agreed.

"I see," the judge replied. "Okay. I'll present that to the other side and hear what they say."

Judge Friedman returned a few minutes later, bearing news about a counteroffer.

"The defendants propose a more modest settlement without admission of wrongdoing," he said, showing us the figure on a piece of paper. "Will you accept their offer?"

Before he could even finish the question, I blurted out defiantly, "No way!"

The judge paused, staring at me with a hint of a smile on his face. Then, he stood up and left the room to go back to the other side.

As soon as he left, my attorney leaned over to me and said, "I cannot believe you spoke to a federal judge like that!"

But I was so irritated with the whole situation, it didn't matter who I was speaking to. I wanted justice, and my guess was that the judge knew where I was coming from.

Judge Friedman went back and forth between our room and the Allen-Bradley attorneys all morning long with what seemed to be little progress. He certainly got his exercise, if nothing else.

We adjourned for lunch, then immediately resumed the same process for almost the entire afternoon. Just when I thought the mediation was going nowhere, something changed.

"Well, they didn't want to budge on their last offer. But, I explained that they had taken significant income and sales staff from PSI, and that they were going to have to offer something reasonable in return," the judge explained.

"Did they make another offer?" I asked.

"They proposed a larger cash settlement," he replied. "It's your decision, but I think that might be the best they will offer."

I know a good salesman when I see one. Judge Friedman was, in fact, one of the better salespeople I had encountered. He knew how to make both sides in the mediation feel like they were getting a bargain. The attorneys from Allen-Bradley felt that they had to offer a sum of money in order to avoid a bad trial outcome, and the judge made me feel as though their offer was to my advantage. He had allowed the normal mediation process to take its course throughout most of the day, but as the process dragged out, his sales abilities kicked in.

I took the offer and by about five o'clock that afternoon, both sides had come to an agreement. The judge called all of us back into the courtroom at that point and restated the details of the agreement in front of both parties for the stenographer to take down. He then completed the agreement and had us sign it, making it official. The case was settled.

My attorney and I casually walked down the marbled corridors, toward the exit of the courthouse. I was feeling content because my company had acquired a nice sum of money in the settlement, and I felt pretty good about getting my point across. It was a classic case of the independent business owner winning the battle against the big corporation.

But my outlook was the only thing that was bright. The weather

outside was still dreary. We both reached for our umbrellas, but as we did, a familiar voice spoke to us from behind.

"Pretty miserable day, gentlemen," Judge Friedman stated.

"It's sure pouring," I replied, turning his way.

"Where are you parked?" he asked.

"In the lot at the end of the block," I answered.

"C'mon. I'll give you a lift. I'm parked right outside."

All three of us huddled under our umbrellas then jumped into the judge's car. We chatted briefly about my company and the city of Detroit as he drove just a few hundred yards to the end of the block. Judge Friedman proved himself to be just an all-around regular guy. Rodger and I got out of the car and thanked him for the ride then we headed back to the office.

"Damn, Bill," Rodger said. "I don't know how you pulled that off."

"What do you mean?" I asked.

"First a federal judge mediates your case himself, and then you get him to give you a ride to your car! Luck was on your side in this one."

Actually, I don't think luck had anything to do with it at all. I think Judge Friedman was simply a fair-minded man, and he knew I was standing up for what I thought was right. My guess was that he held some level of respect for the determination and guts I showed in taking on the big company of Allen-Bradley.

I hadn't known if I had any chance at all of being treated fairly, but I did know that what they did was wrong. Fortunately, I had a judge who must have shared my opinion, as well as a very fine attorney. (In subsequent years, Rodger went on to become successful on a national basis and was at one time appointed to a position with the United Nations.)

Most importantly, however, I had justice on my side.

CHAPTER 61

Making Machinery and History—The Sciaky Family

Behind every successful business is a good story. Companies like mine don't just happen overnight. There's planning involved, pitfalls, evolution. There is a time when you're about to break into success and other times when you're on the brink of bankruptcy. Decisions are made, fortunes lost, countless jobs on the line. Businesses mirror a changing world and sometimes have the scars to prove it.

Starting my own business was an enterprise and an adventure. And at one point, it became intertwined with another family's story—one that bordered on epic.

By 1994, Phillips Service Industries had been through many changes—its name, for starters.

PSI was involved in the aerospace industry, the automotive industry, the mining industry and the petroleum industry. Then, by the time I had enough experience in all of these areas, the manufacturing of various machines, rather than their repair, became a stronger focus of the business. I was keeping up with the times and keeping ahead of the changes, like other successful businesses before me.

One person who always keeps ahead of the times and industry changes is Warren Buffett. I have always admired him. Among his philanthropic endeavors and other accomplishments, he is revered

for his ability to identify solid corporations and heavily invest in them. Coca-Cola, Dow Chemical and General Electric are just a few. His philosophy is to purchase companies with great value and let them continue to operate as they have been.

In 1994, I decided to begin making some investments in corporations myself, but my philosophy was a little different from Buffett's. My strategy was to identify corporations within my area of expertise that had good foundations yet were struggling due to poor management. Since I had gained success in both repairs and manufacturing, I decided to investigate potential acquisitions that I could improve. In other words, I sought to find failing companies that I could turn into successes.

This is where the story of the Sciaky family comes into play. My relationship with the Sciakys represents the evolution of my success as an entrepreneur. Without understanding the details of their story, the ability to appreciate their family business and my acquisition of the company would be limited at best—not to mention that their story alone is fascinating, anyway.

It began back when the United States became involved in World War II, when the First Ranger Battalion was created. This was an elite group of Army warriors modeled after the British commandos. Though only men who volunteered for the battalion could be considered, very few made the grade to become an Army ranger. Out of fifteen million men enlisted in the armed services during WWII, only 3,000 were rangers.

Six battalions of 500 men each made up this superior fighting force, and with their specialized training they could travel hundreds of miles behind enemy lines under the cover of darkness. Their training included endurance speed marches, mountain climbing and amphibious attacks. These men were the ultimate soldiers and almost unstoppable.

By 1941, Paris was occupied by the Nazis. General Petain of France had surrendered to Hitler's regime in exchange for the establishment

of a mock French government in unoccupied Southern France. This created a big problem for the United States military. Some of the specialized machinery and experts needed to manufacture U.S. planes were located in a suburb of Paris called Vitry-sur-Seine. Somehow, the U.S. needed to get these experts out of France and into the United States.

The manufacturing machines in question were specialized, precision-welding equipment that used electron beams in a vacuum. They were designed by the Sciaky family—a mother, a father and four sons, all of whom were engineers. They had developed their electron beam welding machines in the late 1930s and, at the prompting of the rest of the family, the youngest son had traveled to the United States in 1939 to sell their welding equipment. His name was Mario, and he worked hard at creating a market for their inventions.

Knowing of the progressive war effort rising against Germany, the time to approach the U.S. had been ideal. After the attack on Pearl Harbor, Mario had an attentive audience, and the American military began using the Sciakys' technology to gain a competitive advantage over their opposition.

Mario established the Sciaky Brothers company in Chicago and began manufacturing products for many corporations within the aerospace industry, including McDonnell-Douglas, Boeing and others. In addition, their company provided many parts and products for the Pullman Corporation, which handled government contracts—and which also encouraged the U.S. State Department to take action in rescuing the Sciaky family from occupied France.

After the Germans invaded France, the Sciaky family, except Mario, was trapped within the hostile confines of Paris. There was no chance of escaping on their own, yet the U.S. was in great need of their technological expertise by that time. The decision was made to use the Army rangers in order to get this family of engineers to safety.

From Chicago, Mario made contact with his family in Vitry and

informed them of the potential plan of the U.S. military. And then, everyone simply stayed put and waited.

The elite group of Army rangers made its way from Southern France to the suburb of Vitry, well behind the German front lines. Under cover of night, they landed on the southern shores, where they traveled to the Sciakys' home in the northeast. Their mission was designed for a quick exit because time would be severely limited. Not only was there a significant chance of being caught, but fourteen family members were being rescued—making the mission and escape cumbersome.

Once the Sciaky family was successfully rescued, they were spirited to Southern France, then boarded on a boat to Portugal. Eventually, they traveled by ship to New York. Last, they rode by train to Chicago, where they were reunited with Mario.

Over land and sea, by automobile, boat and train, the Sciakys were safely brought to the United States, where their specialized talents were much needed. Subsequently, they formed Sciaky Brothers, Inc. and enabled the U.S. aerospace industry to maintain its technological advantage over the rest of the world. The family was granted U.S. citizenship by the State Department shortly after their arrival in our grateful nation.

After the end of World War II, the Sciakys' business changed hands a few times over the years. Most of the family stayed in the Chicago area, with the exception of Mario, who decided to go back to France a few years later to rebuild the family business there. He established Sciaky Brothers in France while the other three brothers ran the U.S.-based company. Eventually, the Sciaky family sold the American company to a large corporation named Allegheny International.

After a series of executives were caught embezzling, Allegheny went bankrupt and its holdings, including the Sciaky business, were

purchased by Ferranti International, a British company that later suffered similar difficulties. (I suspect that some of the same people worked for both companies and helped bring about both their downfalls.) Ferranti later filed for bankruptcy and had to sell off its U.S.-based assets. So, in 1994, the Sciaky Brothers company was up for sale once again.

Through several owners, the company had never returned to its glory days and had suffered repeatedly from poor corporate leadership and management.

That was before I bought it and tried to turn this epic tale around.

⁓

Sciaky Brothers was my first corporate acquisition and one of which I am particularly proud. Today, the Sciaky plant, near Midway Airport in Chicago, is a subsidiary of PSI and continues to handle an array of precision-welding needs. The plant itself is 140,000 square feet—about a four-acre building originally sitting on fifteen acres of mostly parking lots (a lot of the land was unnecessary, so I later sold it to a warehouse at a pretty nice profit). The plant focuses on the design, research, manufacturing, testing and even computer-program development for all sorts of welding equipment.

I had to restructure the entire company so that it was once again profitable—and that in itself was no small undertaking. Dealing with employee unions, management and policies took some time, but I made sure to maintain the core values of the Sciaky family's business, not to mention their expertise.

Saving a business with such a rich history gave me a feeling of pride and accomplishment, much more than monetary profits alone could. And, I found out later that the Sciakys shared my sense of pride in their family business and long-held values.

Amidst wars, hostile takeovers, corporate corruption and an

increasingly unstable marketplace, it's nice to know that while businesses must keep up with the changes in the world, some things never change.

CHAPTER 62

Meeting Mario

Though I am quick to make a decision and not waver, I research most things very thoroughly.

Sciaky was my first corporate acquisition, and I made sure I knew as much as I could about the company. I naturally had financial analyses and other market studies performed, but I wanted to get to the bones of the business.

In the process, I learned that Mario Sciaky shared an interest in getting to know the heart, soul and intentions of the new owner of his family's company. This provided a great incentive for the two of us to meet.

Mario was no longer associated with the U.S.-based Sciaky Brothers, but he had heard about me from the company controller, who had worked there for years. Following the acquisition, Mario was hopeful that after so many years of poor management, I would have the ability to restore the company's reputation and good name. I had the same hopes.

———

Mario was an older man, married with two children. He resided near Paris for many years and still operated Sciaky Brothers, Inc. in France. Even though he no longer had any financial interests in

the U.S. company, he still cared about its future. For many entrepreneurs, any business or company they once created represents a piece of their heritage and a part of their being. It's hard to simply let them go sometimes—especially those with a story, like Sciaky Brothers.

So, one afternoon about three weeks after the acquisition, Mario called me and introduced himself. We talked for a little while, and I told him about myself and PSI. We also discussed electron-beam welding and the Sciaky history, which I knew a great deal about by then.

By the end of our conversation he must have felt his family's business was in good hands because he wanted to pay me a visit in Detroit and meet the new owner of the Sciaky company face to face. I realized then that he was more like me than I had previously thought. I liked a man who conducted business directly and not behind a bunch of corporate attorneys and accountants. Such people were increasingly hard to come by.

Three days later, Mario came to visit—like me, he didn't waste any time. He had a strong, French accent but spoke fluent English without any difficulty. Neatly dressed, he presented himself professionally but without any pretense or pompousness. He was a humble man and despite a somewhat quiet demeanor, he was, without question, well educated and very bright.

Mario toured the facilities, observed how PSI conducted its operations, met many of my employees and, later that evening, went out for dinner with Betty and me.

"Bill, I've checked out you and your company," he stated very matter-of-factly. "I am very pleased that you have bought Sciaky. My hope is that you will restore the family name in the marketplace."

"That's my intent," I replied.

"If you do, I will be very grateful."

Mario had meticulously examined and observed everything all day long, since his visit had begun. I knew that, like any businessman

who had put part of himself into his business, he wanted to be sure that he approved of the new owner and the company's direction. Apparently, I had qualified.

Man to man, ex-owner to new owner, Mario was giving me an affirmative nod and his vote of confidence. He was happily passing me the baton. From that moment onward, we shared a mutual level of respect and friendship.

A couple of years later, Betty and I arranged a vacation, including a tour of France. I had been at the helm of Sciaky, Inc. for a while, and the company was showing great success. Throughout, I had kept in touch with Mario, mostly through letters, emails and periodic phone conversations, to keep him apprised. Knowing of our upcoming trip, I gave him a call to see if Betty and I could stop in for a visit.

"You'll be in Paris?" he exclaimed. "You must come to my home. I insist! Will you be bringing your lovely wife?"

"Yes, Betty and I both are coming."

"Wonderful! I will look forward to entertaining you."

Betty and I made arrangements to have dinner at Mario's home in Paris, not far from Napoleon Bonaparte's tomb at Les Invalides.

Weeks later, our car arrived at the impressive Parisian mansion surrounded by immaculate, green landscaping. It was beautiful. We made our way to the large, wooden front doors and announced our arrival with a rap of one of the polished-brass knockers.

"Bill, Betty! *Bonjour!*" our host said upon opening the door.

Not only had Mario made arrangements for dinner, but he had also requested that his children and all his grandchildren drive down from England to meet Betty and me. He was a perfect host, and his home was as striking on the inside as it was on the outside. There were elaborately constructed entryways and moldings throughout,

and impressive pieces of art and sculpture in each room. Betty and I were treated not just as guests but like royalty.

I was excited to be able to meet Mario's entire family, since I had never had the opportunity to make their acquaintance before. Though we didn't spend a great deal of time talking about the Sciaky corporation, it was obvious that Mario and his brothers were pleased with how well everything was going. He was happy to have found someone who shared his vision of the company, and he provided me with one of the most moving experiences of my entire life.

"I would like to make a toast," Mario announced as we all sat down for dinner. "I would like to toast Bill Phillips—a man with a passion for quality, value and service that is characteristic of the Sciaky name, and a man to whom our family owes a great degree of thanks. Thank you for restoring integrity to our family's company and making it possible for its legacy to carry forward into the future. We are proud to have you at the helm of the business that our family first began years ago."

I had never been singled out in a toast prior to that very moment and, in fact, I never have since. Mario stood with glass in hand and looked me directly in the eye as he made his toast. It was a very touching gesture, and I appreciated being recognized simply for who I was. Although we met through business, I will always appreciate Mario for providing that sense of personal satisfaction.

After dinner, he gave me a tour of the rest of his home, and I came across a photograph hanging on one of his walls.

"Mario, what's this picture here?" I asked.

"Oh, that's a picture of my villa near Omaha Beach."

"That's where the Allied troops landed on D-Day," I commented.

"Yes, that's right. You should come and spend some time there when you visit again."

"It looks more like a castle than a villa, Mario. Maybe I could just stay in that smaller, stone house next to it."

"Bill," Mario whispered quietly. "That's where the gardener lives."

"Oh," I replied, laughing to myself. I was glad to see that the Sciakys' epic journey had ended as such a success story.

Although I never got the chance to return to see Mario's villa at Omaha Beach, I always cherished his professional and personal friendship. He welcomed me into his family's business and he welcomed me into his family. For Mario, both were essentially the same thing.

I must admit, I feel the same way about my company as he does. When you pour so much energy and passion into something you create, you want to preserve it and see it thrive. You hope the same principles and values that were its foundation continue even after you no longer guide all the decisions. I fully understand that feeling—and that's why I'm so glad that some of my children have come to work at PSI.

A successful business is quite an achievement. But a successful *family* business is something else: a legacy.

CHAPTER 63

A United Front

I always give credit where credit is due—and my chief operating officer, Gene Lawrie, deserved a lot of credit for helping me land that Sciaky acquisition.

Gene came to PSI from Bray-con International and was employed by Sciaky prior to that. He was, in fact, my link to Sciaky since he was the one the family called about finding someone to buy the business. So I guess he deserved some credit for that, too.

Gene was particularly gifted when it came to acquisitions. He was a good negotiator—partly because he knew where all the skeletons were hidden in the closet. But he also helped build up PSI repair services. We collaborated and I taught him that business from the ground up. Gene and I were a good team. Whatever I didn't think of, he did.

After I made the deal to buy Sciaky, there was one matter of business left unsettled: Who was going to manage it? In the cab ride back to the airport, Gene turned to me and asked, "Who the hell is gonna run this?" I admit I hadn't thought it out quite that far—my first priority was purchasing the damn thing! After all, it was my first acquisition. I immediately thought of Dennis Frank, who at that time was managing one of my other companies.

While the whole Sciaky transaction went rather smoothly, there were a few rough patches—as there are in any business deal. Most of all, there was a union to get around—and Gene helped me figure out a way. We came up with the idea to set up a "separate" company made up of machinists who would "supply labor" to Sciaky and who were, of course, non-union.

When other workers saw how well they were being treated and how good the working conditions were, they wanted to join, too—with or without a union.

The whole idea was perfect—except for one thing. Sciaky had to pay about eighty dollars an hour to its own labor company in fees. Sure, it got us out of union restrictions, but that amount of money was so enormous it could have bled us dry. So, before long, I decided to dissolve the whole "separate" operation.

I told Gene, "Look, I don't care what you have to do, but this is ridiculous. It stops today."

He knew I wasn't kidding so he acted upon it immediately. Normally, when Gene left PSI, he would turn right to go home. After our conversation, I saw him get in his car and turn left toward the airport. He didn't even have an overnight bag or change of clothes!

Regardless, Gene went straight to the airport, got on a flight to Chicago and did exactly what I'd said. He dissolved the "labor company" that next morning and all the workers happily joined Sciaky without a word about a union. By then, they knew that as long as they did their jobs, PSI would look out for their best interests.

Now, that's what I call "unity."

CHAPTER 64

Mountain Secure Systems

Entrepreneurs are a lot like explorers—always looking to break new ground. In exploration, that might mean scaling mountains. In business, it usually means expanding your marketplace. If done successfully, both will take you to new peaks.

The Ferranti Corporation, from which PSI acquired Sciaky, Inc., was undergoing bankruptcy and was required to sell its seven remaining U.S. corporations as part of its liquidation. The whole transaction with Sciaky went pretty smoothly and without too any problems, so, two years later, in 1996, I decided to purchase Mountain Optech from them as well and later changed its name to Mountain Secure Systems.

MSS was a bit different from PSI's other subsidiaries because it dealt with extremely high-tech products. The employees were mostly highly trained and skilled technicians and expert scientists, so we kept almost all of the technical staff along with the purchase. Many of the usual frustrations of dealing with employees during acquisitions weren't present with Mountain Secure Systems. There were no unions and no need for downsizing.

The company didn't have many product lines, but the ones it had

were very specialized. Its premier product line consisted of data-storage devices for harsh or extreme environments. For example, a fighter jet requires a customized data-storage device that can withstand altitude, changes in pressure, turbulence and extreme temperatures. A standard device would operate poorly under such conditions if at all. The company specialized in customizing these devices for such environments and others as needed.

With the purchase of MSS, two significant changes took place. First, while the technical staff was excellent, the management executives were not. In due course, we replaced most of them with new personnel. Secondly, we needed to greatly increase the number of products provided by the company in order to be successful.

I had my work cut out for me.

Though the first year of PSI's operation at Mountain Secure Systems was profitable, the company became somewhat stagnant the following year. Many preexisting programs and projects were coming to a close, and new ones were slow in developing.

"How's our bottom line looking, Lonna?" I asked our comptroller during one of our corporate meetings.

"Not great," she replied. "We're solid for this year but unless we get moving, next year is a concern."

So, that next year, we began developing entirely new product lines and sent our sales force out to make contacts aggressively. We created new systems for rugged terrains and environments, began designing updated in-flight entertainment systems and manufactured hardened data-storage devices that could tolerate extreme altitudes, vibrations and temperatures—all of which we continue to do today. Before long, MSS had multiple contracts with various aerospace manufacturers as well as multiple government contracts involving all branches of the armed forces. Our legacy projects have included

WORM ("write once, read many") drives that withstood exposure to space on the Mir space station. One of the WORM drives has since been placed in the Smithsonian National Air and Space Museum.

Such innovations just go to show that you have to keep changing and staying up to date in order to remain competitive. The business world, after all, is one of the toughest terrains there is.

———

Though several strategies allowed Mountain Secure Systems to become a leader within the area of high-tech data storage products, the greatest source of new business certainly came from sending sales representatives into the field. That's the one thing that doesn't change.

I'm a salesman at heart and still believe that the best way to market is face to face. Although PSI has invested in many forms of advertising, nothing ever worked as well as having a salesperson in the marketplace. It's still the best way to keep your finger on the pulse of your business' market.

Our salespeople would meet with potential customers directly, targeting the people in purchasing. But, they also met with the engineering departments within the companies they visited. In addition to demonstrating how our products worked to the engineering staff, our sales force would often get ideas for new products in this manner or create opportunities for new collaborative design projects. Without making contacts with engineers, MSS would have missed out on many lucrative opportunities. As an engineer myself, I knew enough to send my sales team to the source.

———

Mountain Secure Systems was originally in Boulder, Colorado, and its name reflected the adjacent Boulder Mountains to the west and

south. The products it designed also carried the names of famous mountains all over the world: Alp, Himalayan, Crestone, Olympus, Wasatch and others. Though Mountain Secure Systems has since relocated to Longmont, Colorado, away from the mountains, we have continued naming our products in that way because it symbolizes the need to continue climbing higher in order to keep up with an ever-changing market. Especially in the high-tech industry, change is imperative. It's the only way to reach the top of the mountain.

Today, Mountain Secure Systems operates in a 20,000-square-foot facility and employs about thirty highly trained workers. Recent operations have generated about $10 million in revenues annually. Though it is one of the smallest of PSI's subsidiaries, its position within its market is among the highest.

It may not have looked like much in the beginning, but Mountain Secure Systems has been a success. It fit well in my paradigm of solid companies that needed better management and, before long, it became an integral part of PSI's portfolio.

My acquisition of MSS only reinforced the idea that to stay on top, you have to evolve as your market does. It's a prime example of how constant entrepreneurial creativity and a willingness to adapt can be the crucial difference between success and failure.

In mountain climbing and market shares, the rule is the same: To reach new heights, you have to be willing to acclimate to some pretty tough terrain.

CHAPTER 65

Expanding on a Foundation

So many things in life are simply a series of steps from one point to another: from elementary school to high school, then on to college or the workforce. Foundations are built and then added upon.

That type of expansion has been my experience with PSI. Originally, the company designed hydraulic systems, then attained great success in the service industry. From there, we went on to manufacturing and other, more specialized skills. Because we had a solid foundation, we were able to build upon it. And, along with expanding our abilities, we also expanded the business.

By the early 1980s, PSI was involved in the precision manufacturing and repair of many components of industrial machines. But, there was one component in particular that we hadn't expanded to include in our repertoire. You know how they say always to keep an eye on the ball? Well, I had my eye on ball screws.

A ball screw is a machine part that allows a flat surface to move back and forth in a highly precise manner. Think of it as a large screw with threads, but the nut on the screw contains ball bearings that move through channels, directing them into the threads of the screw. As the nut moves up and down the screw, the ball bearings eliminate friction and allow for precise movements within one-thousandth of

an inch or better. Because of that, ball screws are used for all sorts of precision equipment in the aerospace and automotive industries.

I had long been aware that PSI had the ability to get involved in the repair and manufacturing of ball screws. We had the right facilities, the right engineering knowledge and the right support services within the industry. The only thing we didn't have was an established market.

In the world of ball screws (yes, such a place exists), only two major players were reputable at that time: Saginaw Steering Gear Division of General Motors and Beaver Precision. Beaver was a privately owned company located on the east side of Detroit, originally formed in 1959. I had known about the corporation for many years, but despite my attempts to make contact with its owner about a possible acquisition, I had so far been unsuccessful.

Then, in 1981, another player entered the arena—a local company began repairing ball screws with great success. I tried repeatedly to make contact with that company's owner as well, but he wouldn't speak with me, either. It seemed as though this ball screw repair company was generating significant revenues, which made me want to expand into that area even more. But, I needed another strategy.

After several unsuccessful attempts to gain entry into this field, I made the decision to get into the ball screw repair business from scratch. I'm not much for waiting around once I see an opportunity, so I began placing feelers out for anyone in the industry who might have had expertise in manufacturing and/or repairing ball screws. Because Beaver Precision was having its own internal troubles at the time, it didn't take long for me to get a response.

Gordon Bright was a man about my age who was a bit on the quiet side. He had worked for Beaver for many years and was very knowledgeable about ball screw manufacturing. As a blue-collar worker, he was more of a machinist than an engineer, but he had built on his own foundation of skills and expertise over the years the

same way I had. Essentially, he knew everything about ball screws, and so I was glad when he returned my phone call.

"Gordon," I explained to him, "I'm looking for someone to get onboard and get PSI into the ball screw repair business."

"I can help you with that," he replied. "But, I feel a little uneasy about it."

"Why's that?" I asked.

"Well, it's just that I've been with my company a long time."

Gordon was an honest worker who had dedicated a good portion of his life to one company. And, even though that company was now floundering at the expense of its employees, he still felt disloyal for going to a potential competitor. I liked that about him and from the moment we first spoke, I knew we would get along well.

Ultimately, Gordon made the decision to come to PSI and help me recruit a few other knowledgeable machinists. With these individuals and some newly hired engineers on my team, I was effectively off the bench and in the ball game—the ball screw repair business, that is.

It was another step, another risk and another chance for growth.

From the time I'd entered the Air Force and learned about hydraulics all the way to today, my life has been a series of steps, building from one foundation to another. Every opportunity I took has led me to another.

With each step along the way, my confidence and abilities have grown—and because of that, becoming a major player in the ball screw industry was easier than tackling the servo valve or mining industries. I was extremely used to taking risks by then and wasn't in the business of letting perceived obstacles stop me.

Without question, I have sometimes worried that I might not

succeed in different ventures. But, the fear of missing an opportunity for success always outweighed any fear of failure. Whether I landed on my feet or my face, taking the step from the secure and known into the untried and unknown has made PSI what it is today. More importantly, it has made me the person I am.

CHAPTER 66

Trapping a Beaver

In the animal world, beavers are known for their industrious and efficient work, and for putting up solid structures in a short amount of time.

The same cannot be said about the business world.

———

Within weeks of beginning our ball screw repair services, PSI already received several orders from our existing clients. However, the repairs were often too costly compared to the manufacturing of a brand-new ball screw. It didn't take long to realize that we needed to be in the manufacturing end of things as well. So, we went from doing the repairs internally to collaborating with a few small, private companies that manufactured ball screws.

Once again, the need either to acquire or develop a manufacturing arm for this industry was obvious. The steps required in developing our ball screw repair services had progressively led me to the same conclusion as before—and I knew that the opportunity was still there.

Like many companies that struggle at some point in time, Beaver Precision had been through the ringer. Though it was a solid company initially, the original owner had sold it to another major corporation years earlier—and that corporation had either managed

it badly or found that Beaver Precision was a poor fit for its portfolio of companies.

Beaver Precision had then been sold to another major corporation, where the same thing had happened all over again. It went through three such sales before finally being sold to a private owner.

That most recent owner was a young man who thought he would try his hand at managing a manufacturing company, but his attempt had proven to be unsuccessful. Before long, Beaver was no longer generating enough revenues to cover its overhead. So, with few options available, he chose to factor his invoices, like I had done when I was first starting out with PSI. The difference was that while PSI's reputation was improving at that point, the status of Beaver Precision was in decline. Eventually, the owner defaulted on his factor agreement and the factor took over ownership of the company.

If you think a factor who is in the business of loaning money knows anything about running a manufacturing corporation, you might want to steer clear of placing any bets. Three major corporations hadn't succeeded, and a young entrepreneur had failed. The chances for Beaver Precision to be successful with a factor at its helm were far from good. Once again, I realized that the company's decline was practically inevitable.

A few months after the factor had taken over, someone in the industry told me that he had hired a new manager to help straighten out Beaver's failing business. As the owner, he hoped to have some profitable successes and make something out of the company he had inherited.

Seeing a chance for some success of my own, I met with the new manager, but within a few minutes of our introduction, it was clear to me that the guy was a joke. He had no idea what he was doing. Again, I reached out to make an offer, but no one would return my calls or letters. The place was so disorganized, I wouldn't have been surprised if the messages I left had never even been received—or if the owner or manager couldn't find the phone!

After those repeated efforts, I switched to another plan of action: contacting the corporate attorney who had been affiliated with Beaver Precision. I knew the company was doing poorly, but I also realized what great potential it had. I knew the time was right—I just needed to find the right person to help me pursue the acquisition.

"Mr. Richards, this is Bill Phillips with Phillips Service Industries," I stated to the corporate lawyer on the phone. "I understand you represent Beaver Precision."

"I have in the past," he responded.

"Well, I would like to hire you to contact the owner on my behalf," I explained. "I want to make him an offer. You know him and you know the company. Get me some terms of purchase."

"Alright," Richards replied. "Let me see what I can do and I'll be in touch."

A few weeks later, a conversation took place between the attorney, the factor and me. Finally, I had made contact!

The next step was to see the facilities. I wanted to get a good feel for what was going on within the company and why it had been so difficult to manage. I arranged a visit for later that week with the operations manager at Beaver's facility.

On the morning of my visit, I got into my car and headed east on Interstate 96, and then went north onto Interstate 75 until I neared their large manufacturing plant. It was in the Troy area north of Detroit and was at least 50,000 square feet in size.

I got out of the car around ten o'clock and walked into the reception area of the building. A heavyset, balding man waited for me in the lobby.

"Bill Phillips?" he asked as I walked inside.

"Yes."

"I'm Ted Walker, the operations manger."

"Good to meet you," I replied, shaking his hand.

"Ready to take a look around?" he asked.

"I've *been* ready. Let's go."

Although huge, the plant was well kept. Large pieces of machinery were scattered among several work areas in the clean, climate-controlled space, and dozens of employees worked at various stages in the manufacturing process. It was like almost any other precision-equipment plant I had ever visited, but something didn't make sense. I knew the revenue figures for the plant, and it seemed to me that there was an excess of workers for that level of revenue. Something was off—way off.

"How many employees work here?" I asked the manager.

"We have one hundred and twenty-five workers," he replied.

I quickly did the math in my head. Roughly, a manufacturing facility involved in precision products should generate between $200,000 and $300,000 in revenues per employee. Beaver Precision wasn't even doing half of that figure, given the number of employees the manager had quoted.

"You have too many people for your production," I commented.

"I know," he replied.

"You know? Then why do you have them?"

"Because we're required by the union to have a minimum of one hundred and twenty-five employees at all times," he explained, repeating the magic number. No wonder he knew that exact figure so well.

It became clear to me right then that neither the factor nor the prior owners were running Beaver—the union was. And, unfortunately, it wasn't running it to gain profits. It was only running it into the ground.

The right-to-work laws required a fixed number of employees to be present even though operations didn't justify it. As a result, monthly expenses exceeded income on a consistent basis. I figured the prior owner had defaulted on his agreement to the factor because he was in a no-win situation. The union was bleeding his business dry.

Another thing was bothering me. If several corporations and the most-recent owner had failed to operate Beaver Precision well, how had the factor gotten by for any amount of time when such a deficit between income and output existed?

I got my answer later. As it turned out, the factor had dipped into the employees' pension funds in order to try to make ends meet. He had taken out a huge sum of money and invested it elsewhere, hoping to recoup some of his and the company's losses. You can imagine how well that went over with the workers' union once they found out about it.

To me, it was ironic justice, however, that the underlying cause of the problem lost the most money in the end. The unions had destroyed the company's financial balance sheet from the start, so it was somewhat fitting that the union employees' pension funds were taken by the current owner to partially cover the losses. I'm sure the union didn't see it that way, though.

After my meeting with the operations manager, I went back to my office at PSI and went over all the information and figures with my executives. Purchasing the company then was out of the question. There was no way I would take on its liabilities or the union responsibilities that Beaver Precision had acquired over the years.

Instead, I made the decision to acquire only the assets of the company. In other words, I wasn't willing to take the employees, the outstanding invoices, the contracts or any union agreements as part of the deal. PSI would only purchase machinery, receivables, hard assets and the government side of the business. This was the best way to escape the demands of the union and give Beaver Precision a fresh start. It would also turn out to be one of the smartest decisions I've ever made.

Needless to say, the union didn't like that proposal one bit. First of all, they didn't want the factor to sell the assets because they needed the original company to survive. That was their only hope for getting their pension funds back. Secondly, they knew that their position of control would be jeopardized if PSI purchased the assets away from Beaver Precision. But, in the end, there was nothing they could do about it.

The factor accepted my offer and, within a month of my purchasing the assets, all operations were moved from the old plant in Troy to PSI's facilities on the west side of Detroit. With a new name—and me as the owner—this struggling company finally had the opportunity for a fresh start. With the assets of Beaver Precision acquired, I renamed and restarted Beaver Aerospace and Defense, Inc., in 1997; I had begun my pursuit of the company in 1995.

Of all the companies I acquired, it took me the longest to finalize the deal with Beaver Precision. It seemed like some roadblock appeared every time I tried to make a move. But, I damn well didn't quit. I knew it was a great opportunity from the beginning and I wasn't willing to walk away. Eventually, I found a way to get my foot in the door and made the most of it from there.

Today, Beaver Aerospace is the largest subsidiary of PSI with more than $60 million in annual revenues, and it has several major government contracts. I guess that just goes to show what a great deal of persistence can do for you.

CHAPTER 67

A Not-So-Civil Union

Almost everything in Detroit is tough—from the streets to the cars to, most of all, the residents.

Toughness doesn't stem from a lack of fear but instead from the ability to face fear and take action. Without fear, life would be boring. It's what makes your heart pound, your breathing fast and your attention focused. It's also what makes you human.

But, not letting fear overcome you is what makes you brave.

The sky was already dark outside my office in Livonia, Michigan, as I walked to my car. It was seven o'clock and the end of January, and the sun had set hours earlier. The air was dry and frigid, and my feet crunched the ice and still-remaining snow as I walked through the corporate parking lot. The street lamps were already shining an orange hue onto my Cadillac, which was one of the few vehicles left in the lot.

As I turned to open my door, I saw it. Sandwiched between the wheel drum and the asphalt, my left front tire was completely flat. But, it wasn't a nail or a tiny puncture that had caused it. Along the whitewall, three neat gashes had been cut with surgical precision. My tire had been purposely slashed.

Things were starting to get a little hairy. And, though I caught myself glancing over my shoulder, I knew exactly what had happened and who had done it. The union was starting to raise the stakes to another level. Its members didn't like the fact that I had purchased only the assets of Beaver Precision, and they were letting me know by sending me this message.

I had a message to send them, too: I wasn't going to be intimidated.

The following day, I hired several guards to provide surveillance of the PSI facility. I even had one go to my home, which was fifteen miles from the plant. I knew the union could be ruthless, and I didn't want my family involved in any way. Although I hadn't done anything wrong, I wasn't going to back down. In my entire life, I had never turned my back on a fight.

Since the asset purchase, the union leaders had been extremely disgruntled. I had made it clear that there absolutely would be no union at PSI or at Beaver Aerospace and Defense. I wasn't about to let the same thing happen to my company that had happened with the previous owners. In order to accomplish that, none of the employees from Beaver Precision had been attained directly in the asset purchase. Instead, I was in the middle of conducting interviews in order to get exactly the right people and the all-new workforce we needed.

But how was I going to be sure that I was hiring effective employees and not ones simply interested in reestablishing a union? I handled this issue like I did everything else in my life—hands on. After handpicking my management staff from the existing management, I conducted interviews of all the employees from Beaver Precision who showed an interest in continuing to work there. The

managers identified those employees who had strong work ethics, were honest and so on.

As a result, I ended up hiring about half the employees who had previously worked in Troy. Those selected had reputations for being good workers—and I would see to it that they remained that way. As far as unionization was concerned, there was no guarantee that they wouldn't pursue it. If they believed in a union, then regardless of whether or not they were good workers, they would support union involvement in the company.

As the employee-selection process was taking place, the union was aggressively going after PSI, filing a federal lawsuit against the company for not including the union in our current operations. The litigation cost me many thousands of dollars but the judge ruled in my favor, leaving the union out in the cold. That was when its members started slashing tires and vandalizing our property as scare tactics. All their other avenues had closed. I, however, still had a few strategies up my sleeve.

Despite what many believe, I have found that people don't form lasting relationships with organizations or companies. Instead, they form relationships with people. When corporate loyalty is present, most of the time it's because people feel loyal to the managers and owners of that organization. As loyal as my ball screw guy, Gordon Bright, had been to Beaver Precision, he'd chosen to come to work for PSI because there was no longer anyone left at his company toward whom he felt an allegiance.

Getting to know my employees has always been an important part of my business strategy. And, it was one strategy that helped me keep the unions away from my company.

One evening, after finishing my administrative work, I walked around the plant and talked with several employees. During a conversation with one machinist, I looked over and saw another man lifting an incredibly heavy piece of equipment onto a work table.

"Hey," I exclaimed, "you shouldn't be lifting that. It's too heavy. Why aren't you using a lift?"

"The hoist is being used for another piece of machinery," he replied.

The guy was about my age. I told him, "That's too heavy. You'll hurt yourself."

Then, I bent down and, with great effort, lifted the piece of equipment off the ground and placed it on the table.

"There's no question," I said. "That's too much to be lifting." Then, I turned to one of the managers and said, "Get another hoist in here by the end of the week."

I wasn't trying to show off, but by lifting that piece of equipment, I showed my workers that I didn't expect them to do anything for my company that I wouldn't do myself. That, along with ordering the second hoist for their safety, won me great loyalty among the workers that evening.

By getting to know my employees a little and letting them get to know me, a personal relationship was built—and that is where job loyalty begins.

I also took the time to explain to my employees exactly how the union had brought about the demise of their prior company and that it was a threat to their job security. Because of that, the union never gained any type of stronghold within PSI or any of its subsidiaries.

After the lawsuit was over and the union's scare tactics petered out, it eventually stopped pursuing PSI for a couple of years. Two years later, though, it returned, trying to get enough support to hold an employee vote. This failed as well. By that time, the employees were happy with the working conditions and the progress of Beaver Aerospace and Defense. The proof was there, and the union's message fell on deaf ears.

As I've said, Detroit was no easy place to live. It wasn't easy to grow up there, it wasn't easy to build a business there and it wasn't easy to get ahead. But, I knew I couldn't let fear stand in my way if I

wanted to succeed. The more you summon the strength and courage to stand up for yourself, the more confidence you gain in yourself and your actions. It's like forging steel in a fire: The experience isn't easy or fun, but in the long run, it builds strength and character—and that's what makes people want to work for you and with you.

My employees trusted me to look out for their best interests and not take advantage of them. Because of that, they didn't feel the need to unionize. As for me, I just didn't believe in the union's practices.

But, no one could accuse me of not having paid my dues.

PART VII

Full Circle

CHAPTER 68

The Business of Defense

Every once in awhile, if you're fortunate, the work you do can make a difference. Not just in your life, your family or your community—but in the world.

———

Despite my acquiring the assets of Beaver in 1997 and developing the ability to manufacture ball screws on a large scale, the company struggled to keep its head above water for some time. But, the climate changed for us after 9/11—as it did for everyone else.

As part of a massive effort to review security, the United States Air Force and other branches of the military took a close look at their entire inventory, including everything from weaponry and military bases to missile installations. The Air Force was particularly interested in the safety of the nation's nuclear missile sites.

Scattered across various locations in the U.S., nuclear missiles were housed within deep silos in the ground, which had been there for about forty years. They were part of the Air Force Intercontinental Ballistic Missile (ICBM) Program. If needed, these silos would open and allow nuclear warheads to be launched with near-pinpoint accuracy in an 8,000-mile range. But, in the security analyses of these sites, there was one major problem: The doors that covered the silos

took approximately twelve minutes to open and another twelve minutes to close. If a technician had to go into a silo to service a missile apparatus, a terrorist could also make his way in because the time it took for the door to close was just too long.

That was where Beaver Aerospace and Defense came in.

Lieutenant General William Lord was director of communications and information at the time, and upon learning about the problem with the silo maintenace doors he insisted on the development of a new system that opened and closed within twelve *seconds* rather than twelve minutes.

The lieutenant general's command was a pretty tall order. The openings were sealed with a steel and concrete plug weighing 17,000 pounds, called a B-plug. This was the door that needed to be moved approximately ten feet within twelve seconds.

Not exactly mission impossible, but close.

I got the call to duty when Beaver Aerospace and Defense was contacted by Northrop Grumman. They held the overall contract with the Air Force to correct the silo B-plug problem and wanted to know if we could design and manufacture a process to meet the proposed specifications.

I was involved in the negotiations, as was my son Scott (who was a major player in the project) and the general manager of Beaver. Along with several highly trained engineers, we began to compile a proposal for developing a completely new apparatus that could move the B-plug.

The previous design was slow and cumbersome and could only operate under full power. Our eventual design utilized an electrical drive and a ball screw, an extremely complex design that allowed the ball screw to retract within itself. The telescoping feature enabled the B-plug to be moved more rapidly while simultaneously avoiding

interference with the plug's closure. The system was also designed to store enough energy within itself to open and close twice, even in the event of complete power failure. This was our country's defense we were working on; there was no room for error. We had to get it right.

Plenty of skeptics thought the project couldn't be done—but that didn't include any of us at Beaver. Somehow, we just knew we could design the system—and we were right. Although we weren't the only ones bidding on the project, we were the ones who were eventually awarded the job.

My background in the automotive industry gave me confidence in the ability to solve any problem. Since the assembly line could never stop, you had to think quick on your feet. Aerospace companies are too big and have slow processes, and the same goes for the aerospace industry in general.

Overall, the planning and development phase of the B-plug project took a total of three years. This included designing the system, creating a unit to test, testing it in the laboratory, demonstrating a prototype to the Air Force and Northrop Grumman, and, eventually, performing an actual site test. I had never seen these silos up close before, let alone been in one, so we headed out to Utah to get personally acquainted with them. That's what you'd call the "hands-on" approach.

Once we reached a certain level of development in the project, we went ahead and rolled the dice by beginning manufacturing. Our bid covered the manufacturing of 475 B-plug systems. Once they were completed, Beaver was responsible for shipping them to various regional warehouses near the silo locations. From there, military and civilian contractors installed the units.

Beaver Aerospace and Defense has handled annual revenues of about $60 million since we secured the contract with Northrop Grumman (who named us "Supplier of the Year" three times), and the "fast B-plug" system project accounts for about fifty percent of

that. The project covered an eight-year span and you can imagine how gratifying such a thing was for a company that was not nearly that profitable beforehand.

This project put Beaver back on the map thanks to our ability to design and masterfully manufacture what was thought by some to be impossible. If all the previous owners and managers knew where the company stood today, they would be amazed. And I have to admit that of all the corporations I have acquired, I am very proud of Beaver Aerospace and Defense—not only because we turned it around to make such a profit but because it got us back into the defense and service of our country.

Those silos and nuclear missile sites that my company and I—as well as my son—got into better working condition help to defend the future of the United States. What could make a father, businessman and former Air Force engineer prouder?

But, as I've mentioned, the B-plug project also relates to my own personal history in the military. During the Korean War I was stationed in Newfoundland, which served as a barrier against potential intruders coming across the United States' northern borders. After the war, most of these northern U.S. bases, including mine, were either closed or turned over to the Canadian government.

The connection became obvious to me immediately as I went to work on the B-plug project. When we at Beaver began examining the missile silos, it drove home the fact that the age of nuclear technology, which had arisen as the Korean War ended, had eliminated the need for those perimeter bases since our defense system (nuclear missiles combined with satellite technology) provided us the ability to protect ourselves without them. Those bases where I had served in our country's border defense as a young airman were gone, but there I was, involved once again in homeland security as an established entrepreneur. Not only that but my son—the next generation—was working there by my side.

Between my time in the military and my years involved in aerospace and national defense, I have spent a good part of my life serving the country I love, which truly is the land of opportunity.

Those opportunities are what finally brought me full circle...only to be back exactly where I belonged.

CHAPTER 69

Where's Barzini?

I t's strange how entrepreneurs come upon their knowledge of the business world. We don't all sit around reading how-to books. Hell, we've got businesses to run! Besides, there are plenty of other places to gain solid business wisdom—though some of them might seem unlikely.

By 1997, I had made connections with several business brokers. With the acquisition of the Beaver Precision and Sciaky corporations and their increasing success, I was constantly looking for other companies with potential to turn around. My formula for acquisitions seemed to be working well so far, so I figured, why stop?

One morning, I received a call from one of the brokers. He described a company named Evana in Evansville, Indiana, that manufactured assembly equipment for various corporations. Evana was floundering, and the broker had been contacted by the current owners about finding a buyer. From everything he explained, it sounded like a great opportunity to me.

The company had great potential because of a growing number of possible clients, and it appeared there was room for improvement in their management technique, which was probably the one thing

holding them back. Evana looked like a company that could expand PSI's holdings for a reasonable price.

At that time, my corporate financial officer was a man named Fred Crooks. He had been hired specifically to help with business acquisitions, among other things, and soon he and I both became involved in the process of acquiring Evana.

After Fred had performed some of the preliminary evaluations of the company, I decided to speak to the owners myself. One was a lady named Dee, who had previously been the company's bookkeeper, and the other was a man named Jerry, who had been the plant manager. Other than their longevity with the company, the two had no relationship to each other—and, more significantly for me, neither had much experience with directing a corporation. For the past five years, they had tried to handle the operations, but the business had progressively declined.

I phoned one of the owners to introduce myself and to explore the opportunity a bit further.

"I understand you're interested in selling your company," I stated.

"Yes, my partner and I are looking to sell," Dee admitted. "I spoke with your CFO earlier this week."

"That's what he told me. When is a good time for me to come to Indiana to look the place over and meet you?"

"Let me talk with Jerry and I'll get back to you."

That wouldn't be the last time she was unable to make an immediate decision. I was starting to get some idea of what might have been killing their company.

⁓

Fred and I, along with Gene Lawrie, flew to Evansville the following week. Situated on the Ohio River, it's a comfortable-size town of less

than 200,000 people. The Evana plant itself was like most others I had seen; the 50,000-square-foot facility was climate controlled and employed a little more than a hundred people. Workstations were situated in rows where dozens of technicians attended to their own specific tasks. Everything seemed to be in good working condition and my first inspection seemed to support my hunch that the company had great potential.

"So, how have operations been going?" I asked the owners.

"Pretty well, but contracts with the automotive industry have fluctuated over the years," Jerry replied.

"Well, I'm certainly interested in acquiring it. How about Fred and I begin conducting our due diligence and see what we can do?"

"Okay. Let Jerry and me talk and we'll call you," Dee stated.

After a couple of calls later that week, Fred finally received some of the company's information to review. Financials, production lines, overhead expenses and the like were provided in part. This, combined with my visit, was enough for me to begin the process of negotiation.

But, no matter how hard we tried, Dee and Jerry would never commit to anything, and they certainly had no clue about how to negotiate a deal. Instead of hiring someone to negotiate for them they simply struggled poorly through the process, dragging it out as long as possible. It seemed that instead of attempting to come to an agreement, they had a greater interest in avoiding a decision altogether.

"Jerry, you know I want to buy the company, right?" I asked one day on the phone, trying to cut through all the BS.

"Yeah," he replied.

"Then let's set a date to hash out the details."

"Well, let me get back to you with a good time."

I thought I'd have to cover the mouthpiece to stop myself from screaming into the phone!

This was turning into one of the most frustrating deals I had ever made. I just couldn't understand why these two people who wanted and needed to sell their company wouldn't commit to any decision or move forward with the process. Then, the revelation came one day when Fred was conducting some additional investigations at their facility.

"Bill," Fred said to me over the phone, "I can't understand it. Every time I ask for additional information, the answer is always the same—they have to get back to me."

"You know what?" I said. "I don't think they're pulling the trigger on this."

"What do you mean?" Fred asked.

"You need to find Barzini," I said.

"Barzini? Who the hell is Barzini?"

There is a tremendous amount of wisdom that can be gained from watching *The Godfather*. Whenever my executives get angry or perplexed about certain things, I tell them to go watch that movie again—and pay attention to its messages. It is one of my all-time-favorite films.

In the movie, Don Corleone holds a meeting with the heads of the five mafia families in order to stop all the killings among them. All along, Corleone thought that the Tattaglia family, the Corleones' archrival, was behind the murders. But during the meeting he figured out that Don Barzini was actually the one calling the shots from in the shadows.

When Fred described the situation at Evana to me, it finally became obvious to me that there had to be a Barzini lurking around out there. Someone else was making the decisions for Dee and Jerry. This was why they always had to get back to us. They had to check with Barzini first—but now, we were the ones who had to find him.

"Fred, have you seen anyone else around there?" I asked.

"Well, there's this one guy who comes in for a couple of hours each day," he replied.

"What does he do?" I asked.

"I don't know. He's always dressed in a suit and tie, and he goes upstairs to the office. Then, he leaves a little while later," he explained.

"That's Barzini," I stated, somehow managing not to do a Brando impersonation.

As soon as possible, Fred introduced himself to this man, who turned out to be named Charlie Walker. Charlie was the original owner of Evana; he'd founded the company in the 1960s. Five years earlier, he had sold the business to Dee and Jerry.

However, despite the new owners' mortgaging of their own homes, they had to have Charlie underwrite a bank note to acquire the corporation. In other words, he held the purse strings of the company even though he was no longer the owner. So, every time we posed a question to Dee or Jerry, they had to run it by Charlie before giving us an answer.

We had found our Barzini. I flew down the following week to meet Charlie Walker in person. We got along fine, and Charlie has been one of my dearest friends ever since. He is about ten years older than I am and is a great businessman. At our first meeting, he understood perfectly the situation the company was in.

"Charlie," I told him, "I'm willing to try to make this deal work, but everyone is going to have to take a haircut on it."

"What do you mean?" he asked.

"You, the bank, Dee and Jerry are all going to take some losses in order to make the numbers work."

He got the idea, and with a little artful negotiation we came to a deal that benefited us all—let's call it a deal they couldn't refuse. Dee and Jerry walked away with money in their pockets—probably for

the first time in a while—and so did Charlie. And, I gained another solid company to add to PSI's portfolio.

Since we acquired Evana in early 1997, the facility has not only doubled in size but has been completely modernized. We have progressively expanded the number of industries that we serve, providing automated machines that manufacture everything from sensing devices on automobile airbags to medical devices. And, while patience and persistence helped me accomplish the deal, I'm not sure I could have done it without a little wisdom gained from *The Godfather*.

CHAPTER 70

A Matter of Perspective

Sometimes you have to remind people that Miss Manners never wrote a business book.

That's because the basics are pretty simple: You treat people with respect, you don't take advantage of anyone, you stand up for yourself and you always tell the truth. Other than that, it's pretty much no holds barred. You do what you can to look out for your business and try to get ahead.

And yet, it's always been interesting to me to see what some people find offensive. We're socialized into thinking that some things are unacceptable, others are tolerable and others should be completely ignored. With all this judging of other people's behavior, priorities get a little out of whack, and I'm sure I'm guilty of it as well sometimes, though I try my hardest not to be.

We grow up being taught that some things simply shouldn't be done, regardless of the reasons behind them. Such was the case that caused the loss of one of my most tenured employees.

———

Fred and I had almost finished with all the details of the Evana acquisition when one last issue arose.

"Bill," Fred began, "what do you want to do about the life insurance policies?"

"What life insurance policies?" I asked.

"Dee, Jerry and Charlie all have pretty big policies owned by the bank," he replied.

"Really?"

"Yeah. We can transfer ownership to PSI, or we can let them go. If we keep them, we'll have to pay the premiums, though."

"Let's keep 'em," I said.

When Dee and Jerry bought the company, a sizable portion of the purchase had been financed by the bank and cosigned by Charlie. As a result, the bank had insisted that all three of them obtain $2-million life insurance policies, with the bank listed as the owner. That was its way of trying to protect its assets.

Evana had paid the premiums on those policies prior to our acquisition and if any of them died, the bank would be the beneficiary. Now that we were buying Evana, I saw no reason why we shouldn't have taken over as owners and beneficiaries of the life insurance policies and kept them active. But, I think I might have been in the minority on that.

"Dad, you mean if any of them die, the company gets the money from the life insurance?" asked Scott, my oldest son.

"That's right," I replied.

"Don't you think that's kinda ghoulish?"

"Ghoulish?" I responded. "I don't think it is."

"It seems wrong to me somehow to benefit from their deaths."

To me, it seemed practical.

Scott is an engineer and has been president of PSI for a long time, and though I admit I'm biased, he is a brilliant man. He's mostly quiet, always pleasant to be around, and his engineering abilities are exceptional. But, for whatever reason, he didn't have much of a stomach for taking over the life insurance policies of the Evana owners. To him, profiting off of someone else's death was offensive.

Still, I decided to stick with the rules of business and do what

was best for the company. We completed the acquisition and began paying the monthly premiums on all three policies.

A few years later, a review of the insurance premiums showed that we might have been able to lower our payments. So, Dee, Jerry and Charlie all underwent physical exams in order to see if they qualified. Amazingly, Charlie, who was around eighty years old at the time, passed his physical, but both Dee and Jerry didn't.

A few months after that, Dee died from cancer. By that point, she no longer worked with us at Evana. But, even so, we were notified of the unfortunate news of her death.

At the time, Evana was bringing PSI's bottom line downwards. It had been a rough year for all of PSI's corporate subsidiaries and we were looking at a million-dollar loss for the fiscal year. The recession of 2001, a result of the collapse of the dot-coms, multiple accounting scandals and 9/11, had brought dismal returns to many corporations. And PSI was no exception.

But, within thirty days of Dee's passing, the life insurance company mailed us a check for $2 million, which was completely tax-free. PSI went from being a million in the red to a million in the black just like that.

"Scott, I want to show you something," I said, walking into his office shortly afterward.

"What's that, Dad?" he replied.

"Take a look at this."

I handed him the insurance check and he studied it for a moment. Then, without a word, he handed it back to me.

"Do you still think it's ghoulish?" I asked.

"I suppose it'll be alright," he said with a slight grin on his face.

Score one for practicality.

I continue to keep in close contact with Charlie today. We go to lunch occasionally when I visit the facility in Evansville, and once I even convinced him to let me fly him in PSI's company plane to visit his family out west. But, I had not spoken to Jerry since his contracted time at Evana had expired after the acquisition.

After Dee's death, I wanted to be sure we would be notified if anything ever happened to him, so I called the company controller into my office one day to discuss it.

"Randy," I began, "I want you to get in touch with Jerry's family and ask them to notify us should anything happen to him."

"That seems a little strange," he replied.

"Why? We need to know. We own his life insurance policy. I want you to offer them two thousand dollars each as an incentive to update us on that kind of information."

"You want me to offer to pay them?" he asked in astonishment.

"Yes, I do. That way, I know they'll call us."

I could tell by the look on his face that he didn't like the idea, but I made it perfectly clear that I wanted it done. I probably should have followed up on the issue a few weeks later, but I didn't. I figured Randy had done what I'd said.

More than a year later, I realized that I'd never seen any memo or written document that verified an agreement with Jerry's family about notifying me of his death. So, I called Randy back into my office.

I had a suspicion that he had shirked his responsibility, but I hoped that wasn't the case—and I was going to give him the chance to tell me that.

"Randy, where's the agreement we have with Jerry's family?" I asked bluntly.

There was an uncomfortable pause.

"There isn't one," he replied quietly.

"You didn't call them, did you?" I asked.

"No."

"Why not?"

"Because I thought it was crude," he said.

I stood up and walked around to Randy's side of the desk.

"I'll tell you what's crude! When you tell your wife tonight that you're out of a job, that's gonna be crude! Get your stuff and get outta here."

Randy had been with me for more than twenty years, but I fired him on the spot. The two things I despise most are dishonesty and someone messing with my money. He had done both, and I wasn't going to tolerate it.

Randy was potentially costing the company $2 million simply because he'd thought it was rude to ask Jerry's family to notify us of his death. Well, he received a rude awakening of his own that day.

The bottom line was that there was nothing offensive or crude about having life insurance policies on the owners of Evana, especially since they had signed them themselves for the bank. Nor was it unacceptable to ask for someone to notify the company of their deaths. We were the owner of the policies and had a right to be informed. I certainly wasn't wishing any harm on any of them, but whether or not we cashed in on what we rightfully owned wouldn't have changed the circumstances of their deaths.

However, both my son (at least initially) and Randy had preconceived notions that this was morbid, offensive or in some way wrong. They let superstition or social conditioning cloud their rationality. Randy held on to those preconceived notions to the point that it cost him his job. He had lost perspective on his priorities.

Perhaps I am just more practical, but letting irrational feelings influence how you conduct business just never made much sense to me. My guess is that Randy probably never let his emotions or attempts at etiquette get in the way of carrying out his responsibilities again. It was a hard lesson to have to teach him.

But no one ever said business was easy.

CHAPTER 71

Friends and Favors

"What do you have there, Charlie?" I asked, looking at a manila envelope he held under his arm.

"Oh, it's just some papers I need to show you," he replied casually.

"Well, let's see them."

It was a beautiful day in Evansville, Indiana. I was on one of my routine trips to see the Evana plant, and I always made time to visit my friend, Charlie Walker, if he was available.

We sat at one of the local cafés, having lunch and catching up on what had happened since the last time we'd seen each other. Charlie looked to be in as good health and spirits as always, dressed in his conservative business suit and tie regardless of how long he'd been retired.

Charlie had picked me up from the airport in his blue Cadillac and driven into downtown Evansville along the waterfront. The gambling ferry was traveling from the dock to the center of the Ohio River as we drove past. The sky was a perfect blue without a cloud to be seen, and Charlie even found a parking space right in front of the restaurant.

So far, so good.

Except I couldn't help noticing the envelope.

I had first spotted it in his hand when we'd walked to our table,

and I kept waiting for him to do something with it. But, after a while, my curiosity—and impatience—got the better of me. Even after I asked him about it, he still didn't readily volunteer what was inside. "So, Charlie," I asked again. "What exactly do you want to show me in the envelope?"

He paused for a moment and just looked at me. Then, he answered.

"Bill, I have this insurance policy that I purchased back in 1939," he began. "I bought it from a friend of mine who was just getting started in the insurance business. I thought I'd help him out. It was worth a thousand dollars at the time."

Again, he paused as if he were unsure if he wanted to proceed.

"So, what happened?" I prompted.

"Well, I had forgotten about it until around 1974," he continued. "I needed some money for the business, so I took a loan out against it. But, because of the loan, I no longer owned the policy."

"Who owned it?" I asked.

"Evana was listed as the owner," he replied. "But I didn't know that until last month, when I tried to cash the policy out."

It so happened that Charlie had called MetLife, the insurance company that had written the policy, and asked to cash it out for its current value. But, MetLife told him that Evana, which was now a subsidiary of PSI, really owned the policy.

When the acquisition of Evana had taken place and all the life insurance policies had been transferred over to PSI, this small policy had been transferred as well. And Charlie wasn't too thrilled about it.

"So, how much is the policy worth now?" I asked.

"Five thousand dollars," he answered.

"I see."

"Well, I guess this is yours," he stated, still holding the envelope in his hand instead of holding it out to me.

The $2-million life insurance policy that PSI owned on Charlie,

and which he always knew about, meant nothing to him because he had never personally paid the premium on it, but this small, $5,000-policy meant a lot to him because he'd shelled out $1,000 for it at the start, which was a lot of money in those days. It was if he were parting with some cherished family treasure.

There is something you have to understand about Charlie: He is one of the wealthiest men I know.

You might not guess it from his behavior or appearance, but he is the classic "millionaire next door." Charlie always dresses neatly in a suit and tie, and he has always driven a nice Cadillac, but to say that he throws around his money would be far from the truth. On that day, it wouldn't have surprised me if I'd had to pry the insurance papers from his grasp.

"I'll tell you what, Charlie," I offered instead. "How about I take you for an ice cream when we finish lunch?"

Charlie looked at me for a moment with a half grin, then handed me the envelope and resumed eating his meal.

When lunch was over, we rode in Charlie's Cadillac to an ice cream parlor that looked as if it had been there for decades—if not since the dawn of time. The building was a small kiosk with two windows, one for ordering and one for pickup. It was a pretty efficient model, I must admit.

"Charlie, my treat," I said as he sat in the driver's seat. "What flavor would you like?"

"I'll take one vanilla scoop and one chocolate," he said.

"What kind of cone?"

"I'd like a sugar cone," he said, clearly less anxious about the insurance policy.

I walked up to the window of the ice cream parlor, paid two dollars for each of our cones and brought them back to the car. We sat eating our ice cream outside the shop—and by the time we finished, Charlie had forgotten all about the envelope.

He is an uncomplicated man who has become a success

by adhering to the basics in life: Work hard, protect what's yours and live simply. That's the great thing about Charlie Walker—an ice cream cone was just the prescription to take care of his earlier disappointment.

Of course, he was also a businessman, which meant he understood that I wouldn't give up what was rightfully mine.

$$\equiv$$

Later that evening, as I was flying back to Detroit with my son, Scott, and a few other executives, I turned to them and said, "You know, I bet I'm the only guy on this plane who made five thousand dollars today."

Everyone looked a little puzzled.

"What are you talking about?" Scott asked. "We didn't do any business."

"I did, and it only cost me lunch and some ice cream cones," I said while handing Scott the insurance papers. "Not bad for a day's work, huh?"

This time, Scott didn't seem to have any trouble with it.

Once I was back at PSI, we submitted the policy to MetLife and claimed our money. If Charlie hadn't found out about the policy, we might never have recovered that five thousand dollars. And, that wasn't the first time Charlie had helped me out.

He had been integral in making the Evana deal work, and he had always cooperated when insurance physicals were needed to figure out our premiums. I really wanted to return the favor to him in some way. As wealthy as Charlie was, he didn't need money, so I had to think of some other way I could thank him for his help.

$$\equiv$$

The next time I visited Charlie in Indiana, we had lunch again. During the course of conversation he told me that he was going to be visiting his brother-in-law in Miami the next month, and I saw my opportunity to repay him.

"Charlie, let me fly you down to Miami in our corporate jet," I offered.

"Nah. That's okay, Bill," he answered.

"No, really. The pilot can drop you off and then bring you back when you're ready," I continued.

"That's okay," he stated. "I've already bought my ticket."

"How much did it cost you?"

"Two hundred and thirty-seven dollars," he immediately replied.

"C'mon, Charlie. We're talking about flying on a private jet! Put your ticket on layaway or something."

Try as I might, Charlie graciously refused my offer and traveled commercially to Miami. My guess was that he didn't want to waste the money he had already spent, regardless of the chance to fly on a jet with a crew at his disposal. He never ceased to amaze me like that.

Several months later, Charlie and I were again having lunch in Evansville. We talked about his trip to Florida and his flight, and curiosity got the better of me eventually. I needed to understand why Charlie had refused to fly on the jet. Was it really because of the ticket he had already bought, or was it something else?

"Charlie, I have to know," I started. "Why wouldn't you accept my offer to fly on the jet?"

"Bill, I just don't feel comfortable flying on planes that I don't know."

"Then after lunch, you and I should go out to the jet and let you get acquainted," I suggested.

That was an offer on which he took me up.

Charlie and I boarded the corporate jet and both of us sat on board, enjoying a couple of vodka tonics and continuing to share stories.

At that time, I had a Sabre 80 Sabreliner. In addition to its ability to travel 500 miles per hour, it boasted very comfortable leather seating and was very spacious. After the second cocktail, Charlie began to look around the jet a bit more.

"You know, this is pretty nice," he commented.

"You think you could get used to this? Huh, Charlie?" I said.

"Yeah, I could probably get used to this," he said, sitting back with a smile.

Later that year, he agreed to let me send him to Arizona with his daughter and her family. It took me some time, but eventually I was able to repay him for all of his help. As strongly as I felt about returning the favor, I felt even stronger about sharing my success with a good friend.

I believe that when you give to others, you get it back. It's a cycle, and one you have to keep in mind as you're dealing with people professionally or socially. With Charlie, it wasn't about the five thousand dollars or the private plane or the life insurance policy. It was about showing each other respect as businessmen and friends.

After all, treating people the way you want to be treated is the best policy you can have in life.

CHAPTER 72

A True Team Player

I n sports and business, you always want to surround yourself with
the best. That goes for friendship, too.

———

Like most large corporations, Phillips Service Industries has its fair
share of insurance protection. We have kept the same carrier for
more than thirty years. When you find something worthwhile, it
pays to stick with it.

In the late 1970s, a sales manager for a local Detroit insurance
company came to meet with me regarding their product line. After
several conversations, he and I developed a mutual level of respect
for each other, and it made sense for me to use his firm as our insurance carrier—and that's the one we're still with today.

As it turned out, the owner of the insurance company was a man
by the name of Ralph Wilson. Ralph was a World War II veteran
who had taken over his father's insurance company after the war,
had done quite well and chosen to invest in the Michigan area where
he'd grown up. Not only had he invested in mines and factories
within the region but his company had begun to acquire other enti-
ties such as radio stations and construction firms. Like me, he was a
businessman who received great satisfaction from taking preexisting
companies and making them better.

One of Ralph's more interesting investments included the Detroit Lions. He owned a minority share in the NFL team in the 1950s. But, in 1959, Ralph was notified by Lamar Hunt that a new league, the American Football League, which Lamar founded, was in the process of being formed, so Ralph decided to get in on it. In fact, he was one of the first people Lamar called to join up. He wanted to have a team in Miami, but that franchise had already been selected by another investor. As an alternative, he picked the Buffalo Bills, figuring that the weather in Buffalo was a lot like what we had there in Michigan. Ralph became the team's original owner—and still is today.

The insurance sales representative I had come to know was apparently impressed with Phillips Service Industries and, knowing that Ralph was always interested in other business acquisitions, told him that he should make plans to meet me. Even though I wasn't interested in selling the company, the representative thought the two of us would hit it off—and he was right.

Ralph lived in Detroit and had grown up in the area. From that standpoint alone, we had a lot in common. Shortly after his sales representative had spoken to him, Ralph came over to visit the company and we had lunch together. He realized that I had no intention of selling my business, but we got along well nonetheless. Not only did we share the same interests and heritage but we also shared the same conviction of character. Gradually, visit by visit, Ralph and I became close friends.

Ralph is nearly fifteen years older than I am but from the moment we had our first conversation, it was apparent that we were very much alike. Of course, it helped that he always laughed at my jokes. But, more importantly, Ralph has always been a man of high integrity. If he says he'll do something, he's going to do it. I have known him to pay debts even when it was questionable whether or not they were his to pay. He would say, "I borrowed it, so I'm gonna pay it back." He has always been a man of his word.

Though it's not commonly known, Ralph loaned money to Al Davis of the Oakland Raiders and to Billy Sullivan of the New England Patriots to keep both franchises from succumbing to financial failure in the early days of the AFL. Because that's the kind of guy he is, Ralph has always enjoyed a great reputation wherever he has gone, whether it has been in business or among his NFL colleagues.

One afternoon at the Meadowbrook Country Club, my son-in-law Steve was playing a round of golf with another club member. Neither of them knew each other extremely well, but by the end of eighteen holes they had become somewhat acquainted. As they sat in the clubhouse at the end of the day, drinking beer, the man happened to mention that he was one of the owners of Ralph Wilson's previous insurance company. He and another man had bought it from Ralph a few years earlier.

"You know, there are two men in my life whom I have been completely impressed with," the man stated.

"Who's that?" Steve asked.

"Ralph Wilson and Bill Phillips," he replied. "They are two of the finest men I've ever known."

"Well, I know my father-in-law will be happy to hear that," Steve said.

"Who's your father-in-law?" the man asked.

"Bill Phillips."

Of course, Steve couldn't wait to tell me about this conversation later that evening, and I couldn't wait to tell Ralph. I was flattered to be included in the same category as him.

Ralph was like Charlie Walker in the sense that he had remained the same humble person despite the status and wealth he had achieved. Several years ago, PSI had suites at different sporting venues around

the country. From baseball to football to even NASCAR, I believe we had as many as fifteen suites in different locations. Our sales representatives would entertain clients in these suites at various sporting events. In fact, I was told at one point that we had more suites than any other active corporation.

One autumn day, I decided to go to an NFL football game in Foxboro, Massachusetts. The New England Patriots were hosting the Buffalo Bills, and I spent most of the first half in our company suite with our sales executives and guests. When halftime came I asked my sales reps if they wanted to meet Ralph Wilson. They jumped at the chance, so we headed over to Ralph's suite for introductions. Being the owner of the Buffalo Bills franchise, Ralph was awarded a suite at any stadium his team was visiting during the season.

As always, Ralph was a gracious host and he welcomed my sales staff. After introductions, I began talking to his wife, who was also a lovely person. She and I talked about what was happening in their lives and I brought her up to date about Betty and the rest of my family. Pretty soon, I noticed that Ralph was nowhere to be seen. He had vanished while I had been immersed in the conversation. But, almost as soon as I noticed his absence, he reappeared.

"Ralph, where have you been?" I asked.

"Your employees kidnapped me," he stated with a grin.

"Kidnapped you? What are you talking about?"

"Well, I got to talking with your sales buddies and they asked me if I would go over to your suite and meet their clients," he said.

"You have to watch those guys," I said. "They'd go to great lengths for a sale."

"You know me, Bill. I was happy to do it."

And he was. If it is something within his power, Ralph will happily do any favor for a friend. Everyone who knows him knows that. And while in my opinion it's long overdue, Ralph is so respected that he was inducted into the NFL Hall of Fame. He has been a longtime champion for the league and the honor is well deserved.

At the enshrinement ceremony, Ralph had a great line. As soon as he got up on stage and the applause died down, he thanked everybody for the highest honor one could get in football, then added, "But I have to tell you all…I'm really a tennis player."

Of course, not everything in his managing career went so smoothly. Ralph told me the story about one of the first times he watched the Bills play. After the first half, the Jets were beating them 21-0 and everyone in Ralph's suite convinced him to go in the locker room and give a pep talk to the team. Now, although he has a great sense of humor, Ralph is essentially very understated, but he figured he'd go meet the players and say a little something.

Apparently, he went in there, introduced himself and talked a little about team spirit. Then, he left and watched the rest of the game—which the Bills lost 51-0.

Afterwards, Ralph promised the coach, "That's the last pep talk I'll ever give."

"No, it doesn't have to be," the coach replied. "Just do me one favor. Next time, give it to the other team."

Back around 1981, Betty and I went to Dallas with Ralph Wilson and his wife to watch a game between the Cowboys and Bills. Lamar Hunt, who owned the Kansas City Chiefs, was also there—along with his brother, Bunker.

Bunker Hunt was born in Arkansas; he was the son of H.L. Hunt, one of the richest men in the world at one time, who had made his fortunes in the oil business.

Bunker made lots of money in that industry as well and, in the late 1970s, decided to corner the silver market, just like his family had done with everything else. He spent a hell of a lot of money and bought a hell of a lot of silver, which he was actually flying in cargo planes over to Switzerland.

In a short time, he practically cornered the global market in silver and went all over the world trying to get people to go in with him in buying it, including Mohmar Kadafi.

Bunker amassed $2 to $4 billion in silver speculation—until silver prices ultimately collapsed two months after hitting record highs in 1980. He filed for bankruptcy, settled for $10 million and was banned from further trading in the commodities market.

Newspapers at the time carried the story that Bunker was practically destitute and had to sell his Rolex watch in order to survive. But anyone who knew Bunker knew he never owned a Rolex: He was a sloppy dresser, but a good guy. In fact, he showed up at the game in Dallas with gravy on his tie.

As I was talking to the Hunt brothers in the private suite, I kept remembering the story in the paper about the Rolex and got to wondering about what kind of watch Bunker was wearing. I couldn't figure out a tactful way to broach the subject so I asked, "Bunker, what time is it?"

When he looked at his wrist, I saw it was a Timex.

That's not the only great story I remember from visiting with Ralph. In 2006, Detroit was hosting the Super Bowl and Ralph and I were having lunch at his home in Gross Pointe, Michigan, a few weeks beforehand. As usual, we talked about business, Detroit and even a little football. We shared some laughs and a few opinions. Before I left, Ralph wanted to know if I had any interest in getting tickets to the game.

"Sure," I replied.

"How many do you think you would like?" he asked.

"Well, you know I have a big family."

"I'm aware of that," he said, smiling.

"Would ten tickets be too many?" I asked, thinking I would get one for each of my children as well as for Betty and me.

"Ten!" he exclaimed. "That's a lot."

"Ralph, whatever you give me is fine," I said. "You know me. I'd be happy to have it."

Ralph picked up the phone, called his secretary, Hazel, and requested ten Super Bowl tickets for me without even thinking twice. Then, he hung up and looked over at me, sitting across from him.

"Bill, you tell Betty I can't afford for you two to have any more children," he said with a smirk on his face.

Not only had Ralph arranged Super Bowl tickets for my whole family, but they were located on the fifty-yard line, twenty rows from the field, all ten in one row. As we sat and watched the game, the people around us kept looking at us, trying to figure out if we were famous. Leave it to Ralph to make us feel special.

Just as with business opportunities, there are opportunities in life that you should make the most of. A routine insurance sales call gave me the privilege of meeting one of the greatest people I have ever come to know. When you think of what you might have passed up, you realize the potential that every moment holds.

CHAPTER 73

An Infidel No Longer

"Follow me, please," the guard said in a thick, Italian accent. Betty and I followed.

We made our way through the tens of thousands of people gathered within St. Peter's square. Up the steps we went, toward the statues flanking the entrance to the basilica. The privilege to actually enter St. Peter's was something I had never imagined I would be granted. After all, I couldn't even get married in the main chapel at St. John's Cathedral all those years ago. How would I ever be allowed to enter one of the most revered sites in all of Christendom?

In 1997, Betty and I decided to take a trip through Europe and, as part of our travels, we planned to tour Italy. We had finally reached a point in our lives where we could worry a little less and enjoy ourselves a little more. The children all had lives of their own and PSI was doing very well, including its newly acquired corporations. It was time for the two of us to see more of the world after we had worked so hard.

Time changes many things. In our lives, not only had success come our way but my status within the Catholic Church had evolved. Since my days of being labeled an "infidel" by Father Murphy, I had made great strides within the Catholic religion. Betty and I regularly

attended Mass in Michigan and all of our children had been christened within the Catholic Church and had been taught Catholicism. As a result of my connections within the community and my business success, I'd also become a member of the advisory board for Madonna University, a Christian college. In fact, I was its chairman for five years.

Madonna University is in Livonia, Michigan, where PSI is headquartered. It was founded by the Felician Sisters in 1947. Between Madonna and our local diocese, I had the privilege of getting to know most of the regional priests and bishops for the diocese and beyond. So, when Betty and I decided to tour Italy with some friends, I thought it would be an ideal time to see if we could gain access to St. Peter's Basilica and meet the Pope.

I called the president of Madonna University a few weeks before our trip and asked if she might be able to arrange a visit within the Vatican for Betty and me. Without hesitation, she called Cardinal Edmund Szoka, who had served as the archbishop of Detroit between 1981 and 1990. He had been involved in all the Catholic churches in the diocese as well as the Catholic universities and colleges in the area, and we had become good friends along the way.

In 1997, Cardinal Szoka had become the president of the Governorate of Vatican City State, which meant that he had left the Detroit area to live at the Vatican. His job was to straighten out the financial situation in which the Catholic Church had found itself. This was his sole responsibility for a term of three to four years. So, we would be meeting him when we made our trip.

Our itinerary began in northern Italy. Gradually, from Venice, Betty and I traveled along the countryside with another couple, experiencing the nation's culture, its opera and many fascinating sights before eventually coming to Rome and Vatican City. The grand scope of Vatican City is something to be revered. St. Peter's Square was breathtaking and the intricacies of its architecture were

awesome to behold. The basilica itself had been built on the exact location where St. Peter was buried and his body is believed to lie exactly beneath the high altar inside.

In the first century AD, St. Peter was crucified by Roman Emperor Nero. After his martyrdom, he was buried nearby with a red rock placed atop his tomb to mark the site. A church has stood over this location since the fourth century but the current basilica hadn't been completed until the seventeenth century. Michelangelo, Maderno and other famous Italian artists and architects had spent their lifetimes completing it. Although I was familiar with its history, I didn't get a complete grasp of its awe-inspiring construction until I actually saw it in person.

Betty and I, along with our friends, arrived at the Vatican to meet Cardinal Szoka. We took a limousine from our hotel along the narrow streets of Rome to his freestanding apartment within the Vatican. The cardinal's apartment was like none I had ever seen before. I would guess it was 4,000 square feet in size with an expansive living room, a dining room and a kitchen. The bedrooms were spectacular, and detailed paintings and sculptures decorated every room and passageway. Much of the furnishing had been in place before the cardinal's tenure there but he had also incorporated many treasures of his own from his travels around the world.

Cardinal Szoka showed all of us his apartment, describing many of the interesting trinkets and art pieces, and then we all sat for a wonderful lunch. By the time we left, we had all become well acquainted, and the cardinal told us that tickets to enter the basilica and meet the Pope would be waiting for us at our hotel. Betty was happy and could hardly wait for the next day to arrive. Likewise, I was very thankful that the opportunity to meet the Pope himself was actually going to occur. But even with this anticipation, my imagination couldn't do the actual moment justice.

The next day, Betty and I arrived at St. Peter's Square in our

limousine. Our driver showed the guards at the entry gate our colored passes and they allowed us to proceed to the next checkpoint. We went from checkpoint to checkpoint until the massive crowd of people made it impossible for our vehicle to pass through. Then, we exited the car and were escorted by the guards to the next checkpoint. Altogether, there were six checkpoints, and the color of our passes permitted us to go all the way to the steps of St. Peter's Basilica.

I estimate that more than a hundred thousand people stood within the square that day but Betty and I were part of the twenty-five who walked up the steps of the basilica along with the guards. Approaching the entrance, Maderno's façade—with Christ, John the Baptist and eleven of the disciples—watched over us and the majestic dome loomed overhead. Betty and I stood, along with the rest of the small group, waiting for Pope John Paul II to arrive. It was surreal, to say the least.

The Pope's chair had been placed centrally, in front of the entrance of the basilica. It had a high back with velvet cushioning and was trimmed in gold and ornate carvings. Our small group was instructed to sit on folding chairs arranged in a cluster off to one side; we patiently waited in wonder. In the background was St. Peter's Square, where that hundred thousand people also awaited the chance to catch a mere glimpse of the Pope. Yet, there we were, a few feet from his chair.

While we were waiting, I fell into conversation with the man sitting next to me, who was the current president of the Greyhound Lines bus company. His name was John Teets and he had recently taken over the failing corporation and turned it entirely around. We discussed his experiences and our mutual interest in acquisitions. He was a pretty impressive businessman, to say the least, and I was enjoying our conversation. For a moment, I almost forgot where we were.

Suddenly, though, the doors of the basilica opened and Pope John

Paul II was ushered by his aide to his throne. The crowd immediately started chanting, "*Il Papa, il Papa*" as the volume of the synchronous calling heightened, along with my anticipation. The Pope was wearing a modest vestment with a white, flat cap pressed over his gray hair, despite which he looked very youthful.

He stood at a podium that was situated in front of his chair and began to offer a prayer to the masses that had gathered. After the crowd expressed its own reverential response, it became incredibly quiet. A subdued and serious tone overtook the *piazza*.

Our group was then called up, row by row, to meet Pope John Paul II. Betty and I waited until the Pope's aide opened his hands and indicated it was time for us to come forward. We stood up and walked carefully in front of the Pope's chair as if walking on eggshells.

"Welcome," the aide stated. "Please state your name and where you are from."

"I'm Bill Phillips and this is my wife, Betty. We are from Detroit, Michigan, in the United States of America," I answered.

The aide then repeated the information to Pope John Paul II.

"Oh, Detroit!" the Pope responded.

"Yes, Holy Father," Betty answered.

"I have recently visited Detroit," the Pope said. "Welcome to the Vatican."

Pope John Paul II then allowed Betty to hold his right hand, and he proceeded to say a blessing over both of us as the thousands of people behind us stood perfectly silent. Not even a murmur could be heard. It was if the entire world had stopped and a spotlight was being shone on this spiritual scene taking place in front of the basilica.

Even though it only lasted a couple of minutes, this was one of the most powerful moments in our lives. To this day, Betty contends that the Pope had the softest hands of anyone she has ever met.

When the moment was over, the Pope returned inside and our group was again assembled outside St. Peter's Basilica. A Vatican

photographer captured our meeting with the Pope and we received the results later at our hotel room. That picture now hangs in our home in Livonia and is one of our most cherished possessions.

Our fortunate group received a tour of the basilica after meeting the Pope. We viewed the Sistine Chapel, the high altar, the towers, the narthex and the numerous pieces of artwork that adorned St. Peter's Basilica. The high altar itself was surrounded by an elaborate baldachin, and every nave and cleft revealed some unexpected architectural design. With a knowledgeable guide, we could have spent days in there, learning about the history of the basilica and how it had come to exist in its current form.

The entire experience in Vatican City was the highlight of our trip to Europe. I can see why so many make the pilgrimage to St. Peter's Square and the basilica at some point in their lives. For us, it was even more amazing because we were lucky enough to have seen the inside of the magnificent structure and to have had the opportunity to meet the Pope personally.

Generally, I am not the type of person to be overwhelmed when meeting anyone, regardless of their status, but meeting the Pope was the most impressive introduction I have ever experienced. I don't think Father Murphy back in Newfoundland would have ever expected a former infidel like me to receive such a privilege.

It truly shows that anything is possible.

CHAPTER 74

Damage Control

When you have worked with someone for twenty years, you assume you know them pretty well. That goes for both the good and the bad.

But, sometimes, the bad is just better hidden.

———

I had known Fred Crooks for more than twenty years. He had been the tax auditor with Arthur Andersen, with whom PSI had worked; he had also been actively involved in the selling of the Detroit Tigers for Tom Monaghan and in the purchase of the same team by Mike Ilitch. He had a pretty good track record.

Fred had consistently done a good job for PSI over the years. He was knowledgeable and stayed on top of everything, and we had never suffered any significant accounting errors.

When PSI began making corporate acquisitions in the mid-1990s, I needed to create and fill the position of chief financial officer. The company was large enough that accounting and finance, especially for corporate acquisition analysis, had to be brought in house rather than provided through contract consultants. With his experience and expertise, Fred seemed like a great candidate for the job.

Fred was a short, stocky guy who always wore his hair in a buzz

cut. Like many executives I have met, he wasn't one to keep himself in the best physical shape. Overall, I'd say his appearance was disheveled even when he had on a suit and tie. But, he was easy to work with and rarely showed a temper—though, at the same time, he was very matter of fact and direct in his opinions. Those traits never bothered me, of course, and, in fact, they served him well as a financial director.

I approached Fred with the offer to become PSI's chief financial officer and explained our future strategies regarding corporate acquisitions, in addition to the company's direction in general. He was enthusiastic and gladly accepted the position. Everything seemed like a great fit—so far.

Subsequently, Fred helped PSI handle the acquisitions of Beaver, Mount Optech and Evana, and he managed the daily financial affairs of PSI and all its subsidiaries. During the acquisition of Evana, he came to me with some thoughts of his own.

"Bill, I'm getting up in age," he started. "I'm thinking about retiring in the next couple of years."

"Is that right?" I responded.

"Yeah. I was thinking we should probably get a person in here for me to train," he continued. "That way, in a few years, he'll be ready to take over."

"That sounds like a good transition plan," I said. "Interview some people and find one you think will be a good candidate. Then, I'll interview the ones you like."

We interviewed several good candidates for the position and eventually settled on a guy by the name of Larry Perlin. Larry began training under Fred to learn all the intricacies of PSI. But, three years went by and I sensed Larry was beginning to get restless. Something wasn't going right.

"Larry, how are things for you?" I asked as he came into my office one morning.

"Well, not as I expected," he replied.

"What do you mean?"

"I've been here for almost three years and I just thought I would be advancing by now."

"What seems to be the problem?"

"I've come up against a wall," he said. "Fred doesn't share information with me. He keeps me doing menial tasks."

As I figured out much later, Fred didn't have any intention of retiring. What he intended to do was hire another financial guy who could do most of his work while he continued to earn his CFO's salary. Fred was one of those guys who didn't want to go home yet didn't want to work, either. He was married and had a disabled adult daughter. Understandably, his family responsibilities weren't easy, and I suspect that PSI was a sort of escape for him. But, instead of doing his job, he had been trying to figure out ways to minimize his workload. That was the real reason why Larry had been brought onboard—and it didn't sit right with me.

I called Fred into my office and told him it was time for him to retire. "Fred, you told me three years ago that you wanted to retire," I stated. "That's why we brought Larry onboard. You need to get him up to speed and go home."

"Well, I'm not sure Larry is ready yet," he stated.

"Then get him ready," I answered. "That was your job from the beginning."

"Yeah, but he hasn't progressed as fast as I would like."

"Fred, it's time for you to move on," I stated bluntly. After all, I wasn't there to babysit. "I think Larry can handle it. Get him up to speed."

Our meeting was not harsh or confrontational and, eventually, Fred reluctantly agreed to retire. Within the month, Larry took over as CFO and Fred was out. I had thought that would be the last time I would see him but, unfortunately, that wasn't the case.

Several weeks later, a letter came in the mail to PSI from an attorney's office. Fred was suing the company for age discrimination! Now, after twenty years, his real colors were finally showing through. Unfortunately, it wasn't under my control to decide how to proceed. PSI had general liability insurance to handle such claims, so the attorneys for the insurance carrier decided whether or not we would proceed to court or make some type of settlement. If I'd had my way, we would have been doing battle and he never would have seen another dime from PSI. In my mind, he had been stealing from the company for years by receiving pay while Larry did half his work.

I am still amazed by how, after twenty years of knowing a person and working closely with him, I could have been blind to his real character. At times, it makes me wonder whether I should trust anyone.

But, in the overall balance of things, I still believe that awarding your confidence and trust to those around you is a key to achieving success. No man attains it alone.

Leadership is the quality that encourages success and builds trust between you and your workers. You have to put some of the power in the hands of those you lead, and the best you can hope for is to minimize the effects of people like Fred Crooks along the way.

I just wish I had minimized him many years earlier.

CHAPTER 75

Round Two

"We feel it's best to settle on this one," stated the lead counsel for our liability insurance carrier.

"That's ridiculous!" I exclaimed. "You're gonna reward him for being a thief?"

"Bill, I understand your frustration," he continued. "But from a risk perspective, we're better off settling."

"I say we fight."

"Are you willing to pay extra?"

That's what our legal system has evolved into. Fred Crooks suggested his own early retirement, asked for a trainee replacement and then proceeded to cost the company money because he didn't do his job properly in the first place. Yet, the insurance attorneys felt it was better to give him a paycheck for suing PSI for age discrimination than to fight him in court. They had no principles invested in the case, only financial risk.

And, of course, Fred himself had nothing to lose. I suspect he had an attorney on contingency, so he didn't have to invest anything to play the lawsuit lottery that has become such a popular national pastime.

In 1988, before PSI began corporate acquisitions and before Fred Crooks' time with the company, a young lady had worked for me in Detroit. Over the course of time, her work performance had been poor; she had been documented as being repeatedly late for work and had been in trouble for substance abuse. There were ample reasons to dismiss her from PSI, and so I did.

A few weeks later, I received notice that she was suing the company for wrongful termination and for medical injuries that had occurred as a result of her termination. Reportedly, she had taken eighty birth control pills in an attempted suicide and then gone to the local emergency room for treatment. The effects of the pills on her body and her subsequent medical care were estimated to have cost $15,000 and she wanted compensation for her pain and suffering.

"Bill, I think we should just settle with this girl and be done with her," my attorney at the time recommended.

"Settle?" I said. "You've got to be kidding me."

"She'll win a lot of money in court," he stated.

"Let me ask you something. What do you think about this girl?"

"I think it's terrible. The poor lady tried to commit suicide."

"You feel sorry for her?" I asked. "Do you even know if she went to the hospital?"

He looked at me, puzzled.

"Have you seen her medical records?" I asked.

"No," he admitted.

"I want you to get out of here and don't come back until you know what the hell you're talking about! We're fighting this case, and you'd better make damn sure we have what we need to win it."

This attorney had come into my office without even reviewing any medical records, hospital notes or much of anything else—and then suggested we settle the case in court. Talk about incompetence!

As it turned out, the ex-employee had gone to the emergency room and had been given some ipecac to induce vomiting. After

receiving the medicine, she left and didn't return to the ER. In other words, she left without signing out. The facts supported her irresponsibility not only in her job at PSI, but in the way she'd handled her so-called suicide attempt.

Despite the opposing counsel's encouragement, there was no way I was going to settle this case out of court. I wasn't one to roll over and I will always fight for what is right.

My attorney told the other counsel that a trial was inevitable because his client was "hot tempered." Perhaps I was. Abuse of the legal system and attempts to take my hard-earned money tend to push my buttons the wrong way. And, all the while, my attorney kept feeling sorry for the girl and telling me how bad a trial outcome would be for me. But, it didn't matter what he said. I knew I was in the right.

The day of the trial finally arrived and my attorney and I went into downtown Detroit, to the civil courtroom to defend our position. I was dressed in a conservative suit and tie and represented a corporation; on the other side was the girl, dressed very simply, playing the part of the wounded victim.

The bailiff announced the judge's entrance into the court and we all stood as we watched an African-American woman walk behind the bench. She was distinguished in appearance, middle aged and confident in her demeanor. But, since she was a minority and a woman, I no longer felt that my chances of victory were as high.

The trial proceeded and the woman's attorney pleaded her case, describing her intentional overdose of oral contraceptives, her emotional distress and the devastation caused by her loss of employment. The judge attentively listened to her bleeding-heart story. But, before we had even gotten into the core of the trial, Her Honor paused.

"Let me get this straight," she stated, turning toward the woman. "You took eighty pills, trying to commit suicide, and you believe it's your employer's fault?"

The woman nodded.

"I've heard enough about the facts of this trial," the judge declared. "Young lady, I strongly suggest that you go get some help and get your life together."

The woman again nodded but with a look on her face as if she had been scolded by a parent.

"And you, Counsel," the judge said to the woman's attorney, "I suggest you go find some decent legal work and quit wasting this court's time with frivolous cases. I rule in favor of the defendant. This court is adjourned."

To think that my attorney wanted to settle this case out of court for $15,000! He had misjudged this girl based on appearances, without doing his due diligence—just like I was ready to assume how the judge would rule based on her appearance. But, boy, was I glad I hadn't given up.

———

In the end, my former employee suffered no penalty except for a scolding for starting such a ridiculous lawsuit. She'd had no risk; she'd made a frivolous claim against PSI that we'd had to defend at a significant cost, but once we were found to be in the right, that was it. If her attorney was receiving contingent earnings based on a reward, she paid nothing to roll the dice against my corporation. It was open season.

Unfortunately, I didn't have the same outcome with Fred Crooks. Because the insurance carrier had the deep pockets in the lawsuit, their attorneys were the ones who called the shots. PSI carried a deductible that needed to be paid in any agreement but, by far, the

bulk would be paid by the insurance company. Essentially, it was their decision whether to stand up and fight or lie down and roll over by handing out a few bucks and hoping it would all go away.

Needless to say, the case never even made it to court. During the mediation process, the insurance attorney felt that the risk would be too great if it went to trial and so chose to settle for $750,000 instead.

I couldn't believe it. But, no matter how adamant I was about pursuing a trial, they would hear nothing of it.

Basically, what it boiled down to was that our legal system awarded a deceitful and conniving ex-executive a tremendous amount of money for a fictitious claim that he knew perfectly well hadn't occurred.

This kind of abuse happens every day in our courts and not only does it affect insurance premiums and corporate bottom lines, but it also encourages people to file unnecessary lawsuits and tie up the system and keep it from addressing real issues. Why not take a chance on earning free money when your risk is essentially nothing? What have you got to lose by lying and trying to take the easy way out?

I still believe that if we had gone to trial, a judge with good sense, like the one in the previous lawsuit, would have found Fred Crooks to be a fraud, and he would have walked away with nothing. But, it wasn't my call to make.

The only silver lining was that it would be the last time that man would ever drag the company down. He got what he wanted: an easy payday.

I guess some people prefer that to the difficulties of earning money and respect.

CHAPTER 76

Negotiating
With the White House

"Bill, this is Thad," the familiar voice said on the phone. "I've got something to ask you. Something of national importance…"

Thad McCotter was one of my long-time acquaintances and a current U.S. representative from the state of Michigan. I had known him since his days as a county representative and had helped his political success all the way from the local to the state to the federal level. He had always been a supporter of local business and, as a result, I had given him my support through political contributions.

I didn't know what the call was about, but I couldn't wait to hear.

"What do you think about President Bush coming to visit the Beaver Aerospace and Defense plant?" he finally asked.

"Well, I suppose I would be honored," I replied, letting the idea sink in.

"He's looking for a location to talk about his tax reform policy. I thought your facility would be a great location."

Having President Bush speak at Beaver Aerospace and Defense would, without a doubt, be a huge honor to me. It also wouldn't hurt Thad's reputation to have the president come and speak in his home state.

I was all in—except for one thing.

It was the summer of 2003 and President George W. Bush was speaking on behalf of his recent Jobs and Growth Tax Relief Reconciliation Act. This act was intended to accelerate the tax relief stipulations previously passed in the Economic Growth and Tax Relief Reconciliation Act of 2001. The prior one had lowered income taxes on capital gains and dividends for individuals, but the implementation was originally over a nine-year period. The more recent act accelerated that timeline significantly.

As a means of highlighting its positive effects on American industries and businesses, Bush was seeking an appropriate platform from which to deliver his national speech. What more fitting place than Beaver Aerospace and Defense, a homegrown industry?

A few days after getting Thad's phone call, I was contacted by one of President Bush's top aides. Skip—he preferred to be called by this nickname—was an attorney originally from Alabama but hardly had any detectable Southern accent. Our initial phone conversation consisted of a few questions about my company, the Beaver Aerospace subsidiary, and some polite small talk about my family and me.

But, before we ended the discussion, Skip did want to verify that Beaver Aerospace was indeed a profitable corporation. I presumed a failing company might not have been the best place for President Bush to speak about job and growth-tax reform. Fortunately, I was able to say that we were definitely operating in the black.

Although other locations were considered, my manufacturing plant was ultimately chosen as the venue for President Bush's presentation. Skip and some of the other aides made arrangements to visit our facility in Detroit, to meet me as well as to examine the layout where the president would deliver his speech.

Several conversations took place with my son, Bob, about making the arrangements onsite, but they understandably wanted to see the facility in person and verify my approval before proceeding with the final details.

When Skip finally arrived, I could tell that despite his youthful appearance and nickname, he was a man firmly in control. He impressed me with the way he handled himself: pleasantly yet decisively. Nothing was left to chance.

"Tell me about your family life, Bill," he said.

"Well, I've been married to my wife, Betty, for forty-seven years, and I have eight children," I stated. "You've already met my son, Scott."

"Yes, I've had the pleasure," he replied. "Tell me a little about your current business here at Beaver Aerospace and Defense."

"Beaver Aerospace has been part of PSI since 1997," I answered. "Our expertise is in ball screw manufacturing, which services many industries, including the military."

"Tell me a little about your close business and personal colleagues." Question by question, Skip learned the details he needed to ensure that our location was the best choice for the president—and I'm also certain that everyone involved was investigated to some extent by the Secret Service. Not only did they judge me by my personal and professional background and my company's history, but also by the company I kept.

The meeting with Skip lasted a while, with various interruptions occurring throughout. Phone calls, people entering the room and urgent messages made for a fragmented visit. After all, I had a business to run. But, eventually, Skip had asked everything he needed to ask. Then, it was my turn.

"I have one issue," I said. "I would like my wife to be there when I meet President Bush."

"I'm sorry, but I can't promise that," Skip said. "That might be cumbersome."

"Cumbersome?" I responded. "This woman helped me build this company, and it's costing me one hundred thousand dollars in operational downtime to have this visit. Now, I want to proceed with

everything, but I want my wife to have the opportunity to meet the president, too."

"I just don't know if that will be possible," Skip stated again.

"Let me put it another way," I said. "Either it's possible, or there's no presidential visit happening here."

Skip paused and looked at me. I assumed he knew I wasn't kidding.

"Okay, Bill."

He met with Bob, Mike Fitzpatrick and several other employees during his tour of the facility and spoke again with Scott to finalize plans. On his way out the door, Skip turned around one last time and asked all of us if there was anything else we needed to cover. I was ready to reiterate my insistence on Betty's being there to meet the president when Skip spoke up—he must have anticipated my comment.

"I know, I know, Bill. Your wife will meet President Bush."

With that, he smiled and left.

———

I was very proud that a United States president wanted to visit one of my facilities, but at the same time I was still the same person as always—and my sense was that it was only fair that my family, especially Betty, enjoyed the moment with me.

Sometimes, you have to be willing to let some things go if they are contrary to how you feel. Meeting the president would have been nice, but my family was more important to me and I had to speak up for what I felt was right.

Fortunately, Skip assured me that having Betty and the rest of my family there wouldn't be a deal breaker. Otherwise, I would have had to stand my ground—and the president would have had to hit the road.

When it comes to backing down, PSI isn't the right place.

CHAPTER 77

Hail to the Chief

The White House staff was busy making preparations for President Bush's visit to Beaver Aerospace and Defense.

That's something I'd never dreamed about saying when I first started out.

⟞⟐⟝

A stage was assembled on the floor of Beaver's manufacturing plant and, as is routinely done, the president's people arranged to have their own electrical generators put into place for power. They weren't taking any chances.

On the day of the president's arrival, I sat in a conference room with Secretary of Commerce Don Evans, waiting for President Bush to show up. Though our conversation was nice, just knowing that the president would be arriving at any time was something of a distraction.

I felt a little anxious but, like always, managed to make the most of my time. Secretary Evans and I had many things in common and hit it off very well during our hour-long meeting while waiting for President Bush. Evans had been born in Houston, and I had been stationed in Texas for a period of time during my Air Force training. I had also operated the PSI facility in Houston back in the 1970s, so we had some common ground.

Additionally, Evans had spent a great deal of his life on oil rigs and had eventually become the CEO of Tom Brown, Inc. before taking on the role of secretary of commerce. Tom Brown, Inc. dealt with natural gas and crude oil exploration and development, so we also had some similar business experiences to talk over.

"So, what are we going to do about this recession?" I asked him, directing the conversation toward economics.

"We have to get China to raise their labor rates," Evans stated. "Our businesses aren't on an even playing field."

"Really?" I said, surprised by his response. "You think you're going to convince a country with over a billion people to raise their wages?"

"What are your thoughts on it?" he asked.

"I say give American businessmen the tax breaks and financial incentives to create new products and services," I replied. "We'll take care of the rest."

American entrepreneurs have always been able to create solutions through ingenuity and determination—I was an example of that. All we have ever needed were the right tools. If there's an opportunity for a product or service to be provided for a profit, the American entrepreneurial spirit has always come to the rescue.

Since I was young, I'd heard story after story of how creative opportunists (and I mean that in a good sense) have generated success for themselves and their families within the framework of our country's capitalist structure. The freedoms we enjoy and a competitive market enable anyone to succeed.

Some of the most unusual and ingenious products and services have launched the careers of many innovative spirits. Take away the constraints and let creativity do the rest—then, stand back and watch the results. For example, consider the story of Alfred Taubman and Herbert J. Hoelter.

Taubman was a well-known real estate developer, especially in the Detroit area. One of his biggest successes came when he revived

Sotheby's auction house from its financial woes. After he took over the company in 1988, Sotheby's reclaimed its status as a solid and reputable business. However, in 2002, Taubman was found guilty of violating antitrust laws and was fined $7.5 million and imprisoned for a year. In short, he had fixed commission rates with rival company Christie's, which subsequently implicated him as the instigator.

As it turned out, Taubman's corporate jet was located in the same hangar as PSI's. I was at the hangar the day he was being transported to Minnesota to begin his sentence, and I struck up a conversation with one of his assistants. Interestingly, after his conviction, Taubman had hired consultant Herbert J. Hoelter, who specialized in teaching executives how to survive in prison.

It was Hoelter's responsibility to educate Taubman on how to behave and cope with the changes he was about to experience so that he could survive in his new circumstances. And Taubman, I'm sure, was willing to pay handsomely for that service. Hoelter also assisted moguls Michael Milken and Martha Stewart to prepare for their times in the big house.

Where there's an opportunity for profit, you will find an entrepreneur who, like Hoelter, is ready and willing to provide the solution. With a master's degree in social work and an extensive history with the judicial system, Hoelter and his colleagues found a unique niche for their talents. I'm certain that when they were children, they didn't expect to teach white-collar criminals how to adjust to prison life. But, the opportunity came, and they took it.

Where one businessman failed due to dishonesty, another succeeded due to ingenuity.

***

Secretary of Commerce Evans and I were speaking about the recession of 2001, which hardly compares to the recession of 2008 in severity. But, in essence, I still feel that the solutions are very much

the same. In order for Americans to compete, all we need is to enable the entrepreneurial spirit to thrive within our country. Time and time again, Americans have been leaders in technology and business. Just supply them with the tools and incentives, and the rest will follow.

While I understand the purpose of raising tax rates on the wealthy to help bail the country out of tough economic times, I am concerned about how this will constrain business. The wealthy are the ones who primarily invest in businesses and other ventures. And, if tax rates increase, these investments will certainly decline. Likewise, taxation on businesses hinders their ability to compete globally. Such financial handcuffs will limit companies' abilities to be creative and competitive in the long run.

My thought is to provide all businesses, small and large, with tax breaks and other incentives to stimulate what I feel is the ever-present backbone of America's success: creativity and ingenuity. Our freedoms and culture invite diverse and original ideas. This is the real solution that is congruent with our people, our culture and our "melting pot" philosophy. That is what Americans have thrived upon and always will.

The answer, then, as I told Secretary Evans, is within our own country, not outside it.

The hour I spent talking with Secretary Evans passed quickly and, before I knew it, the president had arrived.

White House Chief of Staff Andrew Card ushered President Bush through the back door of our facility. Along with Scott and the general manager of Beaver Aerospace and Defense, the president was escorted to where Secretary Evans and I were waiting.

"Bill Phillips, allow me to introduce you to the president of the United States, George W. Bush," Andrew Card announced as he entered the conference room.

George W. Bush was immediately behind him, and both Secretary Evans and I were on our feet by the time the president reached out to shake my hand.

Though a few words were exchanged, all I really remember was that the interaction was very brief; less than a minute later, the president was walking toward the staging area on the factory floor. Every major media network was on hand to cover the event, and everyone present was excited and honored to be hosting a presidential speech.

Scott and I stood off to the side of the stage as Secretary Evans formally introduced President Bush to the crowd. About 200 employees were on hand as well as many invited guests, and Betty and most of my children were sitting in the front row of the audience. Cameras were flashing, videos were recording and dozens of news reporters were capturing the occasion. The entire event felt surreal.

A United States president was standing in the middle of one of my corporations, delivering a national address about tax reform in the same town where, as a boy, I'd delivered newspapers detailing the same type of events. I must admit it was both mind boggling and humbling.

President Bush mentioned my name and the Beaver Aerospace and Defense manufacturing plant many times, graciously thanking us for the use of the facility. And, he associated our company and our employees with the national support all Americans were providing to the U.S. troops in Iraq. President Bush echoed a good portion of the conversation I had with Secretary Evans about American entrepreneurship. He first thanked all of us at Beaver for producing the stabilizers on Air Force One:

> First, let me just say I appreciate the hardworking folks here at Beaver Aerospace for making sure that Air Force One functions properly. Otherwise, it might have been a long flight. I appreciate what you do for America's

defense. I appreciate your hard work. I appreciate your talent. I appreciate your help in making this country strong.

Then, President Bush spoke about the importance of entrepreneurs—and our employees—in making America the world leader in both efficient and effective industries:

> *You know, one of the great things about America is the entrepreneurial spirit of our country. And Mr. Phillips is an entrepreneur. And one of the things we've got to do in America is keep that entrepreneurial spirit alive and well. And Mr. Phillips knows what I know—you can be an entrepreneur, but without good workers, good, dedicated, hardworking people willing to run the machines and show up on time and work hard, the entrepreneurial spirit is kind of empty. And so, first of all, I want to not only thank the Phillips folks, I want to thank the people who work here in this facility. Thanks for making America go.*

Finally, after touching on the tax breaks that he was enforcing, the president said the result would mean a savings of $70,000 for small businesses such as Beaver Aerospace. And he had a very good understanding of how we would put that money to work for us:

> *And that means more money that goes into research to develop new products. And that's important. If I were a worker here, I'd want to be on the cutting edge of new products. I'd want the people who run this company thinking about how best can I use my talent and my skills to build a new product to stay competitive.*

It seemed that President Bush really understood that entrepreneurs—and not just "big business" corporations—make up the backbone of America and keep our country on the cutting edge when it comes to industry and innovation.

After that, the bulk of his message highlighted the benefits that the tax breaks and stimulus checks of the recently passed legislation were having on the recession, and the manufacturing facility provided a good forum for this message.

When the speech concluded, the president went through the audience, shaking hands. I was beginning to get concerned that Betty might not have the opportunity for a personal, face-to-face introduction, but just as the thought entered my mind, one of President Bush's aides approached me.

"Mr. Phillips," he said, "the president would very much like to meet your family."

"We would be delighted," I replied. "Where's convenient?"

"Let's meet back in the conference room," he answered.

One by one, I introduced my entire family to President Bush. He was friendly and had a very down-to-earth personality that made everyone feel at ease. We hardly noticed the entourage of staff and Secret Service agents as we spoke with the commander in chief.

"Mrs. Phillips," the president said to Betty, "it's very nice to meet you."

"May I give you a kiss on your cheek for your mother, Barbara?" Betty asked.

"You certainly may," he replied.

Betty moved closer and kissed his right cheek, leaving an imprint of lipstick on it.

"Oh, let me wipe that off," Betty said.

"No, no," President Bush insisted. "I'm going to leave that there."

"I have always admired your mother...and you as well," Betty said. "And, your father is a wonderful man."

"Yeah, he's a pretty good guy," the president commented as he smiled at my wife.

We all talked for a few more minutes and, throughout the conversation, President Bush impressed me with his humility and personable nature. I hadn't been sure what to expect, but I was pleasantly surprised that he was so approachable.

"I need to find out where Laura went," President Bush said, turning to one of his aides. "She was supposed to leave for Glacier National Park with some of her friends, but we were notified of a forest fire there this morning."

"Did she cancel her plans?" I asked.

"I believe so, but I had to leave," the president continued. "I'm not sure where she was going."

"You could call her on that red phone there," I said jokingly, pointing to the phone the Secret Service had carried into the room. Apparently, it travels wherever the president goes just in case of a national emergency.

"You know, I sure would like to meet up with her," President Bush said thoughtfully. "We should head to the ranch for the weekend. Yep, that's what we should do."

With that statement, he said his goodbyes to all of us and left. The occasion had been momentous, to say the least, and certainly an experience I will always remember. It was also nice to know that the president was as concerned about his wife as I was about mine.

Afterward, I stepped out into the hallway of the conference area where my pilot, Frank, was standing. We both watched President Bush as he made his way to the presidential limousine.

"Hopefully, he can meet up with Laura for the weekend," I commented.

"Yeah," Frank said in a serious voice. "I guess it's always about being with your lady...even for the president."

We shared a good laugh about that, but Frank's joke highlighted what a regular guy President Bush seemed to be.

About two weeks after the president spoke at our facility in Detroit, my son-in-law Mike attended a local business luncheon where Secretary Evans was speaking. After the talk, Evans walked into the audience and shook hands in a receiving line, greeting each of the attendees. Eventually, Mike made his way to the front of the line.

"Good afternoon, Secretary Evans," he said. "Mike Fitzpatrick, chief counsel at Beaver Aerospace and Defense."

"Beaver?" Evans said enthusiastically. "Great to meet you, Mike. I enjoyed my visit there."

"Thank you. My father-in-law is Bill Phillips," Mike stated.

"Ah, he's quite a guy. We had a really great conversation. Be sure to tell him I said hello."

I don't know if any of my thoughts about national policy and economics had any influence over Secretary Evans, but at least I do know that I made an impression on him nonetheless.

I believe in American ingenuity and creativity, and, no matter what, I think these characteristics will always enable us as a nation to surpass any obstacle. Though some of my children are devout Republicans, I have always tended to be more objective, embracing some Republican platforms as well as some Democratic concepts. As usual, I suspect the answers lie somewhere in the middle. But, having climbed the ladder of success one rung at a time, I will always be biased in favor of the American entrepreneur.

As a businessman starting out from very humble beginnings, I'd had the honor of meeting the Pope as well as the current United States president. While both men were extremely powerful and worthy of great respect, they were still simply men. Seeing them as real people and fellow human beings made me realize that we all have greatness within us—it's just a matter of letting it express itself.

If I could stand in their presences after overcoming the odds, anyone could. And that's what's truly great about our country.

CHAPTER 78

Making Up Stories

The morning after President Bush's visit to Beaver Aerospace and Defense, I was walking outside the manufacturing plant, enjoying a quick break. It wasn't long before I saw a van pull up to the main entrance.

It wasn't any ordinary cargo van, either. It was equipped with a small satellite on its roof, and the bold letters on its side referred to one of Detroit's local television news channels. When the van came to a stop, a young lady and two men stepped out onto the sidewalk. One man carried a camera, and the woman had a microphone in her hand.

I didn't know what they were there for. But I was pretty sure it wasn't good.

I walked over quickly and was able to intercept them before they entered the building. The woman carrying the microphone was tall and attractive, with long, blond hair—she was clearly ready to go on the air. Her sidekick started his camera as soon as I approached. The other, older guy, who was wearing a bowtie, wasn't doing much of anything, as far as I could ascertain.

"Is there something you need?" I said as I walked up to them.

"Yes," the lady answered. "We would like to interview one of the employees here."

"Who?" I asked.

"We want to talk to the man holding this small flag," she said,

showing me a photograph. The picture was of a Beaver employee holding an American flag that President Bush had signed the previous day.

"No, you're not going to interview any of my employees," I stated.

"We have an expert on the desecration of the American flag with us," she said, pointing to the man in the bowtie. "We just have a few questions."

"What exactly makes him an expert on flag desecration?" I asked.

"He's a World War II veteran," she replied.

I was astounded. President Bush had come to give a talk and meet the employees—whom he thanked on behalf of the country for their hard work. But, this news channel was trying to put a completely different spin on the story, focusing on alleged flag desecration. Was this supposed to be investigative journalism or a way to stir up trouble—and ratings? I checked the side of the van again to be sure they weren't from one of the national tabloids. Their story seemed to rank right up there with some make-believe celebrity encounter with alien abductors.

The last time I'd had any significant contact with the news media was in 1991. One of the executives from Martin Marietta had contacted one of our executives at PSI on a Friday afternoon with a sudden emergency: a machine that needed urgent repair. Those things always happen on Fridays. It seems to be a rule.

Essentially, the machine he described to us manufactured weaponry for the military—and this was when we were in the middle of Operation Desert Storm. Everything had to be placed on hold until this machine could be fixed.

The problem was with a ball screw. Our manager and executives

of the ball screw repair services division accepted the task. What was newsworthy about it was the fact that many staff members who actually completed the labor volunteered to work without pay over the weekend to make sure the job got done.

Soon, word got out about their generosity and patriotism, and the local news channels all decided to cover the story. Even CNN ran it, after asking my permission to air clips from the local stations. One of the television news reporters came and interviewed me onsite—but unlike this "news" crew that was searching for an obscure and controversial angle, that interview had stayed on target and gotten to the heart of the story.

"Mr. Phillips, were you surprised that your employees volunteered for the task?" the reporter had asked me.

"Our employees are good people and are very patriotic," I'd stated. "I'm not surprised at all."

"You obviously have a good relationship with your employees."

"I have always had good relationships with people who've worked for me, but things like this show just how good they really are."

One week later, a lieutenant general in charge of all military parts acquisitions came to visit our plant in response to that story, and the local news covered his visit as well. Subsequently, we received commendations from the state of Michigan and the U.S. Congress. Everyone wanted to be a part of such a feel-good event.

But, the crew that wanted to interview the employee holding a miniature flag that our president had signed had no intentions of making anyone feel good. In fact, they were going out of their way to find something to implicate President Bush in some kind of wrongdoing, and get my company entangled in the process.

As I listened to what they had come there to accomplish, I wondered what type of person lay awake at night dreaming up such sensational *non*-stories. Did they have nothing better to do with their careers? Or did they lack respect for their viewers so much that they couldn't be bothered reporting real events?

Sadly, the news media is no longer what it used to be. Investigative journalism has "evolved" into an entertainment industry. What used to be found only in the supermarket tabloids is now on the front page of almost every newspaper, and cable TV is saturated with sensationalized controversies, from the local news to the dozens of syndicated shows that cover—and distort—whatever topic is in vogue. "The news" is no longer the trustworthy entity it used to be. When they're out targeting celebrities or politicians, they don't care how many honest and hardworking people get implicated in their storylines.

I wasn't going to let that happen there.

<hr>

"You're not going to interview any employees in my company," I repeated. "The only thing that happened yesterday was that a lot of people came together to hear a speech, have a good time and meet the president. That's the only real story here."

With that, I sent the television news crew on its way.

Even though they still decided to run a small piece on President Bush's possible violation of the flag's sanctity, it carried absolutely no weight. Like most news stories today, it was forgotten long before the next day's newscast took place. Like the old saying goes, today's newspapers will wrap tomorrow's fish.

But, examples of sacrifice, enthusiasm and pride in one's work and country will always serve as inspiration to Americans.

CHAPTER 79

Trust

I have always been proud of my relationships with my employees and the people with whom I work. I believe in giving them the benefit of the doubt, getting out of their way and letting them do their jobs. That's what I pay them to do, after all. Besides, qualified workers don't need or appreciate too much handholding.

I will put my trust in anyone who has earned it—at least until they prove otherwise.

Then, I show them the door.

In December of 2007, I was invited to a dinner reception in New York City to honor David Brandon, a good friend of mine and the chairman of Domino's Pizza. I was told I could bring some people along, so I invited several of my top executives to make the trip with me, as well as Jack Kirksey, the mayor of Livonia, Michigan, and some of his staff. This didn't require much more than putting on a tux and enjoying the evening.

A few people made speeches in David's honor and then the man of the hour spoke himself. After the ceremony was finished, everyone stayed and mingled. For me, that meant getting to know some new people, but it was also one of those times I could talk with my executives outside the confines of PSI's facilities.

Bart was one of the executives I'd invited; he served as the chief operating officer of PSI. Bart was a smart, high-energy person who seemed to be on top of everything. I had long suspected that he might have overmanaged his employees too much for my liking, but for the most part he seemed to be diligent, effective and extremely busy. But on several occasions, I had cautioned him about micromanaging.

Truth serum may not actually exist, but for some people alcohol serves the same purpose. Bart couldn't handle too many drinks, but through the course of the evening he had a few and began to loosen up.

"You know, Bill," he started at one point, "you really handle the employees well."

"What do you mean?" I asked.

"I mean you stay involved."

It was a nice compliment—and it was also the truth. But I had another question. "How would you know that?" I asked.

"Because I tell them to report to me about what you say," he told me.

"Are you kidding me?" I asked, amazed. "You require the people under you to tell you about my conversations with them?"

"Well, yeah," he shrugged. "You knew I did that."

"The hell I did!"

After that, I kept a close eye on him for the rest of the evening. All it took was a few more drinks and some more discussion, and it became all too obvious to me that Bart was overbearing and smothered his employees. He was the classic micromanager who couldn't let people do their jobs without being involved. He didn't want anything happening that wasn't under his control—even if it involved me.

Now, I knew that that kind of control kept employees from doing their best work. Creativity doesn't flourish when someone is always looking over your shoulder, and it also makes you lose focus. That kind of "tight grip on the reins" mentality is inefficient

and constraining. I thought about all the time he spent monitoring the employees' conversations—and what he could have been doing with that time instead.

A few months later, I promoted Mike Fitzpatrick to manage the repair services division. Mike's an interesting and well-qualified guy; he initially obtained a law degree and had acted as PSI's corporate counsel in the past. But then he made the decision to get his MBA and pursue a career in business. When the opportunity for the manager position opened in the RSI division, Mike was chosen for the job.

He turned out to be an excellent manager, and his knowledge of law and skills with people helped him become a good leader among his staff. He knows how to motivate those working with him and encourages everyone to take pride in their work.

One day, he submitted a requisition with my consent to print some baseball caps and polo shirts with his division's logo on them. He thought it would not only create a team atmosphere but also show his appreciation for the employees' dedication and service to the company.

But some time passed, and Mike still didn't hear anything more about the requisition. He didn't know if it had been received, denied or accepted. So, he contacted the chief operating officer—Bart—and asked about it.

"I did receive it, but I just haven't had time to look it over yet," Bart told him.

"No problem," Mike said. "When do you think you might get to it?"

"To tell you the truth, I don't know. But as soon as I do, I will let you know."

A week passed and Mike still hadn't heard anything about his

order. He was beginning to think that the cost of the requisition might be the problem, so when he found shirts from another subsidiary that could be used for free, he decided to contact Bart again.

"Bart, this is Mike," he said over the phone. "I've got some good news. I found a hundred shirts in the marketing department that we can use for our employees."

"Oh, yeah? That's great," Bart replied.

Mike waited for a definitive answer. When one wasn't forthcoming, he prodded, "So, what do you think?"

"Well, I'm still thinking it over," Bart stalled. "I'm not sure it's worth the expense, but I haven't made any final decisions."

A few more days passed and eventually Mike became frustrated with the process. He wasn't one to pull rank, but after being repeatedly put off, he talked to me about the situation.

I listened to his idea about the caps and shirts, and for the minimal cost, there was no question it was a great idea. Employees need to know they are appreciated, and they need to be proud of their work. Nothing makes productivity fall more quickly than a bunch of employees who feel as though they are being taken for granted and have no stake or standing in the company. So Mike's idea made perfect sense. I signed the requisition order for the shirts and caps and sent it through our purchasing department.

The next week, I met three of PSI's executives at Meadowbrook Country Club in Northville, Michigan, to play a round of golf. I was putting pretty well—until I was interrupted by my cell phone.

"I'm really sorry to bother you with this," Mike said when I picked up, "but I have some information. The order for the shirts and caps was stopped."

"Why?" I asked.

"I don't know. I only know that the COO put a stop on the order."

"I'll take care of it," I said, snapping the cell phone shut.

I wasn't sure exactly what had happened, but I had a pretty good

idea. I put away my club, walked off the green and went right over to where Bart was standing next to the golf cart.

"Did you cancel the order for the RSI caps and shirts?" I asked him directly.

He paused briefly, realizing that no matter what answer he could give, it wasn't going to be a good one.

"Yes, I did," he replied.

"Even though you knew I approved them?" I went on.

"I…I wanted to take a longer look at it," he stammered.

"I'm telling you to release the requisition right now," I exclaimed. "You've held on to it long enough with your micromanaging. You've been sitting on it for two months! Get on your phone and order those caps and shirts now. We'll deal with the rest later."

Bart was on the phone before I even finished my final sentence.

The shirts and caps were printed and shipped to Mike's office within a few days. Still, that didn't change the fact that Bart needed to control every little thing under his command. It made me question how many other employees had brought great ideas to the table only to be squashed or left unacted upon. Bart's need for control was compromising the future and productivity of the company.

The next week, I called Bart into my office and repeated everything I had said on the golf course—and then some! Though the issue of the caps and shirts was not the only problem, it did epitomize what was wrong with his executive management style. He was the COO, not the company gatekeeper. Although he didn't need to be in on every little detail, he didn't seem willing to relinquish authority or trust his employees to do their jobs on their own.

After he left my office, I knew exactly what I had to do. I contacted our attorney and arranged for a meeting. The following morning, I went into Bart's office with the attorney and the head of personnel—and with only one objective in mind.

"You haven't been making your numbers, and your microman-agement techniques don't belong in this company," I stated bluntly,

staring Bart directly in the eyes. "Get your stuff together. You're done here."

I offered him a severance package, which he took, and that was the end of it.

The last I heard, Bart was working for a company based in North Carolina, managing a much smaller number of employees. Though he is likely making less of a salary, I suspect he is happily able to continue with his micromanagement style. But for PSI, Bart was a poor fit and it was time he moved along.

After an executive or employee is fired, everyone seems to come out of the woodwork to express how horrible that person was. This fact never ceases to amaze me. I don't know if people fear losing their jobs, fear changes in their work environment or simply prefer to avoid conflict, but no one ever acknowledges the problem in front of me until that employee was gone. As soon as Bart was out the door, the same thing happened. Countless people expressed how relieved they were that he had left.

Awarding trust to people is one of my biggest strengths, although some may claim it's a weakness. It allows me to delegate authority to others, which in turn lets the company grow and opens the door for creativity and expression. Don't let Donald Trump or any of those guys fool you: No one has ever built a large, successful business entirely on their own. In fact, many companies have suffered from stagnation as a result of owners or executives maintaining too much control over every part of the process or small detail. Micromanaging is a sure way of limiting a business' potential.

Sure, giving up some aspects of control can be difficult and may sometimes come back to haunt you. But once I find out that my trust has been violated or someone's actions don't fit well with the philosophy on which I based my company, I have no problem making the tough decisions and acting upon them.

I manage from a distance and with trust in my employees—unless they do something to make me get up in their face.

CHAPTER 80

"Plane" and Simple

A couple of year ago, I had to fly out to Colorado to check on some trouble with my business. A few of my key executives were with me. They were all younger guys with no military experience among them.

About halfway through the flight, we heard a loud *pop* on the private jet—and to anyone not used to aircraft, that sound is scary as hell.

My pilot, Frank, who had been with me for twenty years and had flown a chopper in Vietnam, wasn't too worked up about it and neither was I. The same couldn't be said for the other passengers.

The rest of the flight was fine and we didn't hear any other noises. But, when we got on the ground, Frank and I immediately got out to check—and were flanked by the other guys.

I saw a hole in the bottom of the jet and knew exactly what happened.

"The refueling door snapped," I said. "It's bent all the way in."

The executives turned pale as they stared at this hole in the plane.

"What do you want me to do?" Frank asked.

"Why don't you try the usual?" I said.

"Okay," Frank answered casually. "I'll get the duct tape."

The executives' expressions were equal parts horror and disbelief.

"You're going to fix that with duct tape?" one of them asked.

"Sure," I said, checking my watch. "Let's get to that meeting."

Fixing aircraft with duct tape wasn't at all uncommon in the Air Force. Often, it was the only resource you had—and it could mean the difference between having to stay grounded in Greenland after a run or returning to the relatively comfortable base in Newfoundland.

So, needless to say, I was no stranger to the quick fix.

After taking care of business, the executives and I returned to the airport, where they immediately ran to check out Frank's handiwork. They were staring at the duct tape suspiciously, their mouths hanging open, but they weren't saying a word.

"If you want to fly commercial, go ahead," I told them. "But I'm getting in."

They all looked at each other, and then one of them spoke up. "No, if you're going to go, so are we."

He didn't sound too sure of it, but I guess they couldn't let a couple of old Air Force guys get the better of them.

When we landed safely, I could tell they had a whole new kind of respect for me.

But, in my point of view, it wasn't anything unusual. I'd built an entire business by looking for simple solutions.

If there's one thing you learn from both military service and the corporate world, it's that you do what you have to do to survive.

CHAPTER 81

Character

I'm a down-to-earth guy who tries to keep things in perspective. Though I've had opportunities to meet presidents and the Pope, sports legends and business leaders, I didn't let myself get so overwhelmed by the experiences that I forgot to appreciate the people behind the titles.

After President Bush visited the Beaver Aerospace plant in 2003, it seemed as though the location was placed on the map of political destinations. In 2008, I once again received a phone call from my congressman, this time asking if I would like to have a visit from Senator John McCain as part of his presidential campaign tour.

While meeting McCain was something I wanted to do, hosting political talks at the plant was incredibly expensive. Shutting down the machines and business operations for the day cost tens of thousands of dollars. Although I did agree to have Senator McCain speak at the facility, the decision wasn't without serious consideration.

Accompanying Senator McCain was Senator Lindsey Graham, who represented the state of South Carolina. Not only was he funny, but he was also a realist. After initial introductions were made, Senator Graham said to me, "I bet this is going to cost you a lot of money." And indeed it did.

The fact that we were hosting some of the nation's most politically powerful officials didn't cause me to ignore the costs involved. I was still very grounded and focused on business. But, I was enthused about Senator McCain's visit.

My son Bob had read a great deal about the senator prior to his trip to Beaver Aerospace, and he'd learned that the plane McCain had flown in the Vietnam War had flight-control applications made in part by our manufacturing facility at Beaver. The ball screws for which the Beaver Aerospace plant was well known were key parts of the flight component. Though this had occurred before PSI had acquired the company, the historical importance in light of McCain's visit was definitely noteworthy.

After Senator McCain made his speech, Bob walked onto the stage with a plastic model of the exact ball screw that Beaver had made for McCain's plane.

"Senator McCain," Bob began after taking the microphone, "we would like to present to you this model of a flight-control component made here at Beaver Aerospace many years ago. This replica is identical to the one that was in the plane you flew during the war."

Senator McCain took the replica and shook Bob's hand in appreciation.

"Thank you," McCain stated. He studied the model for a moment, and then he looked to the audience. "It had nothing to do with this flight control, but I must say that was a bad day to fly," he said with a grin.

It was a great experience to meet Senator McCain, and I was honored that he visited one of our company's subsidiaries.

But, I also have been honored to meet many not-so-famous people.

Recently, I had an opportunity to meet Jamie Dimon in Detroit while he was speaking at a luncheon in the Ritz-Carlton hotel. Mr. Dimon is the chairman of JP Morgan Chase and someone I have respected for a long time. He is an extremely honest man who works

very hard, leading by example and intelligence. His employees respect him and enjoy working for him, as do his executives. He is simply someone I admire, and I easily relate to him as a business leader.

After the luncheon, I introduced myself and we spoke for a while. During the course of the conversation, the topic of meeting important people came up.

"You know," I commented, "my wife tells me I have met the two most powerful men in the world: the Pope and the president."

"Who do you think is more powerful?" Dimon inquired.

I thought about that for a moment. "I really don't know," I stated. "I guess the president, since he has all the ammunition."

I have thought about that question and my answer since then, and I don't really think anyone could know who carries more power. They both have tremendous responsibilities and resources at their disposal, but true power doesn't necessarily come from that alone. Power comes from other people respecting you and believing in your leadership skill.

So, a person's principles and basic character—not title or position—are what truly gives him or her power. With that, we can all achieve great things.

PART VIII

Family Matters

CHAPTER 82

Tales From Alaska

I love business. I love talking about it, thinking about it, developing business strategies, acquiring businesses and creating new business ideas. I've been an entrepreneur from the start and I wouldn't have it any other way.

But, I'm also someone who enjoys getting away from it all once in a while and exploring the world. Believe it or not, I do know how to relax—though I never completely leave the business behind. It's my passion and it's in my blood. If I didn't still enjoy it, I wouldn't still be doing it.

Of my many outside interests and activities, fishing is one of my favorites. I routinely escape to the upper peninsula of Michigan a couple of times a year to fish or hunt and, since 1980, I have been to Alaska eight different times on fishing expeditions. To me, nothing is more simultaneously relaxing and entertaining than great fishing. Especially when you hook a big one!

My favorite fishing spot is Wood-Tikchik State Park, located in the northwestern portion of Alaska. With more than 1.6 million acres and a series of lakes up to forty-five miles in length, the park boasts some astounding fishing and scenery. Once you're among the serene, snow-peaked mountains, you become completely immersed in the environment. Plus, I always take some of my family along, which makes the experience that much more rewarding—not to

mention more fun. My son Sean said that these trips opened his eyes to nature, and that's a pretty special gift to be able to give to the next generations.

In July 2008, my oldest son, Scott; his son, Zane; my grandson Andy; my son-in-laws Brent and Steve; my good friend Mike Morse; an engineer at one of my companies, Ron Fukui; and I decided to go on another excursion to Alaska. We boarded the airplane with our gear and left from Michigan, heading to Dillingham, Alaska. There isn't much in Dillingham other than a small runway, a few houses and an old hotel. As soon as we disembarked, we realized we'd left civilization far behind. The crisp, dry air, the surrounding woods and the overall silence all welcomed us upon arrival.

From Dillingham, we drove from the lower Nushagak Bay to a lake about twenty minutes away, and then we boarded a float plane that flew us the additional hundred miles north into Wood-Tikchik State Park. The plane dipped and dove along the way, negotiating the jagged mountain peaks and coursing through wedge-shaped valleys. The landscape was so vast that the journey seemed endless and without a final destination. And that's coming from a former Air Force man!

Looking out over the terrain, we couldn't make out any buildings or homes; hardly even a roadway could be detected. All we could see were miles and miles of evergreens and occasional lakes dotted among the rolling mountains. Then, out of this seemingly uncharted terrain, we finally arrived at our destination: Tikchik Narrows Lodge.

I have stayed at Tikchik Narrows Lodge many times, but on every trip, I am amazed by its appearance. The lodge sits at the very tip of a narrow peninsula that separates Tikchik Lake and Nuyukuk Lake. The thin channel of water between the peninsula's tip and the far shore is what defines Tikchik Narrows. The lodge itself is made of stone and cedar, and a circular, glass-encased dining area sits up high, overlooking the lakes and the mountains in the background.

This rustic scene might not be everyone's idea of paradise, but it comes pretty close for me.

We got settled into our cabins and woke up the following morning at six o'clock so that our guide could fly us in the float plane to one of the nearby lakes. This wasn't the type of vacation where we slept in, lounged around a pool and read the newspaper. But, as soon as we were flying among the Alaskan mountains and casting fishing lines from a boat into a pristine lake, any thoughts of stress or feelings of tiredness evaporated entirely.

My grandson Zane had just turned thirteen years old, and he had already become quite good at fishing. His father, Scott, is an avid fly fisherman and travels all over the country each year to test his own skills against those of the fish. I'm sure Zane picked up some of his father's talents along the way. My son-in-law Steve and my grandson Andy, are also knowledgeable fishermen. They were all there to see how they would fare fishing for king salmon, rainbow trout, grayling, Arctic char and a variety of other local fish. We'd come to the right place: Alaska offers some of the best fishing in the world.

On this particular trip, we were all patiently waiting and casting when Zane suddenly felt a pull on his line. For the next forty-five minutes, he struggled with a fish as big as he was, pulling and releasing repeatedly, trying to coax it into the boat. A couple of times he wanted to give up, but Scott encouraged him to keep at it. Finally, he was able to gather a net around the fish and drag it into the boat. It was a huge king salmon.

"Zane, that fish is as tall as you are!" I exclaimed.

"How much do you think it weighs?" Zane asked.

"Forty-five pounds," I stated with authority.

"How do you know, Grandpa?"

"Because that's how many minutes it took you to get him into the boat."

About fifteen years ago, I had caught a king salmon about the

same size, and I had asked my guide the same exact question. His answer had been the one I'd given Zane.

All of the guides I have ever had in Alaska have been impressive people. During the summer, most of them work there as fishing guides but their duties involve much more than just fishing. Most have pilots' licenses in order to fly float planes for their clients, and all of them know how to handle the unexpected.

Ten years ago, while I was fishing in Alaska, casting and reeling off the lake's shoreline with eight other fishermen, the guy in front of me suddenly hooked a large salmon on his line. As he began to reel the fish onto shore, a brown grizzly bear came running from the woods, charging directly toward the man with the fish. Before any of us could react, the bear had ripped the salmon off the hook and headed back into the woods. Everyone froze. Our guide pulled out his gun just in case the bear decided to charge our party, but the rest of us simply stayed very still.

After a few minutes, all remained quiet, so, like true fishermen, we naturally resumed fishing. As soon as our lines were cast, the brown bear appeared out of the woods again. He wasn't running this time; instead, he meandered toward the shoreline to check things out. The bear had found an easy way to score a meal—or so he thought. But, without a fish on anyone's line, he soon lost interest and went back into the woods.

"You know, this is worse than before," our guide stated.

"Why's that?" I asked, a little concerned.

"At least when he was on the shoreline, we knew where he was," he said with a smile.

One of my favorite guides was Ray Loshie—a true outdoorsman, an Alaskan man's man. He had a scar from where a bear had taken a chunk out of his arm, and he told stories about how he'd had to fight

off grizzlies with knives on several occasions. Ray served as my guide on many of my trips to Tikchik Narrows, and all of those times I never knew exactly what to expect from him.

For most guides, working in Alaska was their summer job. When the winter months came, many headed to South America, where they got jobs as guides as well; Argentina and Brazil were some of the more common destinations. One evening at the end of my trip, I was sitting around a fire with several of the guides. Ray was there, and they all began talking about where they would be heading soon, after the season was over.

"I'm taking my plane and heading to the Baja peninsula," one of the guides said.

"I'll be in Patagonia, Argentina," another stated.

"Where will you be heading, Ray?" I asked.

"Oh, I'll be heading south as well," he said in a very matter-of-fact way.

"South where?" I inquired.

"All the way south to Spokane, Washington," he replied with a grin.

Ray wasn't much for venturing outside of his domain, but he was definitely skilled and absolutely without fear. Those were good traits to have anywhere, but particularly in Alaska. Or in any part of the business world.

⁓

Zane and the rest of us caught a lot of fish that week and, as always, the trip was incredible. Every evening, we returned to the lodge, unpacked our gear and then got ready for dinner, which was prepared for us in the main dining area. In the summer, as many as forty other guests were usually there, and in a crowd that size, there were always a few characters ready to entertain everyone.

Our trip in 2008 was no different. One man who had been

Detroit. He was a banker and had to be back sooner than we did. So much for bankers' hours.

So, Betty and I sent the couple back and decided to fly commercially for the remainder of the trip. We took a short flight from Barbados to Puerto Rico for what we hoped would be a more relaxing vacation.

We arrived at Puerto Rico's airport and took a taxi to our hotel, but as we entered through the revolving glass doors, we received an unexpected and not-so-pleasant surprise. The entire lobby was packed with people, many of them camped out on the floor or sitting on their luggage. It looked as if Betty and I had entered some kind of impromptu sit-in. This didn't bode well for us.

Apparently, one of the large cruise ships had been delayed due to weather or technical difficulties, and all the passengers were refusing to give up their hotel rooms until the ship arrived. That meant that all the other guests arriving with reservations were stuck out in the lobby. One look around the front of that hotel and Betty and I chose to keep on moving. Both of us got the message then: It was time for us to go home.

Direct flights to Detroit from Puerto Rico didn't exist in 1977, so we had to catch a connecting flight in New York. Unfortunately, we weren't the only ones with that plan. The line at the airline counter was a serpentine mass of humanity inching forward one body and one piece of luggage at a time. We waited patiently at first, moving our suitcases forward to secure our place behind all the other unfortunate travelers. It was turning into the trip from hell, and I didn't think we would ever get home.

Inching up in line, I noticed three men standing off to the side. None of them were actually in line, and every so often they spoke in Italian to one another while glancing in our general direction. As Betty and I moved forward toward the airline's counter, I noticed that those men were stepping forward as well. Soon, it became all too

obvious to me that they were trying to cut in line like students in a grade school cafeteria.

Given the type of day Betty and I were having, the last thing I was going to put up with was anyone inconveniencing me further in order to save themselves some hassle and time.

"Listen," I said to the Italian man closest to me, "do you speak English?"

"Yes," he replied with a thick accent.

"If you and your buddies move your suitcases forward one more inch, you're gonna wish you hadn't," I stated. "It's not a good day to mess with me."

That was enough for them. They picked up their luggage and left.

Our saga, however, was far from over. Betty and I finally boarded a plane to New York—and found ourselves squashed between two large women traveling with what appeared to be all their worldly belongings. We somehow survived the three-and-a-half-hour flight and finally arrived in New York City, only to have to catch another flight then to get home. Take my word for it: Detroit never looked so good!

Considering our first vacation experience to Barbados, it's a wonder Betty and I had any desire ever to return.

Over the next few years, we sampled different vacation destinations each winter. The first year, we tried the American Virgin Islands. Our trip was alright but lacked anything close to quality service. The following year, we tried the British Virgin Islands, but they seemed too quiet for our tastes. A lack of interesting destinations and golf courses made them far less than appealing to me.

We then tried the Dominican Republic, which was too laid back

in some parts and too dicey in others. No matter where we went, we couldn't seem to find the vacation spot that was just right for us.

But, in 1985, I found myself on a layover in LaGuardia Airport and across from me on the concourse was a small travel agency. In vivid color, an advertisement for a beautiful, tropical villa seemed to be calling out to me. After a few weeks of winter's chill, the images of pristine, warm waters and white beaches certainly grabbed my attention. I went inside without hesitation and gathered information about the villa.

It turned out to be located in Barbados, and its landlord also owned one of the island's hotels. He lived in the actual advertised villa, which was named Bachelor Hall, but every winter he left Barbados to visit London for six weeks or so. The arrangement couldn't have been any better. Six weeks was the perfect amount of time for Betty and me to have a winter getaway, and the season on the island was ideal as well. I talked it over with her when I got home and we agreed to give Barbados another try.

Bachelor Hall was a great place; rather than being on the Atlantic side of the island, the villa was located on the Caribbean side. The waters were calmer, the beaches were nicer and that area of the island had many activities that were ideal for Betty and me. Our trip couldn't have been more relaxing and enjoyable—though I did manage to get in a few business calls.

Since that year, we have traveled to Barbados every January for our winter break.

Many of our family members have joined us there over the years. All of our grandchildren have very fond memories of Barbados. We also had close friends who would often come and go during our stays there.

We rented Bachelor Hall from the same guy for ten years. But, in time, he had to oversee some major renovations at the hotel, which meant he would be staying in his villa instead of renting it out. For Betty and me, that meant finding a new spot on the island of which we had grown very fond.

I asked our landlord at Bachelor Hall if he knew of any other villas to rent and he put me in touch with a friend of his from London who also vacationed in Barbados. The following week, I contacted her. The friend's name was Hazel Sapcote, and she was a pistol—a very attractive woman with an entertaining personality. A former flight attendant for British Airways, she had connected with a wealthy English businessman during the course of her travels. The two eventually married, and they shared a villa in Barbados.

Hazel was excited to meet Betty and me; we had lunch with her while visiting London later that year, and the next winter we rented her villa, which was spectacular. It was fully staffed with household personnel, and the accommodations and location were exceptional. The only problem we ever encountered was with her butler, Arnold. He was all too familiar with the rum shop across the road and was often late for work—not to mention a little intoxicated when he finally did show up. Hazel had decided to make Arnold her own personal project, hoping to cure him of his addiction, but I questioned whether he wanted to be cured. Betty and I only stayed at Hazel's villa once, but our experience there only furthered our love for the island.

Sam Mahone was the manager of the agency who rented Hazel's villa. One day while we were there, Sam approached me about another villa owned by yet another Englishman. He and I walked down a sandy path, through a patch of trees across from a beautiful beach. Hidden behind a wooded area, a set of gates opened to reveal a magnificent villa. The layout, the staff and the butler were exceptional.

For the next twelve years, this villa, St. Helena, became our destination when traveling to Barbados. And, of all the places we stayed, it was easily our favorite. We shared many wonderful memories there, just the two of us and with our children and grandchildren.

Because of the number of trips we made to St. Helena, Betty and I became acquainted with some of the other people on the island of Barbados. Two men we came to know especially well rented the villa

adjacent to ours. Their names were Allen and Ray, and they were also from Britain.

Allen was slightly heavy, Ray much thinner. It was a little like looking at Laurel and Hardy. Both men had become successful despite their very humble beginnings; they'd grown up poor in the United Kingdom. Allen told of times when, as a child, he'd collected lumps of coal that fell off the railway cars so that his family could have heat. Interestingly, both of them had subsequently made fortunes in the coal mining and trucking industries. See what I mean when I say that all things happen for a reason?

The villa in which Allen and Ray stayed on Barbados had a tennis court, so Betty and I occasionally played a few matches with them. However, more often, all of us would go golfing on some of the great courses that the island had to offer—especially the Royal Westmoreland, which was one of my favorites.

One of the highlights during our winters at the St. Helena villa was always the Valentine's Day party that Allen and Ray hosted. Being very social people, they would invite everyone residing along the beach to attend their party each year. During the afternoon on Valentine's Day, they would get things started with a party for the local Barbadian kids; activities included sack races, games and even sailboat rides.

Once the sun went down, the two men would welcome their guests for the evening. It was always a costume party, and people wore all sorts of elaborate getups. The parties were always guaranteed to be loads of fun. Betty, of course, was especially fond of the celebrations since Valentine's Day has always been her favorite holiday.

After a few years, Allen and Ray decided to travel to another destination, choosing to spend their subsequent winters in South Africa instead of Barbados. But, Betty and I were glad to have met them. They were generous people who were always happy to share whatever they had, and we became good friends throughout the years. It just went to show that friendship is what really makes life richer.

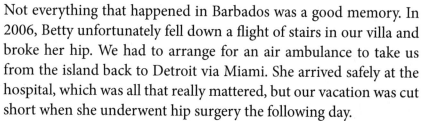

Not everything that happened in Barbados was a good memory. In 2006, Betty unfortunately fell down a flight of stairs in our villa and broke her hip. We had to arrange for an air ambulance to take us from the island back to Detroit via Miami. She arrived safely at the hospital, which was all that really mattered, but our vacation was cut short when she underwent hip surgery the following day.

The next year, again at St. Helena, one of our grandchildren suffered a less severe injury. The owners were fully aware of our series of accidents but, despite our having stayed there every year for more than a decade, they never contacted us during those times to see how we were making out. Since I was accustomed to common courtesy, their lack of communication bothered me, so Betty and I chose not to return to St. Helena after that year.

The following January, the accommodations we rented were less of a villa and more of a mansion. The house was not on the water, and its layout wasn't all that great for children; it just didn't work out well for us. So, we went back to searching for a place to stay. For the next two years, we rented a home on the beach, but it was too close to the road and was quite noisy.

Next year, we will again be looking for the ideal villa destination.

Despite a few drawbacks, Betty and I have been perfectly happy with Barbados for the past twenty-five years. For two months out of every year since 1985 it has been our home away from home. In fact, this year we were notified that we are eligible for honorary citizenship!

Without question, Betty and I have many special memories of our time spent on the island, as well as memories of friends and family who have visited us while we have stayed there. Barbados has become not only an important part of our history but also a rich part of my children's and grandchildren's travel experiences. Hopefully, it

will be a place they enjoy as much as Betty and I have for many years to come.

My success in business has made it possible for me to escape the business world every so often. More importantly, it has given me quality time to spend with my family and friends. Now, who says business isn't personal?

CHAPTER 84

Island Night Noises

Because members of our family often come to stay with us in Barbados, at one point Betty and I arranged to have a night watchman for our villa. Crime doesn't run rampant in Barbados but some security still seemed reasonable. Though we had a few different night guards over the years, one in particular, a man named Frank, was more of a character than the rest.

Frank had somehow gotten hold of an old Barbados police uniform—the cap, the suit, the whole nine yards—which he wore to work every evening. He also carried a wooden baton similar to a police nightstick. I don't think he ever used it, but it was part of his normal attire. Though he appeared a little unkempt, he was proud of his uniform; he even walked down the driveway on his arrival every evening with a bit of a strut.

A classic Frank idiosyncrasy was his signature way of greeting everyone in the house. He would come on duty in the evening, so, naturally, saying "goodnight" was more appropriate than "good morning." But, instead of a simple "goodnight," Frank would always wish everyone a melodic "night, night" as he made his rounds. The combination of the singsong quality of his speech and his Barbadian accent made it fun for the kids to imitate. In fact, even the house staff at the villa had noticed it and did a pretty good imitation of Frank on occasion.

One year while we were in Barbados, my daughter, Amy, her husband, Mike, and their newborn baby, Jack, came for a much-needed getaway. After the first weekend, however, Mike had to return to Detroit to handle business, leaving Amy and Jack behind. I figured that since we had Frank at our disposal anyway, I might as well use his services to keep an eye on them.

"Frank," I said as he came in to work one evening, "I have an important job for you to do."

"Yes, Mr. Phillips?" he replied enthusiastically.

"My daughter, Amy, and her baby are here. They're staying in the bedroom on the first floor. I want you to put a chair there and take a post outside their room."

"I'd be glad to, Mr. Phillips," he replied. "I'll take care of it."

That evening, Frank took up his position outside Amy's room just as she managed to get her newborn to sleep after much effort. If you've ever had to coax an infant to sleep, you know that the ensuing silence and peacefulness is certainly something to relish—and that any noise might erase all your efforts and place you back at square one, with a screaming baby to boot. But, all was quiet and Frank was on guard, so what could possibly have gone wrong?

A little after midnight, Amy was sound asleep. The room was dark and the hallway barely shed a sliver of light beneath her doorway. Everything was perfectly quiet. Then, in the midst of the tranquility, there was a loud and sudden noise.

Clank!

The same, sharp sound rang out again and then a few more times afterward, decreasing in volume. Shortly, the quiet returned. In the aftermath, Amy, wide awake, could hear Frank rustling in the chair outside her door. She didn't know what the noise was, but she felt comforted that he was keeping watch. Fortunately, the baby hadn't woken up, and Amy gradually went back to sleep.

About an hour later, the house had again become perfectly still. Then, once again, the silence was interrupted.

Clank!

The noise sounded again, with the same echoing ending as before. Amy sat up in bed and looked at the crib for any motion or noise. But, the baby remained silent except for the soft sounds of his breathing. Again, she heard Frank moving around in his chair. She lay there in bed a little longer, trying to figure out what the noise had been, but eventually she went back to sleep without a clear answer.

At three o'clock in the morning, the same loud disruption happened again. This time Amy lost her patience—and finally figured out what the noise was.

"Frank!" she exclaimed. "Lay the nightstick on the ground!"

He didn't reply, but we can assume he did as he was told since that was the last interruption of the evening. The noise had been his wooden stick hitting the marble floor repeatedly as he'd drifted off to sleep. Every time he'd dozed in his chair, the stick had struck the ground, serving as his alarm clock. Unfortunately for Amy, it had woken her up as well.

Well, at least it was good to know that Frank was alert and on guard!

By the time Amy and Jack woke up the next morning, Frank's shift was over and he had gone home; he worked from seven at night until seven in the morning. When my daughter and grandson came to breakfast, she detailed the events of the previous night and we all got a good laugh out of Frank's trusty nightstick and his apparent inability to stay awake. By the time breakfast was over, even Amy was laughing about it.

Believe it or not, Frank was actually one of the better night guards we had in Barbados. All of the night staff, especially the guards, were notorious for dozing off during their shifts—though Frank's enthusiasm helped make up for his nighttime naps. He was always smiling and loved to be around small kids. Betty and I have a photograph of him sitting with our granddaughter, who was five years old at the time, and the picture shows his easygoing personality.

Not all of our night watchmen were as entertaining as Frank. When Betty and I stayed at the villa, Hazel insisted that we have a guard at night to help watch the place since our grandchildren were visiting. She arranged for Arnold, the head butler, to find someone who would stand guard outside the villa at night.

After dinner one evening, I was sitting on the veranda overlooking the backyard. The moon was full and, combined with the night lamps scattered along the walkways, lit the lawn fairly well. The night was quiet except for the chirping of bugs and the sound of the ocean.

Soon, I saw three shadows appear in the middle of the yard. One was Arnold, whose figure I knew well; the second was our new night guard; and the third was a smaller shadow attached to a leash. This turned out to be a German shepherd—our first line of defense against any intruder.

As I sat on the back patio and watched, Arnold and the other man tied the German shepherd to a small post in the middle of the backyard. The dog was attached to a rope that allowed him to roam in a circle with a radius of four or five yards. Once that was finished, Arnold led the other man toward the laundry room located near the back of the house. I didn't quite understand why Arnold was showing him that area, but at the time, I didn't think much about it. I figured he was just getting the guard acquainted with the lay of the land.

Some time later, I went upstairs, read for a while and eventually fell asleep, assuming I would have a peaceful night's rest on the island with nothing to worry about. But, at two o'clock in the morning, I listened as the German shepherd barked continuously for more than ten minutes. I finally forced myself out of bed. From my window, I could see the problem: The poor dog had made several laps around the post to which he was tied and gotten tangled up in his leash. He could barely move at all, having knotted himself pretty well against the post.

I looked around the backyard through the bedroom window. No one else was around except the dog. Then, I made my way downstairs to see where the night watchman had gone.

"Guard! Guard!" I yelled as I walked out into the yard.

There was no answer, only the sound of the barking dog.

"Get out here and take care of this dog!" I yelled.

Still, no one appeared. I shouted a few more times, then considered trying to loosen the animal from his trap, but I didn't think approaching a worked-up German shepherd in the middle of the night was the best idea. Finally, I gave up and went back to bed, but I was none too happy.

The dog settled down and finally became quiet. Or, so I thought. When I got back up to peer out over the lawn, I noticed that the German shepherd was gone. The guard, who had most likely avoided my shouts, had waited for me to leave before taking the dog and hightailing it out of there. It suddenly occurred to me then why Arnold had shown him the laundry room in the first place: That was where he would get a good night's sleep while the dog did his job.

The guard must have figured it was better to leave after I had returned to bed than to stick around for the aftermath the next morning—and he was very much right about that.

Of course, back home at my place of business, if I had caught people sleeping on the job, there'd have be nowhere for them to hide. I'd have found them and made sure I gave them the proper send-off before escorting them out the door myself. I hadn't earned the nickname "Thermonuclear Bill" for nothing!

But, this was Barbados—a different world. And, a few night-time interruptions on rare occasions weren't about to ruin our time there.

That guard had just better hope he never finds himself in Michigan, looking for a job at PSI.

CHAPTER 85

It's in the Genes

I've often heard entrepreneurs described as "self-made men." That's an interesting trick. True, they might have started their own companies, but I'm fairly certain someone else had a hand in their existence here on Earth.

Regardless of the successes I've achieved, I understand the important role of family in my life.

One thing is for certain: You can't escape your family (not that I'd want to!). Whether direct influences or inherited traits affect who you become, your family is with you one way or the other. My most significant influences came from my own parents. I've already illustrated my father's inventiveness in the story about the lawn sprinkler he designed and we sold together, and the fact that he was willing to move our family around to find the best opportunities for us showed that he was anything but risk-averse.

But, my mother's influence was equally important not just on my business but on my successful relationships with my own children. She was a sweet, Southern lady who used to have my kids over for some traditional Southern fried cooking (which they'd jokingly referred to as "health food") in order to give Betty and me some time to ourselves.

To my mother, I was always "Billy Tom." Almost everyone else was "baby."

"Be sweet, baby," she'd tell my kids as they left her house—and

that simple phrase would stay with them for the course of the day. My daughter, Terry, told me that when she had a choice between doing something sweet or not so sweet, she'd think about what her grandmother had told her and take the right action.

I'd like to think that I inherited my mother's generous, loving and kind traits when it came to my own close-knit family. And, while I wouldn't necessarily use the word "sweet" to describe how I conducted myself in business, I always tried to do the things that would make her most proud.

For example, one of the biggest repair contracts we had at PSI was with General Motors; it accounted for about one-third of our business at the time. When their contract went back up for bid, the competitors lined up—despite the fact that GM only wanted to pay thirty-five dollars an hour, which wouldn't have been enough for any company to turn a profit. Our competitors' plan, I suppose, was to inflate the amount of hours they spent on the projects in order to make up for the low hourly rate. PSI could've done the same thing.

In the end, GM wanted to remain with us. The only problem was, I wouldn't falsify the hours to make us more money. For one thing, it wasn't honest. For another, it would send my workers the message that it was okay for them to pad their hours. What kind of employees would I have then? To me, it just wasn't a smart business move.

So, I let the contract go. It was more important to me to do the right thing. That has always been the criteria for my company. Everything we do is bounced up against that. I guess that's just how my mother raised me.

My mother was pregnant with my sister, Gail, when we first moved to Michigan. Although Gail wasn't born in Arkansas, I have to admit that she turned out more than alright. She is a good friend to Betty, who helped her with her homework—and life in general—when she was still in high school. I also maintain a close relationship with Gail despite our age difference and the geographical distance between us (she now lives in California).

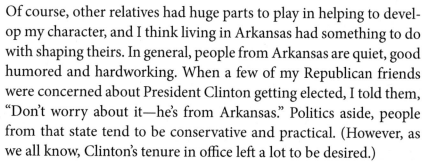

Of course, other relatives had huge parts to play in helping to develop my character, and I think living in Arkansas had something to do with shaping theirs. In general, people from Arkansas are quiet, good humored and hardworking. When a few of my Republican friends were concerned about President Clinton getting elected, I told them, "Don't worry about it—he's from Arkansas." Politics aside, people from that state tend to be conservative and practical. (However, as we all know, Clinton's tenure in office left a lot to be desired.)

I'd say that my paternal grandfather from Jackson County, Arkansas, made the strongest impression on me, especially at a very early age. I spent a great deal of time watching him run his farm, and his work ethic, eagerness to learn and creativity made quiet impressions on me that have helped me greatly as an individual and an entrepreneur. Had I stayed in Arkansas for a longer portion of my childhood, the influence of this impressive man might have been even more profound.

Among my grandfather's greatest qualities were his patience and sense of calm when things didn't go smoothly. I am certainly more reactive than he was, but his temperament still taught me the value of stepping back to examine a situation. During some of my corporate acquisitions, such patience and persistence made the difference between my success and a lost opportunity.

When I was a boy, my grandfather had a horse that he liked to ride. It was nothing fancy like a stallion or thoroughbred—just a solid saddle horse, jet black in color and as spooked as any animal I had ever seen. The slightest movement or noise caused it to jump. One day, as I sat on one of the farm's fences, I watched my grandfather attempt to get up into the saddle.

"Whoa! Whoa!" he said soothingly as he placed his left foot in the stirrup.

But, the horse began to step up and down nervously while my

grandfather pulled the reins tighter and tighter. The harder my grandfather tried to swing his other leg over the horse, the more the horse spun around. Before my grandfather knew what had happened, the horse had somehow gotten its right rear hoof caught in the right stirrup and was balancing on three legs. Meanwhile, my grandfather had his right leg halfway over the horse, trying to straddle it. The two of them teetered precariously in that position without toppling over. But, instead of yelling and panicking, my grandfather responded calmly, as always.

"Look, ol' boy. If you're gonna get on, then I'm gonna get off!" he told the horse as I laughed out loud.

No matter what, I never saw him visibly rattled. The few times I did see my grandfather get angry or upset, he walked off quietly to be by himself. To me, that's a man of control. I guess you could say he taught me how to lead by example and hold on to the reins in spite of everything that might be happening around me.

My father had four brothers and one sister and he described my grandfather as being hard, particularly on his sons. (That was something I tried to avoid with my own children; I put everyone through their paces equally and taught them that we were all in this together.) My oldest uncle was named Lawrence and though I hardly knew him, his success as an entrepreneur was well known. The few times I saw him, he was driving a new car and lived in a nice, stately, brick home in Little Rock, Arkansas. It wasn't a mansion, but I could tell that my uncle lived very comfortably.

Lawrence wasn't really too close to any of his family members, but I often thought of him as I came to realize my entrepreneurial nature. He'd used his experience on my grandfather's farm to provide farming equipment to customers, which was how he'd become

successful. I wish I had known him better. I believe he could have taught me a great deal.

On my mother's side of the family, her brother, Sylvester, had the greatest influence on me in terms of success. My mother had grown up initially in the Ozark Mountains and, in 1928, her father had moved their family into the delta region of Arkansas. The Ozarks were too mountainous for farming, so my mother's family migrated to better terrain. They ended up living in Tuckerman, Arkansas, and the family survived by farming corn, cotton and a few other crops. Even on the farm, however, Sylvester couldn't help but become a talented entrepreneur.

Uncle Sylvester—or Vester, as we called him—had a fleet of trucks that hauled various equipment and materials from one place to another. This was his profession throughout much of my childhood. He subsequently owned some small grocery stores and eventually developed a stave mill. Staves are the individual wood strips that are curved to form wooden barrels, and Vester did very well with this endeavor. Each of his businesses enabled him to tackle larger projects. In essence, with each business came new opportunities.

Vester's big success came when he got into the business of making charcoal. In 1959, he opened a charcoal mill, Keeter Charcoal, and shortly afterward landed a contract with Safeway Corporation to supply them with bagged charcoal. Safeway owned stores on the West Coast and eventually grew to become a national chain. Vester became wealthy literally overnight.

Vester had not only survived in a competitive business; he'd succeeded even though he had started with nothing. When I struggled during my early years with customers, business decisions and partners, it was Uncle Vester who gave me good advice...and took me fishing in the Ozarks on occasion.

Another relative who has played a major role in my life is my cousin, Hal Keeter. We often go hunting and fishing at my lodge

in the Upper Peninsula, and I always enjoy any time we spend together.

Both of my parents' families gave me excellent opportunities to learn from their examples and experiences—and, somewhere in there, I'm sure genetics played a part. The entrepreneurial spirit seemed to have been passed on to me through the generations. And it's a heritage I'm happy to have.

CHAPTER 86

Family Business

No matter how big it grows or how far advanced it becomes, PSI is, at its heart, a family business.

As far back as 1972, I had some of my kids pushing brooms, cleaning bathrooms or scraping wax off the floor at my first office early on Saturday mornings. Lynn, Donna, Lisa and Terry were my original janitorial team; in succession, Scott, Bob, Amy and Sean joined in, too. They got about five dollars each for their work, which wasn't a bad day's pay. The point was to teach them to pitch in and work out any problems among themselves. In fact, that's my philosophy with family: You include everyone and you work it out.

But, the lessons didn't stop there.

Instead of giving my kids the actual five-dollar bills, I would have my secretary hand them each a check made out for the amount. Then, I'd bring them to the bank where they could cash their checks. That way, they'd learn about earning money and where it really came from. I didn't go as far as withholding taxes, though. I figured they'd learn that from the government soon enough!

Just like in the corporate world, my kids could get fired for not getting along, trying to pass the buck, being lazy, making excuses or complaining too much. In that case, they would have to go sit in the car until their brothers and sisters finished their work. If you think that was the easy way out, remember that it gets pretty cold in

Michigan in the winter—and they'd still have to suck it up and come back the next Saturday!

The upside is that they also got promotions. As my company grew, most of my children came in to do secretarial work, repair jobs, accounting, sales, tech and hydraulic teardown (which they referred to as "being grease monkeys") during their high school and college years or later. My daughter Terry ran a side office for me until it was integrated into the main business; after first working at PSI, she decided on a business accounting major in college and is now on our board of directors.

My daughter Lynn took care of the Houston plant for a few years and my youngest, Sean, worked for a while in Mountain Secure Systems in Colorado until he decided, much like his father, that he had a driving desire *not* to work for anyone but himself. Though it would be nice to have him onboard, I can't help but respect his decision.

My oldest son, Scott, started as part of the janitorial crew, then moved on to equipment repair, sales, engineer and design work on systems and machines, management, and his current position as president of four of our companies. Today, my son Bob is the vice president of marketing and advertising. I thought it was important that, like everyone else, they start at the ground floor and work their way up. That way, I know my business is in the best possible hands.

My son-in-law Steve, who is married to Terry, is my customer service manager and my son-in-law Mike, married to Amy (who got her degree in advertising), is the president of RSI and serves as general counsel. My sister, Gail Johnston, has three daughters living in Michigan, and one of them works for PSI. I'm also proud to say that a third generation has started here, too: my grandsons Ben and Andy. And, with twenty grandchildren so far, I expect a few more will help keep the family business running well into the future.

Not only does each member bring a lot of individual talent to the

table, but customers also like to know the family behind the company. For me, though, the greatest satisfaction is seeing my children and grandchildren sharing in what I built. That's more a measure of my success than anything else ever could be.

———

Compared to most families today, having eight children might seem uncommon and overwhelming—in fact, it could qualify us to get our own reality show! But for us, a large family was quite natural.

Betty was raised Catholic and I later became Catholic. So, why shouldn't we have had the traditional Catholic-sized family and helped out with the church's head count? Seriously, though, I have always believed that people are what make life truly rich, and nothing has proven this to me more than my children.

With eight kids, we had the recipe for a tight-knit family or an all-out brawl. Fortunately, in our home, it turned out to be the former. Everything was well managed and ran pretty smoothly, and the older siblings automatically helped out with raising the younger ones. That's not to say that our household was rigid or overly restrictive, just that it was structured around respect and responsibility.

For instance, even though I take education extremely seriously and made sure that all of my children got college degrees, I never got angry about their grades—though I did check their citizenship scores closely to see if they were behaving well, paying attention in class and getting along with others. To me, that said more about who they were as people than how they did in phys ed or home ec.

When my kids were young, they would hand me their report cards and I would ask one simple thing: "Did you do your best?" That sense of accountability stayed with them all through school because they knew they were going to have to answer that question eventually—and that their answer to me better have been a "yes." They knew

I believed in commitment and character and didn't approve of doing things halfway. If they tried their hardest and failed, fine. Then, it wasn't a failure after all; it was a challenge they attempted to meet.

Of course, that same principle applies to business as well, and I have to admit that I learned a few things from my family on that front. Providing my children with a certain lifestyle was a motivating factor for most of my life; it gave me an even stronger sense of purpose and a deeper understanding of what achievement could mean. I wouldn't have been half as successful without them.

When our first child, Lynn, was already about six or seven, I was still struggling to make ends meet in business. Still, I decided to surprise Betty one day by buying her a dress. To this day, I remember the look on her face and our daughter's face when they saw it—that is, until the purchase showed up on my credit and I realized I couldn't afford it. Having to return that dress was one of the more difficult things I've had to do, but it didn't deflate me. Instead, it made me that much more determined.

Success to me isn't about hoarding money—it's about living. I want the people closest to me to partake in the good things in life without the kind of hardship or struggles that I saw my grandparents and parents go through, and that I had to overcome myself. Life is about other people, anyway. And, I'm grateful to be able to have so much to share with my family.

Sure, part of that's financial. I have a private plane that I use to bring the grandkids to me or to go see my son and daughter's families in Colorado. I have Heart's Content, the cottage (which my kids call "the compound") in Michigan's Upper Peninsula so that we can all have family vacations and fish together. I give my grandchildren debit cards for birthdays and Christmas so they can budget the balance throughout the year and learn the value of money. Money is freedom. It allows us to enjoy these things together with fewer restrictions.

But, money isn't what's most important. Without family, my jet would be spending a lot more time gathering dust in the hangar and Heart's Content would be nothing more than a nice name for an empty cabin in the wilderness.

In their own individual ways, all of my children have flourished both personally and professionally. They are all great people in their own rights.

Knowing that we have provided well for our family and seeing our children thrive as adults is very gratifying to Betty and me. More than anything, that has given us the greatest comfort and sense of pride. That, to me, is the definition of success.

And, I have my kids to thank for it.

CHAPTER 87

Teach Your Children Well

Any parent will tell you that kids don't always listen. But, believe me, sometimes they're listening when you don't even know it. And, they pick up a lot more by example.

Family life and the business world both have that in common: Your actions speak louder than words.

———

Take, for example, my daughter Lynn's conversation with her attorney about some investment options: "I'm gonna go with my father's advice," she told him. "Never take a partner and never run out of cash." Those are my golden rules! And, how good it was to hear that my children were not only paying attention but were actually putting them into practice.

When my son Sean went into business for himself, he had to take on partners for financial reasons. But, he was sure to keep fifty-one percent of the ownership. That one percent made all the difference, since having control reduces risk. That was how he'd always seen me run my own company.

———

The area in Herman, Michigan, on the Upper Peninsula, where we eventually built our cabin, used to be nothing more than empty, overgrown land and a trailer. My sons were involved in creating trails there and the only road to get to the lake was on our property. It was the perfect spot. Or, so we thought…

It turned out that we had built our cabin a mere three feet onto state land. I offered to buy that property, but the bureaucrats weren't having it. After they rejected all of my proposals, it became clear to me that there was only one thing left to do: move the mountain to Mohammad. So that's what I did: lifted up the entire structure and shifted it a hundred feet.

It sure cost me enough, and the state lost out on a chance to make some money, but there were three things I wanted my family to know: Never suffer foolishness. Don't make unnecessary compromises. And, find a way to solve it—no matter what.

The goal is to get it accomplished, not to sit around worrying about the workload or focusing on the obstacles.

That wasn't the only time my family saw that same principle put into action. My daughter Lisa and her family live out in Kalamazoo, Michigan, so it's sometimes hard for them to make it to family functions or holidays with the rest of us. One time, she told me that they were trying to get to our house for Christmas but there was fourteen inches of snow on the ground and they had to turn around. She said her teenagers were so disappointed about not seeing Grandma and Grandpa.

Well, I wasn't going to let that happen again.

The next holiday, I chartered a huge Indian Trails tour bus and brought the whole family out to Kalamazoo! When we arrived, I told her, "You can't say we weren't there."

My wife and I both make sure that's something our children and grandchildren can never say about us. Betty has always been there for our family. She shows up. And my children tell me that they can count on me to step up to the plate as well.

After our youngest daughter, Amy, had her baby boys, Betty and I came over to help out. She said that ever since she and her siblings were young, they'd seen how important family was to us—so it became important to them as well.

That's a trait I definitely see in each of my children. They work as a team, they look out for one another and they solve problems together. They've even driven halfway down I-94 in Michigan in order to meet and take each other's kids for the weekends so the cousins could spend time together.

I've also seen it each year—for the last ten or fifteen years—at our traditional Thanksgiving family football games, which even our college-aged grandkids look forward to. My son Bob had the idea to print up Phillips family sweatshirts each year and hand them out to everyone on the field. Okay, so maybe there's a little healthy competition—which helps in sports and business, after all, since you can't be afraid of conflict. But, what I see most of all is teamwork.

The same principles that keep our family close are what account for the senior group of workers who stay at PSI: loyalty, accessibility, camaraderie and honesty. It works the same with eight kids and twenty grandkids as it does with 600 employees: You don't lie, you don't back out of a deal, you be there when you should be and you do what you say you will.

Those are the basic rules in life that have made me a good salesman, a good businessman and—most importantly—a good family man.

CHAPTER 88

Giving Back

They say that charity begins at home and I believe it. After all, if you can't be kind to and help out those you love in whatever way you can, where does that leave you?

I've got an answer: It leaves you alone in this world as one selfish S.O.B. That wasn't a rhetorical question.

~~~

My philosophy is "Live a good life, but don't screw up the end game." So although charity does begin at home, it shouldn't end there. It should extend to your community—your neighbors, friends, co-workers and customers—as well as to your company. From a business standpoint, a strong, healthy community benefits everyone; that's why each branch of PSI employs people from the surrounding area and spearheads a variety of local charitable programs.

Success isn't about money; it's about living. If you use what you have to help impact the lives of others, you can really change things for the better. That's why most of the entrepreneurs I know got into business in the first place: to make a difference.

Of course, I am a businessman, so I know that anything that affects your bottom line can't be taken lightly. But, for me, life is good—I have a wonderful wife and wonderful children and a more than fair amount of success. Why shouldn't I want to share? I believe that

when you give back, you get something back in return. Sometimes, it's just a good feeling, and sometimes it's something more concrete.

From a personal perspective, I choose to make donations to Madonna University. The Felician sisters took what was originally a one-building liberal arts college and turned it into the thriving university it is today. That's the kind of gumption and perseverance I feel should be rewarded.

In appreciation, Madonna University presented me with an honorary doctorate, which I cherish as a symbol of how seriously I take education. I have served as chairman on their board and they have also provided me, indirectly, with many fine, well-educated employees.

Next to the school campus is Angela Hospice, a patient care center that serves the community of Livonia and neighboring areas. It was started by Sister Giovanni, a registered nurse who began caring for terminally ill people in their homes. The hospice soon outgrew its one-room office and today provides care for over 1,500 patients annually.

Clearly, Angela Hospice filled a need in our community. I respect that as an entrepreneur and admire it as a Catholic. For those reasons, on the spur of the moment, I decided to try to meet some of *their* needs through a financial donation. That action followed my business philosophy: Do what's necessary to make an improvement or find a solution.

Though the hospice acknowledged Betty and me with a plaque in their lobby, I wasn't looking for recognition. I am, however, honored to be associated in any way with such a fine institution.

St. Mary Mercy Hospital in Livonia has been providing outstanding care in our neighborhood for over fifty years. The Felician sisters saw a necessity for such a hospital after a fire broke out at the General Motors plant in Livonia in 1953. They struggled for six years to finally get it open. Unfortunately, it's a place I've come to know all too well.

Betty ended up in St. Mary several times, after a few falls and broken bones. Although she's always received excellent attention there, I wasn't happy about her having to share a room. I felt she would have been better off with more privacy, especially when family members came to visit.

When it comes to my wife, I'll do whatever it takes, so I approached this as I would have a business transaction: I asked the doctor in charge how much it would take to make my request a reality.

Let's just say that since then, Betty has always gotten a nice, private room—as well as a road named after her next to the hospital, hospice and university complex. But, to me, Bridget Drive is more than a street sign. It's a reminder of what really matters in life: taking care of the people you love and those around you.

CHAPTER 89

Giving Thanks

Just because I started my own business doesn't mean I always had to go it alone.

I was lucky to have a supportive family and friends who pitched in however they could, especially in the early days of PSI.

As for my employees, I couldn't have gotten along without them—except for the ones I couldn't get along *with*.

I've had workers who started with PSI at eighteen years old and stayed with me for over thirty-five years. For the most part, however, I feel that executives can only work for someone else for a certain amount of time—eight years, on average. After that, they either get complacent or get the idea that they're running the show.

One secret to starting your own business is to begin with a bunch of characters who can't get a job anywhere else. They're willing to work for less and be loyal, since they know you're the only one who'll have them.

But, I've been fortunate on that front, too. I've had some great employees over the years and I'm grateful to them for their hard work, their friendship and the contributions they've made to my company and my life.

Marvin Smith was a leading technician in the field of hydraulics when he came to work for me as a young man, shortly after I'd first started PSI. He helped build the business by building and designing the machines that I sold and also by managing the shop.

Norma Lipar was my second secretary—and I was "her guy." Nothing was going to get past her and get to me unless she let it. She was a great assistant and a pretty tough lady—with one weakness: poodles. After she retired and the business became more successful, I sent her a thousand-dollar bonus check each year. Then I'd inevitably get a call from one of her kids telling me that their mom spent the money on a poodle.

They'd say, "Mr. Phillips, that's very nice of you, but you have to stop sending her checks. She doesn't have room for any more poodles."

But, I told them to let her spend it on whatever made her happy.

I "borrowed" my current secretary, Jill Sak, a few years ago from another division of my company. It was supposed to be a temporary arrangement, but she's proven to be too good to let go.

Then, there was Ray Rosbury, who helped me out with some money in the early years by buying stock in PSI. Ray was a World War II bomber pilot who wasn't into diplomacy. One day, as he was touring the factory, he saw one of our workers sitting on a stool as he assembled some equipment. Ray walked over, kicked the stool out from under him and shouted, "This isn't a rest home. Get to work!"

Since then, I'd have to say that my "no partners" rule has served me well. Ray wouldn't have been the easiest person to work with. But, at least he was a man of action!

As always, however, the person I'm most grateful to is my wife, Betty. She's the one partner I'd never get rid of. Not only has she been a great companion and a wonderful mother to our kids, but she's also helped me quite a bit in business: It was Betty who taught me how to "read" men.

I don't know if she just has a strong sense of women's intuition or if she can recognize a tell as well as any professional poker player; whichever the case might be, her talent has served me well throughout the years. There has not been one single executive that I considered hiring without having him meet my wife first.

Within minutes, she has a pretty good sense of the person's character. By the end of dinner, she can practically list someone's negative traits as clearly as if she were reading from a police record. Let's just say that any time I didn't take her advice, I've regretted it.

Throughout my career and my life, I've been grateful to meet a lot of extraordinary people—and to marry the most extraordinary one of all.

Realizing how many people helped me along the way is what keeps me humble and helps me realize how blessed I've truly been.

CHAPTER 90

How Business *Can* Be Personal

As I've mentioned before in this book, I'm a big fan of *The Godfather* movies. You can get a lot of valuable business information from them, even if you're fixing hydraulic systems instead of putting hits out on someone. But, there's one thing those films got totally wrong. While "it's not personal, it's just business" might be a memorable line, it's also a lot of B.S.

Business *is* personal, especially for an entrepreneur. I poured so much of my own time, sweat and energy into turning my ideas into actualities and making my company a reflection of my own principles. With three generations of my family working at PSI, you'd better believe that business is something I take personally.

The man who sits behind the desk at PSI is the same one you'll find sitting at the dinner table with my family. My principles don't change in any situation, and my experience base is what guides me in everything I do. All the lessons I learned from the family farm in Arkansas and growing up in inner-city Detroit, my time in the military, my struggles to start my own company and my promise to myself to provide a better life for my family have made me who I am—and that's not just something that I can switch on and off. That's why I apply the same code of ethics to both my professional and private lives, which are, in fact, ultimately inseparable.

Two basic rules are pretty simple, really: Never welsh on a deal and never back down from a fight.

First of all, when you make a decision, it's either yes or no—you give your word and then live by it, whether it's to your kids or your clients (even *The Godfather* reminds us that "a man that doesn't spend time with his family can never be a real man"). Secondly, you can't be afraid of conflict. It will find you—especially in the business world. If not, it means you're probably doing something wrong, since no one's taking notice.

My sales background also informed a lot of how I ran my subsequent businesses. To me, winning means getting the other guy's money. And, that usually involves taking risks. To make the sale, you always have to be *seeking* opportunities—and *seeing* opportunities where others don't. Personally, I've had to figure out the angles in order to keep my family—as well as over 600 employees—fed. Now, that doesn't mean lying, selling a bad product or giving substandard service. That means being the best at what you do and separating yourself from the pack somehow. Oftentimes, it means running an honest business where customers trust your word and your work is enough to set yourself apart from the competition.

One of my sons once told me, "Dad, the one thing you're unable to do is lie." That was one of the best compliments I have ever received, and it is true both in and out of business. Because I've lived an honest and candid life, I've never had to second guess what I did or said and I've always been confident in my words and actions. Honesty helps eliminate many barriers that prevent success. Trying to conceal a prior indiscretion is like wearing handcuffs—you no longer enjoy the same freedom you once had.

Honesty is what allows me to look myself in the mirror and look everyone else straight in the eye.

Of course, in every transaction, you've got to know who's buying and who's selling. So it's always important to stay in control of every situation. But you can't force anyone into buying or bully them into seeing your point; it requires complete confidence in yourself, your character and your product instead. That's why you should never be

afraid to ask for what you're worth and always take what the market will bear.

Good sales skills don't end with the customer; they also apply to your own employees. An effective salesman is accessible and knows how to make the client happy. A good boss does the same things by being available to his people and keeping up morale. When I visit the work floor, I'm just as concerned about my employees' well-being as I am about my company's bottom line.

No one in the corporate world ever made it big by doing things halfway. Bill Gates, Sam Walton, Jack Welch, Warren Buffett, even Donald Trump, like him or not, put their personalities and their passions into their professions. To be successful, you have to invest yourself in what you're doing and be willing to give whatever it takes, which requires an enormous amount of individual dedication and sacrifice.

As Michael Corleone would say, that's "just business." But, it's also extremely personal. And, it's your choice to determine whether or not you've got it in you.

PART IX

The Future of PSI

CHAPTER 91

Lean, Green...

Heading into the second decade of the new century, it's more important than ever for PSI to keep up with the changing demands of the marketplace, the increasing complexities of the world and the escalation of the global trade wars. In fact, keeping up is no longer good enough. We have to stay ahead of the curve on all fronts.

Toward that end, from an operational standpoint, PSI has implemented changes in our system of enterprise in order to streamline the business and speed up productivity. If there's one thing that working for a car manufacturer taught me, it's never to let the assembly lines stop moving. Quality and output are the only ways America can stay ahead of its competitors.

The Lean system we employ has helped us to get each company operating in its prime—with the best practices of the industry applied to all aspects of business. It has allowed us to increase our product flow, from simple changes like getting rid of clutter to more major areas such as streamlining our quality systems and communications with our customers all over the globe. What's best is that the operational changes we've already made will only become more pronounced over time, making PSI that much more viable and visible in the future.

But getting "lean" is only part of it. PSI is also going green.

Evana is working on a new assembly system for solar panels

that will vastly increase the number of panels made in America. The way we heat our houses and run our cars will change in upcoming years—decreasing our dependence on foreign countries' fuel supplies in the process. So it's not only good for global resources but for the specific well being of our country as well.

In addition, we're repairing wind turbine components in order to make wind power a more practical source of energy in the foreseeable future.

PSI's repair companies are also providing work for Air Force bases on equipment that is no longer repaired by the original manufacturers. These "sustainment services" we offer are not only saving the government—and taxpayers—hundreds of millions of dollars, but they also cut down on the need for disposal and unnecessary waste. For instance, the B-52 bombers that I first saw in 1953 are slated to fly until 2030—and PSI is partly responsible for keeping them up in the air.

Fifty-three years after I left the military, my company is charged with overhauling silos that house the Minuteman missiles that made Air Force bases such as the one where I was stationed in Newfoundland obsolete. It gratifies me that my son, Scott, led the charge on this complicated project.

It's funny to think that I started PSI with my knowledge of hydraulics, which I gained in the Air Force. But, just as the military changed and diversified by incorporating missiles into our defense system and decreasing Air Force bases, my company has shifted from only hydraulics to a wide range of high-tech services.

Sustainability is key, but so is diversity. PSI is spearheading sweeping changes in a variety of industries, which is all part of a diversification plan that I have always practiced. But, there is a synergy among our projects and our people. We are working toward building a better future.

Strategic planning tells us to develop a grand vision, set our targets high and make plans to get there, constantly monitoring and

adjusting along the way. I, for one, have never shied away from setting audacious goals and doing everything in my power to get to a better place. There are no limits! That's the guiding principle that powers PSI as we look toward—and shape—the future: one year, three years and five years at a time.

We're committed to making PSI four times its current size in the next five years as we continue to make America a safer place with more-sustainable resources.

And, that commitment is something you can count on, even as the nature of business changes.

CHAPTER 92

Fighting Machines

Innovations that would have been unthinkable a mere ten years ago are now a major part of our product line. We tackle the government contracts that few other companies could handle—and find the solutions that our armed forces need.

For the Navy and Coast Guard, we are customizing data collection devices for P3 sub-hunter aircraft, which patrol our coasts in search of enemy submarines, dropping sonar buoys, devices that blast waves into the water to detect the presence of submarines.

Beaver is also focusing on a major redesigning of components for U.S. submarines. Currently, hydraulic equipment is used to move surfaces in order to dive and climb, as well as to open gates and valves. We are working on an electromechanical system, which is cleaner, lighter and takes up less space. The result is improved efficiency and less maintenance.

Mountain Secure Systems is working on data storage and control on anti-ICBM systems as well as the targeting pods for F16s.

Our products can also be found on Mars, on the appropriately named Spirit and Opportunity expedition. We made the pinions in the lander's legs that ensured that the rovers began their journey properly. Had they tumbled over, it could have resulted in untold costs for the U.S. government and set the Mars exploration program back years.

But our work on the Mars project isn't our final frontier.

Sciaky is currently developing a new technology called Direct Manufacturing. Sciaky's process is called freeform fabrication and it involves computer-aided design (CAD) and electron-beam (EB) welding. This precision component-manufacturing system is a complete reimagining of the mechanical development process. It is now being applied to aerospace innovation, bringing Star Trek technology to life.

A component is designed on a CAD system and the program is downloaded into Sciaky's control system. A fully articulated electron beam gun follows the computer model, using a layer-additive technique to deposit metal layer by layer until the part has been built to specification in much less time than required by traditional methods of manufacturing. Because the part is built from nothing but a computer model, there are fewer material costs involved and absolute minimal waste.

Because the process must take place in an absolute vacuum, the applications were obvious to us—as was the enormous impact it could have on America's space program.

Using this system, replacements for damaged or malfunctioning parts can be manufactured onboard space shuttles, allowing almost immediate repairs to be made on-site, in open space or on other planets.

Although Sciaky has been perfecting its freeform fabrication system for nearly a decade now, changes to the aerospace industry occur slowly and with much caution. The cutting edge has to catch up with us.

———

Many of the opportunities I've taken in life have led me down a path where I could continue to serve my country long after my time in

the military had ended. I started PSI with little more than a sales background, an entrepreneurial spirit and the aeronautics education I gained in the Air Force. The fact that my company is assisting all ranches of the U.S. Armed Forces makes me extremely proud as both an American and an entrepreneur.

Though PSI is currently working on some top-secret projects I'm not at liberty to discuss, there are two things I *can* tell you definitively: Going into business for yourself is one of the most liberating choices in life. But, choosing to be of service to your country and community is among the most meaningful.

CHAPTER 93

Looking Ahead

I recently watched a TV interview with Warren Buffett in which he was asked his thoughts about the future of America's economic status. Would the U.S. continue to be the dominant force that it has been over the decades?

His answer echoed what I have always believed to be true: America's system has proven to be by far the best in the world at fostering excellence and creativity. From electronic technology to medicine to defense, Americans have always been able to set themselves apart. In short, we live in a culture where entrepreneurship flourishes—and that is what will continue to ensure our country's future as a world leader.

America is still a land of opportunities. And, entrepreneurs like me are the ones who make the most of them.

———

My humble beginnings in rural Arkansas and the rough neighborhoods of inner-city Detroit didn't provide me with a clear roadmap to success. I wasn't born with a silver spoon in my mouth—not by a long shot. I faced so many obstacles and challenges that made success often seem out of reach. But, those struggles strengthened

me and forced me to discover, develop and depend on all of my talents and see value and opportunities in things that other people were quick to dismiss.

I truly feel, however, that my dreams and desires were no different from those most people held. I also don't feel that my circumstances were all that much different from those of many Americans. So, what allowed me to achieve success where others have not?

That is a question many have asked me over the years, and one I have tried to answer through the stories you've just read. These are not merely chapters in a book; they are chapters of a life that has come full circle.

At a very basic level, my most reliable guides have always been commitment, hard work and, most of all, honesty. Those were the points on my compass even when my path wasn't entirely clear.

I also innately harbor an entrepreneurial spirit that encourages me to take risks, set audacious goals and do everything in my power to meet them. Many others give up too early or too easily on their passions and lose faith in themselves along the way.

Sure, there have been times when I worried if I'd ever become successful or whether or not my company would survive during tough times. But, fear never made me lose focus or belief in my values and myself.

I always took the risks, searched for solutions and sought out opportunities. That's not just part of a business plan—it's a big part of being alive!

I also believe that things happen in life for a reason. I know I was stationed at Newfoundland for many purposes, none of which were more important than meeting my wife, Betty, and starting our family. My Air Force training also gave me the opportunity to enter the field of hydraulic repairs at just the right time. And, some of my early struggles prepared me for larger ones later in life.

As a child, I saw success as the freedom to choose the life I

wanted for myself, which I have been fortunate enough to create. But, money alone was never a goal; it simply allowed me to provide comfortable lives for those around me without the worries and fears that my parents and grandparents suffered.

The people in my life are a large part of my success. They are what make me wealthy.

Through my business, I have come to know some exceptional people and have become a better person myself because of that. I cannot imagine going through life without close friends—and this, of course, pertains to my closest friend, who also happens to be my wife.

We are so intertwined after more than fifty years of marriage that I can no longer envision our lives apart. Without her, our financial success never would have occurred—but her presence in my life has been a greater gift than any amount of money.

Thoreau wrote, "Most men lead lives of quiet desperation." I am not one of those men. The jets I worked on in the Air Force weren't quiet. The fights I got into to defend what I earned weren't quiet. I'm not quiet when I tell stories or laugh at someone's jokes.

And, as for desperation, I don't believe in it. Desperation is the absence of hope. At times in my life, hope and self-confidence have been all I've had.

The life I'm living is one of service—to my country, my community, my family, my customers, my employees and their families, and charities of my choice. I'm not saying that I haven't served myself in the process on occasion, but hell, I've worked hard enough for it.

I'm very grateful to be where I am in life and have enjoyed myself along the way—otherwise I wouldn't have considered myself successful. But I'm also an entrepreneur, which means always looking

out for that next opportunity, that next sale or the solution that no one else sees. Am I done with all of that?

Don't count on it.

It's in my blood, part of who I am. And I wouldn't have it any other way.